TimE, Fate and Spider Magic

Turn, Turn, Turn
Verse, Verse, Verse

Please ReCycle this Product
Please ReProduce this Cycle

Time, Fate and Spider Magic

A Brief HerStory of tiME

A feirb Hirstory fo emit

with 3 keys
Open 3 Gates
aWait: 3 Fates...

Written and Illustrated by

Orryelle Defenestrate-Bascule

TimE, Fate and Spider Magic

Time, Fate and Spider Magic

All Text and Illustrations (except where otherwise credited herein) inc. cover copyright © 2014 Orryelle Defenestrate-Bascule
All rights reserved desrever stfel llA

Published by **Avalonia**

BM Avalonia
London
WC1N 3XX
England, UK
www.avaloniabooks.co.uk

Originally published (earlier versions before revision and expansion) as the 100-copy HECATE Edition under the title **'Emit fo yrotsreH feirB A'** in 2003; then in 2006 under the title **'A Brief HirStory of TimEmit of yrotSriH feirB A'**, both by **iNSPiRALink. Multimedia PRESS.**

ISBN 978-1-905297-90-0

Design/layout by Orryelle

British Library Cataloguing in Publication Data. A catalogue record for this book is available from the British Library.

All rights reserved. No part of this publication may be reproduced or utilised in any form or by any means, electronic or mechanical, including photocopying, microfilm, recording, or by any information storage and retrieval system, or used in another book, without written permission from the author.

Acknowledgements:

Heartfelt Thanks to:

Giselle Sybil for support, inspiration & the Secrets of the SphinX

Tegan for fireside flourishes & finishes in Relojero

Tesssa, Bex Hexabranchus, Nema, Jan Fries, Aion 131 and Kenneth Grant for magical resonance and impetus

Evan Flux, Justin Patrick Moore and Marios for input and kcabdeef

Sorita D'Este for midwifery of the new strands in the web

Ra'en Fisher Wolf for 8 Gates, inspiration and aid with translation...

...And of course to **Kali-Arachne-Moirae**, the Great Spider Goddess Herself who has impelled this Work...

On the sacred Pentacle
Turns the Wheel of Fate
Determining our path
Within the Lemnisc-8

Clotho:

'Spin the Wheel of Fate
My sisters await
The wheels spin
The journey begins
Implant the seed
And what you sow
So shall ye reap
For from it shall grow
The fruit you eat
I'll spin you in, Begin, begin...'

(Lyrics from the 'ROTA' track of Mutation Parlour's
'LABYRINTH' CD.)

THE FIRST GATE

TimE, Fate and Spider Magic

Time crraaaawwwwwlllsss...
...and creeps off its

Imagine Time as a *S*pider's Web -a *S*piral, with intersecting rays. As a magical model or map, this simple design can be used for potent path-workings and astral timetravel, for mapping and re-routing Fate.

But before progressing to such possibilities in ritual context, we must examine the f a r - r e a c h i n g concepts behind this model.

Time is not as linear as 'history' would have us believe. That name itself, 'His-Story' gives this bias away -this artificial chronology of the written word is only a part of the story, as recorded from a patriarchal perspective, a perspective that has dominated western culture for the last two millenia or so (from a linear perspective) and is only just beginning to change...

*Her*story is another matter - timemit is also flexible, cyclic, Spiralling...

Time is ultimately the domain of the feminine. It is She who creates it's eternal cycles of Birth and Death. She who is also traditionally the mythic archetype of Fate, that sense of irrevocable inevitability which is so intrinsically entwined with Time's domain - as this tome shall explore.

Fate or Destiny is not a popular concept in the modern world -we like to think we have more control over our lives, which is one of the reasons we have such a constrictive sense of time and its

management. Yet if we move beyond fear we may meet and befriend Fate, align it with our wills rather than combat it as some looming and uncertain yet unavoidable spectre.

In the modern world of big business, overzealous ambition (often with little consideration of who or what gets trampled in the manic stampede of so-called progress) and materialistic

pursuit, it is ever more vital to take some v e e r r r y de e ep breaths, slow down and not only hink about but f e e l how malleable this thing we call Time really is. For when we breathe deeply, we may find that time seems to have s l o w e d ...

Try it now, please. This a grimoire not an academic textbook, and requires some co-operation to experience its more subtle layers.

At least 8 d e e e e p breaths, right down into your belly, and fully emptying your lungs on each long, calm and s l o w exhalation...

… … …

Feel better? Or at least a bit different?

In India Time has always been intrinsically associated with the Breath (we will explore this more later). This is a far cry from the western outlook of 'Time is money'. Money is merely an abstract means of manipulating material goods and services, breath is our very life-force without which our most primary material assets (our very bodies) would not be animated...

How much of western civilisation's hasty and often destructive endeavours are the result of our constrictive views of time? Every good businessman wears a watch, and while thinking he is using its mechanisms to order and 'control' his life, is actually often a slave of its order, the constructed **12:60** time pattern of the Babylonians –the same culture which was responsible for the Tower of Babel/Babble and the beginnings of cultural division via fragmentation of the Logos. This advent of imposed Hierarchy was demonstrated concisely in their own story by the different levels of the Tower which lost communication with each other instigating its collapse.

This Babylonian 12 (hrs):60 (mins) system -especially in its modern corrupted form- is a very solar and masculine time system, and even as such is less accurate and true to the great cosmic clock of the solar system than the similarly solar calendars and systems of civilisations such as the Mayans and Incans. The Gregorian calendar we use - introduced by the Christian fundamental patriarchy- is out of synch enough with natural time that the very Equinoxes and Solstices - basic seasonal markers of most ancient cultures- fall on a different date every few years. So perhaps it is time to look again at how the pagan and matriarchal cultures who were suppressed or deleted by this imposed hierarchy viewed time...

Such cultures based their experience of time on practical matters such as when to sow and when to reap the crops, as well as the celestial cycles of the sun, moon and planets. For them, time was something quite perceivable from the natural elements –the rising and setting of the sun at different seasonal apexes -priestesses looking up at the moon and feeling its resonance with their wombs and the womb of the Earth; or direct observations of the patterns of the Great Wheel of the Stars- not some imposed artifice represented by 'precise' (yet inaccurate except on its own arbitrary terms) mechanisms designed to keep people's lives segmented and orderly in a world of synthetic light and even synthetic moods.

Time is as much about intuition as reason, and it is these fundamental feminine aspects of its spiralling course which I wish to examine in this book. Included are states apparently 'outside of' time which the ancient shaman or modern magus are familiar with in the realms of ritual and perception alteration. Some of these may not seem 'logical' to those of a scientific stance. That is part of the point: logic and reason and their goals of functionality over aesthetics and magic have been too dominant in our society over intuition and sensibility (which comes from the senses and direct experience rather than just intellectual mentation).

Behind the waking-day conscious ('solar') world of outer events that have occurred throughout time's course, there is ever a shifting dreamscape woven of ideas and concepts, images and archetypes - subconscious ('lunar') realms reflective of the waking world and yet also feeding back into it, the imagic undercurrents from which our manifest timestream is distilled. It is this shadowy *'HerStory'* I wish to explore in these pages...

And yet while this book focuses primarily on intuitive and mythic or poetic time as a necessary counterbalance to the dominance of the patriarchal perspective prevalent for the last two millennia or so, I do of course use Reason myself as a faculty to organise such expressions (as does any employment of the written Word to at least some degree) and to offer practical ritual frameworks for its apprehension.

Being genetically male myself (though having explored my anima thoroughly on both spiritual and physiological levels, as shall be explained) I would not dare deem to be able to write from a purely female perspective either. So ultimately this HirStory of Time merges the 'masculine' (*Chokmah/ 'Wisdom'*, Sephira **2** on the Qabalistic Tree of Life) and 'feminine' (*Binah/ 'Understanding'*, Sephira **3** on the Tree) apprehensions of time in 'hermaphroditic' transcendence of such dualities, beyond the TAROTA Wheel to **ARCANA 23**, the trump outside the cycle of 0 the Fool to 0 the Fool, beyond the confines of ordinary time.

For I have progressively discovered that the only way to truly go beyond time is by going right into it, understanding it thoroughly enough to master and alter our perception of its inevitable domain- our existence in the world of Form.

So let us now explore the **Hirstory of TimemiT of yrotsriH** - the inner mythic and archetypal conceptions of Time and the closely-related concept of Fate, rather than just the history in terms of outer events- in various cultural paradigms.

This will eventually lead us back to the Present, through **THE SECOND GATE** into contemporary perspectives of such ancient arcana, and what is being done now to apprehend the underlying concepts in new ways which integrate their timeless hirstory and mythic mystery.

Much was made (before the date occurred) of the December Solstice 2012 and its imp-ending 'paradigm shift'. This was the time when the epic Mayan long-count calendar ended and our sun re-aligned with the centre of our galaxy, the dark rift called by the Mayans Hunab Ku or the 'Womb of the Great Mother'.

The significance of this time was propagated primarily by the psychedelic guru Terence McKenna with his '*Timewave Zero*' software and by the 'Dreamspell' people. The latter use calendrics that are only very loosely based on actual Mayan calendrics and are really more the artistic creation of their founder Jose Arguelles.

Branching from this meme were various other New Age angles on the idea, many of which seemed more about commercial enterprise than genuine spirituality (why one would bother accumulating wealth for the purported 'end of time' eludes me); and a few more sincere considerations such as the astronomical and astrological research of John Major Jenkins.

In all the hooha about this 'end of the world' or 'end of time' on Solstice 2012, very little was said or speculated about what awaited us in 2013, and beyond...

Late in 2012, as this anticipated and/or dreaded **'Omega Point'** in the history of human civilisation was suddenly almost upon us, I began to consider what 2013 might signify. Was it a new 'Alpha Point' if there was a significant shift at the end of 2012, I wondered, or - and more importantly by that stage - *what* is to fill that great void of expectation? For perhaps disappointment may ensue if nothing much did actually 'happen' on the 2012 Solstice and life went on as 'normal' on planet Earth...

Indeed, the 'end of the world' -as many misinterpreters of the Mayan calender-end believed it would be- did not occur, and while personally I feel there have been some significant though subtle shifts in human consciousness happening around that time, on an extant level it certainly seems that life and culture on planet Earth goes on as usual.

Our culture seems to love the idea of an Apocalypse (whether the Biblical Rapture of the *Book of Revelations*, the spiritual 'alternative' of Mayan end-times or simply the collapse of the materialist empire), even while often dreading and fearing it. Global havoc and disaster, alien abductions, cosmic revelations or spiritual saviours are much more exciting prospects than the gradual disintegration of our ecology and thus our economy (well duh! perhaps the latter is ultimately based on finite resources rather than abstract credit after all). This was already happening in its own slow (well compared to an apocalypse, but quite rapid from a historical perspective) and easily-ignored-in-the-affluent-west decline…

But, to begin to avert the real disaster of this more gradual disintegration perhaps we need to perceive Time differently. To reconsider this idea that a peak experience of catastrophic proportions is the only thing that can wake us from our collective stupor (as then of course it may be too late).

Apocalypse memes are entwined with a linear perception of Time, and its associated concepts of a burgeoning 'progress' which looks at the future only in a very short-term-profit based way while attempting to escape the past at breakneck speed.

The 'Mayan Dreamspell' movement propagated the idea of a more natural system of time and this is, I think, vital within itself. It is perhaps a shame they got caught up in their own intricate system of calendrics which, being based on erroneous interpretations of Mayan cosmology, has lost credibility. Besides, it is far too complex for most people to even consider as an alternative to their regular timekeeping processes.

What is more important, I think, is changing our general perspective of Time rather than specifics of computation which may just replace one precise 'clock' with another, albeit one more in tune with natural cycles and seasons.

It is precisely these seasons and cycles which are the essence of the changed perspective we need to reconsider. Simply, the basic idea that time is actually based on such things, rather than through a somewhat arbitrary construct created by human regiments and systems of socio-political-religious governments intent on controlling their populace.

Interestingly in terms of all the hype surrounding the transition between the years 2012 and 2013, the numbers 12 and 13 are of great significance in relation to this shift of perspective of Time…

> The sun of reason turns clockwise
> And the moon of intuition turns anticlockwise
>
> Are you clockwise or are you anticlockwise?
> Are you clockwise or are you clockfoolish?
> Are you a solar-tock or a lunar-tick?
>
> *(Lyrics from Orryelle's 'Chaos Clock')*

Twelve is a very solar number. It is the number of solar months in our year. It is also the number whereby we calculate time in our time-obsessed and linear society.

Thirteen is a lunar number. There are thirteen moonths (lunar cycles) per year. It is ironic that our word mo(o)nths of course comes from this, since we have constricted them into twelve. Correlating this with the solar year has been a difficulty for calendar-makers for millennia, but our current contrivances are merely practical solutions, which unfortunately sway the collective consciousness towards solar dominance.

Now let us consider in relation to this timekeeping the nature of the sun and the moon and what they have symbolised and represented throughout our history, and perhaps more importantly now because it has been so overlooked -our Herstory.

In many of the oldest cultures on our planet the solar-masculine and lunar-feminine associations we commonly hold today were originally reversed.

The Egyptians, the Chinese, and the Australian aboriginals for a few examples had Sun-Goddesses and Moon-Gods. Some (e.g. the Ancient Egyptians) had both masculine and feminine deities of each. Even specific Gods have had their roles reversed in relation to these cosmic bodies, e.g. Isis and Osiris via the Graeco-Romans are usually thought of as Moon-Goddess and Sun-God, but originally Osiris (Usire or Asar to the Egyptians) as an agricultural deity related to the moon through the myth of His being torn apart by Set (Darkness) into 14 pieces which were then reassembled by Isis symbolised the waxing and waning lunar cycle (together the complete 28-day moonth).

Nevertheless, these days -largely through the work of the Medieval Alchemists and of Carl Jung with such archetypal energies- we generally associate solar energy with the masculine and lunar energy with the feminine. This correspondence does seem to make some sense: the male as relating to outward energy, ambition, reason, logic, science and such powers of the bright and conscious mind, and the female lunar current in contrast delving into the shadows of the subconscious, of intuition, the inner, reflective and artistic. Of course any metaphor taken to an extreme is absurd, and men and women have all of these attributes, and in some cases men may have more of the 'feminine' qualities expressed above and women more of the 'masculine'; but as a statement of general tendencies these correlations work.

So perhaps the dominance of our linear solar clock and calendar are indicators of the overtly 'reasonable' yet often intuitively-retarded civilisation. Perhaps it is high time for a more lunar approach to time? -An increased awareness of Syn (an Assyrian MoonGod)- Chron (Chronos is the Greek God of Time) -icity...

Thirteen of course has a bad reputation. But from whence did this superstition come?

It is a very feminine number, associated with the lunar currents and thus also the reflective menstrual cycles of women. It has been prominent in the agenda of the patriarchal priesthoods for millennia to vilify and demonise women. They are the most obvious thing to project the blame onto when men 'fall prey to their baser instincts' i.e. the natural appetite of sexual desire which the mainstream religions have denigrated in their perverse separation of spirit and flesh, or macrocosmically of heaven and earth. And so we have the 'unlucky' number thirteen, and Friday the 13th is of course especially wicked as the witch's number is combined with the only day of the week named after a Goddess (Freya) rather than a God (with the possible exception of Mo(o)nday, although that's more ambiguous).

The Babylonians created the 12:60 time system which we use today, so it is interesting to reflect how some of its core mythology reflects the kind of fragmentation this system has spawned:

The primal feminine Chaos Serpent **Tiamat** was divided in twain by the sword (the weapon of the air and the mind in western occultism) of the solar hero Marduk. Thus we have the division of fluid and chaotic natural time (ever the dragon of the tide-driven sea) by solar and patriarchal cults into artifices of calendric calculation to control civilisation.

In the ancient *Enuma Elish* Babylonian creation text, this division is related to the separation of the Earth and the Sky, in much the same way as Geb (the earth) and Nuit (the sky or space) were separated by Shu (the air or atmosphere) in Egyptian mythology, allowing form to proliferate upon the planet.

Tiamat's very name is reflective in the same way as earth and sky may be viewed as microcosm and macrocosm: Often pronounced TiamaiT or even TeyamayeT, its division reveals two reflective wor(l)ds, and the similarity to TimemiT is considerable.

In the splitting of this serpent into Sky and Earth/Sea, did we lose sight of the connection between these vast bodies?- that the cycles of flora and fauna of the land echo the seasonal cycles of the heavens, even as the tides of the sea ebb and flow with the moon's wax and wane.

If the name of Tiamat is further divided beyond its basic reflective palindromic properties, we get 'T-I-am-at': The I am At of when we are located in time: which day, hour, minute or second am I at? Thus the timestream is dammed into a sequence of small partitions, and with all the stops and starts (getup gotowork lunchtime backtowork...) we lose the flow and forget about the why in the what.

So if we've managed to stretch our 12-trained brains to 13 moonths, perhaps we can now take a step further and extend beyond 12 o'clock to 13 o'clock in the microcosm of our day.

Midnight has often been called the *'Witching Hour'* and with good reason, or rather beyond-reason. It is the apex of 'normal time' and thus a window beyond... To fit a thirteenth hour on our nicely-symmetrical and mechanically-ordered clockface, we will have to warp it somewhat, Dali-style, and the hands may spread out at every oblique angle or simply fall off this melting edifice. We find ourselves in a timeless space, a magical crux as the business and duties of the day slip away into dreaming, where time indeed behaves quite differently. Even science has shown that we have hundreds (at least) of dreams every night, and only our conscious recall filters this. We seem to often experience long dreams in 'real-time' (by normal waking perception) and yet they may have actually occurred in the mere fluttering of an eyelid.

There are of course some who make use of this witching hour - which of course extends beyond the parameters of the clockface's mechanical contrivances into a fluid 13- while awake. Witches, magicians, artists (of all kinds not just visual) and sorcerers have long used the dead of night, when the collective work-a-day mentality of the general populace is usually soundly asleep and a psychic peace descends, to find the trance which transcends humanity's usual constrictive time-consciousness. They seek the spaces in-between, the stretch or warp of time in creative or/as magical trance, bridging the subconscious (dreaming) and conscious parts of our brain. When we get lost in the activities of unmitigated creation, we forget the clock and venture into unmapped 'territory'.

Thus the 'myths' of Faery where somebody disappears for but a night, yet when returning to the world of men it seems that many years have passed though he remains un-aged. An accurate tale of how magical trance's altered perception of time alters also how time affects us. We are, after all, 'only as old as we feel' -just ask this 33.3recurring-year-old (more about that 'later')...

In addition to magical ritual and artistic or musical creative trances, meditation too is useful for transcending linear time -in the process of stilling our mind, time seems to cease along with our activity and our thoughts, until eventually we return to its stream refreshed.

'Territory' is enclosed in quotation marks above because time is not space; yet we are constantly mapping time onto spatial planes to try to understand it and regulate it. Really time is more fluid than space, or at least more amorphous than the matter which fills space.

The clockface is a cultural recension of the sundial and the calendrical cycle. Beneath its circular mask and turning cogs is a far more ancient Wheel, inexorably turned by six spindle-fingered hands which also weave the threads which spiral twixt the great spokes, the loom of Fate, She who is Three…

Of course now we have square and rectangular clocks with digital displays. At least mechanical cogs and gears were round; but our modern society's obsession with straight angles takes us even further from the wheel. The cyclical nature of time is disguised in boxes of curveless functionality, even as time itself has become a mere linear regulator for structures of control and imposed order in our lives, rather than the rhythmic ebb and flow of seasons and tides.

The Witching Hour is only one gate beyond conventional time-perception, of course. While the psychic space in the middle of the night and beyond is a potent portal, the true adept can with a bit of effort access the trance of Thirteen o'clock from anywhen.

And so it is with calendars. If we are to go 'beyond time' at the end of 2012, surely this 'has already happened', since beyond-time cannot be constricted to the artifice of time's parameters. This is the problem I have with the idea of time 'ending' at a certain point, in time! I do hope, however, that more of us can collectively move into a more fluid and natural perception of time and into the Dreamtime beyond solstice 2012…

In the ancient language of Hebrew letters have numerical values which are qualitative rather than merely quantitive -i.e. they have meaning and magical significance. By this system of Qabalistic *Gematria*, the word **'Achad'** has the value (when adding up the values of each letter) of Thirteen.

Achad means Unity or one-ness. Thus are the Twelve Tribes woven into One, the global *Thirteenth Tribe* which -according to Hopi Indian prophecies -unites all the peoples of the World.

The model of Twelve and a Thirteenth who is One who Unites them is prevalent throughout many cultures: All-father Odin and the Twelve Aesir of Asgard, Dionysos and the Twelve Gods of Olympus, Jesus and the Twelve Disciples, and King Arthur (or the Fool Parzival?) and the Twelve Knights of the round table. The last of these is reflected in the landscape of Somerset UK (centred in Glastonbury) where much of this mythos apparently played out. There we have the shapes of various creatures mirroring the constellations above -the geomantic Glastonbury Zodiac. There is an additional thirteenth sign, which now looks (somewhat unfortunately) like a dog (and its tail is wyrdly a place called Wagg) but apparently once resembled a unicorn. For more about this and **The 13-Tribe Weaving** on Glastonbury Tor, see **APPENDIX D**.

In his book **'Arachne Rising'** *(MW Books, 1977)* James Vogh posits a rather different (but equally magical) zoomorph for the mysterious Thirteenth Sign of the greater (rather than geomantic) starry Zodiac -the Spider.

Vogh's in-depth exploration of this 'missing sign' has been revealed as a hoax (more about that later), however some of the real hirstory he presents as a foundation for his speculations is significant, particularly the thirteen-tree calendar of the nature-worshipping Druids.

Despite its historical validity or Not, the connective nature of the Spider does ring true as representative of a missing sign, since such a 13-sign Zodiac would be lunar. The spider's web connects earth and sky, even as the sea ebbs and flows with the moon. She is aware of every subtle vibration along Her delicate creation's silken strands. Deep ecology, anyone?

Astronomers (rather than Astrologers) have since posited the presence of a Thirteenth zodiacal constellation in the form of the Snake-handler, **Ophiuchus**.

Snakes and Spiders: what do they have in common? Creation Magic. The Serpent features in the creation myths of almost every culture, and usually symbolises Time. The Spider as the archetypal weaver is almost universally representative of Fate, that intricate tapestry of life. Time and Fate are ever entwined, even as the pattern of the spider's web echo the serpent's spiral, the spiralling golden mean that enlivens sacred geometry at every fractal level of nature's vast loom.

Besides 13 there is great magic in the numbers 23 and 33, also in 9 (symbolising eternity to the Norse) which is 3 x 3.

23 has been posited as the 'number of synchronicity' by Robert Anton Wilson (in his '*Cosmic Trigger*' and other tomes) and many others. Although it has been disputed that any given number will seem to do that if you pay more attention to it, 23 does seem to have a wyrd resonance, and Chaos Magic is often considered the '23 Current'. For me its real significance on a symbolic level was exemplified by Nema's articulation of a mysterious *23rd Arcana* in the Tarot. The traditional 22 Trumps (0-XXI) represent the Fool's (Arcana 0) cyclical (actually progressively spiralling) journey uponT**the Wheel of Fortune** (Arcana X, the X-roads or aXis of this cycle). So it seems **Arcana 23** is 'off the wheel' or as Kenneth Grant expressed it in his book of the same name, '*Outside the Circles of Time*'. So this further resonance of 3 is another kind of '13 o'clock' applied to Tarot symbology, where again the usual cycle (time) is transcended to find a kind of 'dreamtime' trance beyond the confines of sequence.

The symbols Nema discovered for this Arcana 23 are suitably surreal:

**The ballet dancer* -pirouetting on the axis of eternity one supposes

*The clown -the inherent humour in such states, and the Last Last Foundation of immortality

*The frog -the voltiguer or 'leaper in between' due to its amphibious nature which traverses diverse elements and dimensions

*The Wing-ed Eye -the flights of fancy or visionary journey such spaces take us upon, time being more flexible -and even oft unapparent- on the astral plane

We will be following further the fluttering vision of this last symbol further within…

Then there is **33**, and its nigh-inevitable extension as **33.3recurring**. This is how one-third is expressed as a percentage, and demonstrates the flaws in our so-called logical system of mathematics. The decimal threes can never end for it to be a true expression of a third, they trail on infinitely… This eternal aspect of three is something I figured can be employed magically since it is an apparent illogical glitch (I won't go into the details of this lest it become a mathematical treatise) in what is supposed to be a logical system of numerical law which governs our reality. Therefore one-third of a year after my birthday I began to celebrate my 33.3recurring birthday, which continues to recur quite a few years later.

Before that, our ritual opera **The Choronzon Machine** began as a celebration of the 33.3rd birthday of Evan Flux whose April 1st birthdate made him a natural choice (cast by Fate) for the part of the Fool in that Tarotic drama. However Evan wisely (unfoolishly) celebrated his 44th birthday recently, thereby deciding to age and graduating from (rather than to) *The Last Laugh Foundation*. So it was interesting to discover that the *March EquinoX* was the original Fools Day before the date was adjusted, so he was obviously just an usurper anyway. As the cusp of the beginning and end of the astrological cycle, this date makes more sense in relation to **The Fool** of the Tarot (Trump 0 at either end of the Major Arcana), who rides the Wheel of Fate like some kind of Oroboric Unicycle but is not bound to its cycles.

It was interesting to realise too -upon occasion of the beginning of the recurrence of Kestral Znox's (another Choronzon-Machine co-creator) 33.3rd birthday, that Jesus is also this age. Mr ZNox pointed out that Jesus was 33 when he died -a fact (?) I had hitherto been unaware of- and I then realised that his resurrection at Easter is one-third of a year (4 months) after his Christmas birthday, so it seems we are not the first to exploit this aspect of Eternity within the constricting coils of TimEmiT...

Nine (three threes) to the Norse seemed to imply eternity also, and has etymological similarities to names for none, naught or Zero. It was for Nine days that Odin hung upon the World Tree, after which He discovered the runes which I suspect were woven by the Three at the base of the Tree, those arachnean Norns of Time and Fate.

So it all goes back (and forth) to the **Three**, feminine number supreme. On the Tree of Life 3 is the number of the Sephira *Binah*, the Great Black Sea and the Great Black Mother; also considered the origin point of Time in Qabalistic cosmology, and correlating with the planet Saturn.

3 represents the transcendence of duality -when there are two opposing polarities considered, three arises as a third from their conjunction, ever opening our reality to new potential -it is the Gateway, the realm of birth.

She who is Three -the **Moirae** or **Three Fates** of Greek myth, **Three Norns** to the Norse- and yet One. Probably the oldest known 'triformed' Goddess is **Hekate Triformis**, She who appears as having six arms and two legs in ancient reliefs (therefore eight limbs, arachnean) and sometimes three faces and presides over the transition from life unto death -the cyclicity that is the very essence of time.

That as 3-in-1 She has eight limbs is not the only Arachnean element of the Goddess of the Wheel: The Three Fates are the spinner, weaver and cutter of life's thread. So we have the Goddess as Spider, birthing and devouring. Parallel in the East is the Great Black Goddess of Time, also 8-limbed (though of a singular fearsome visage) : Maha **Kali**.

We are spun upon the Wheel of Fate, our destinies interwoven with those of others in the intricate tapestry of life, and we die when She snips our line. No wonder men love and often fear the awesome power of Woman, She who holds the keys (and Is the Gate) to birth and thus also to death...

Methinks - or rather mefeels- 2013 was the year of the Spider, spiralling us back into lunar consciousness.

Post December 2012, The linear march of progress continues unabated- or does it? Nothing happened?

Nothing happened. Nothing all-ways happens, that is Her play. She the great dark void from which we spring, and to which we ever reTurn...

Feel Her great web, the matrix of life, and its myriad interconnections…

In the Web of Fate different timelines converge, alternate strands of possibility divide and branch out. Is our 'Fate' or destiny the path we have allotted, or do we choose it, forge it with our Will?

A common question, but when one discovers **True Will**, which is the Will of Self in accord and flow with the Will of the Universe, there ceases to become any real difference between the individual Will and its macrocosmic reflection in the concept of 'Fate'.

Thus the decisions and paths we 'choose' are actually precisely in accord with, in fact determine, our 'destiny'. It is a subtle concept difficult to explain with words, but an unmistakeable understanding when experienced. I hope my attempts at resolving the apparent paradox of the fate/will dichotomy herein can at least point the way towards this kind of self-realisation.

Finding True Will is one of (if not 'the') major goals of Magick, being the result of the operation named *'The Knowledge and Conversation of the Holy Guardian Angel'* by Abramelin the Mage.

There are plenty of rites and suggestions for how to contact this 'higher self', from Aleister Crowley's elaborate **'Liber Samekh'** (http://mysteria.com/liber/L_800.txt) to the more simplified (but no less effective for those prepared to be that direct) Holy Guardian Angel ritual in the Level 6 section of Nema's **'Maat Magick'** book *(Samuel Weiser, 1980)* - so I will not add to this source material -for ultimately it is a personal journey anyway and there are already rites aplenty to set the ball rolling for those who wish to do it that way. There are also indications in my own **'Liber Pennae-Ultim-Atum'** and Commentary *(www.horusmaatlodge.com/LPUC.htm)* as to the nature of True Will and its discovery. Suffice it to say here that 'Will' and 'Fate' are but two more apparent polarities which may be United within the self in the Great Work of the *Alchymic Marriage*, and that 'True Will' is their union.

'For pure will, unassuaged of purpose, delivered from the lust of result, is every way perfect'

–A. Crowley, Liber Al vel Legis: 1, 44.

25

The origin of the word 'Fate' relates to the concept of Time as a web. For the 'Three Fates' of Greek mythology were once One, and She who is Three has many arms - the ancient Spider Goddess who spins, weaves and cuts the spiral web of fate and time.

The Three Fates are the primary Ancient Greek source of the neo-pagan archetype of the Triple Goddess. Only recently considered as maiden, mother and crone, the trinity are usually representative of the three lunar phases of waxing, full and waning, as The Fates in their roles as **Clotho** the Spinner, **Lachesis** the Weaver, and **Atropos** the Cutter. These roles suggest the metaphor of time as a tapestry, and their cyclical nature in relation to the moon and reflective menstrual cycles suggest the wheel or circle. So a circular or spiralling weaving is implicit -the spider-web of time on its circular (and rotating) loom of Fate-

ARCANA X (10) The Wheel of Fortune:

The cycles of existence, the Wheel of ROTA/TARO from Arcana 0 The Fool to 0 The Fool. Although cyclical, it is more akin to layers of a progressive spiral than a single circle –thus the spiraling web of Fate within the Wheel. Here the Ten Spokes of Tradition (The ten Sephiroth of the Qabala) are replaced with the ChAOSphere, to demonstrate the shifting nature of Time, Fate and Will according to perception.

The elemental pentagram (fire, water, air, earth, and spirit) is still the foundation beneath. These five arms united with the eight spokes of the sphere/wheel (also implying the eight sabbats of the witches' year, the eight directions, etc) together make the thirteen lunar cycles of a year.

Presiding over these lunar cycles are the Three Fates or Moirae, spinner weaver and cutter or waxing, full and waning moon at the top of the image. The crone's scythe is the waning moon even as the lower rim of the Wheel is the waxing moon. The spinner is the Priestess, presiding over the wheel - and also the **SphinX**, representing one of the three *Gunas* or states of being in the Hindu cosmology: the state of *Sattvas* (enlightenment, calm) at the top of the Wheel, the state attained from that of Activity or *Rajas*, as represented ascending on the left of the Wheel by **Hermanubis** (an alchymical hybrid of the Hermes, Anubis and Hanuman). However the calm state of Sattvas leads back to *Tamas* –inertia and sloth– represented by the crocodilian **Typhon** descending on the right of the Wheel.

This Wheel of time at the CrossXroads (with the World/Universe trump in Ra'en's LemniscAte spread) of the Major Arcana is depicted as a visual paradox to demonstrate the mutability of time:

X

The 3-dimensional illusion of the central ChaoSphere flattens to the 2-dimensional rim, OroBorous the serpent which eats its own tail around the periphery of the web of Fate. The intersection of these 2D and 3D realms offers a Gateway to Arcana 23 – outside the circles of time. The Frog or Inter-dimensional Voltiguer leaps off the Wheel. (The frog is a symbol of Hekate, thus the way off the wheel is implicit within the lunar loom itself, via the path of blood or dark moon.

-from Orryelle's **Book of KAOS Tarot**

We will be looking closer at the Three Fates or Moirae, but first let's examine the archetype that the first of the Three has been conflated with upon this TaRota Wheel of Fortune (Arcana X) : The **Sphinx**, central to the image. She forms a trinity with the other two Fates horizontally above the Wheel, and another trinity 'vertically' (in 2-dimensional representation, though really both trinities are cyclical) with the other two figures (HermAnubis and Typhon) representing the Hindu Gunas upon the Wheel.

The composite creature here depicted is the Ancient Greek Sphinx (*'Sphinga'* in Greek), a feminine figure of mystery and destiny whose origins lie -as with many of the Greek archetypes- in nearby Ancient Egypt.

There the Sphinx was usually depicted as male, at least in the iconography remaining today. However there are indications that mythically the Sphinx was originally a creature of more ambiguous gender in the earlier dynasties of Egypt. S/He remains a composite of human and beast, and forms of this mythic creature also existed and continue to exist in the mythic iconography of Persia, Babylon (Sumeria), and even (to my surprise on a visit there) India.

With Hir composite nature the Sphinx has come to represent the fixed signs of the Western astrological zodiac (which also primarily came from or at least via Ancient Greece): - Aquarius the fixed sign of the element of air, represented by hir human aspects; Scorpio the fixed sign of water as represented by hir eagle wings (in early zodiacs the eagle was used rather than the scorpion); Taurus the fixed sign of earth as represented by hir bull's hoofs in Persian, Babylonian and some Indian versions, or by a snake for a tail; and Leo the fixed sign of fire represented by hir leonine body.

As such a composite, s/he is known as the **Tetramorph** -tetra being Latin for four- and as well as the four elements, four magickal powers of *'To Know, To Will, To Dare and To Be Silent'* are associated with Hir in western esotericism. The fifth quintessential power representing spirit or the element of ether is the combination of all of these. However I have come to realise this is really only half the picture, as 'To be Silent' is the negative reflex of the equally important (at the appropriate times) 'To Speak.' As revealed to me in **'The Book of Going Back by Night'** -an inspired writing channeled from the Egyptian double-sphinx **HruMachis**- the four negative powers are, *'To Know Not, To Will Not, To Dare Not, and To be Silent'* and are just as vital as, *'To Know, To Will, To Dare and To Speak'* :

>The Powers of the SphinX
>Are Double
>Each containing its opposite
>Perhaps I was never here at all
>Can you hear with your deaf ears
>My silent call
>For I am Mystery
>And as much as I am
>So I am Not
>
>One must Know when to Dare Not
>Lest the bones of the Fool
>Be found at the bottom of my cliff
>
>To Will is a Power,
>But to Will Not
>Is of equal import
>Lest One be strangled
>By the excesses of one's desires
>And All should come to Nought
>
>To Know is a Power
>But to Know Not
>Allows the Bliss of discovery
>The Fool's rapture unbound
>In finding strange fruit
>Fallen 'pon the ground
>
>Can you Know Not?
>Allow yourself to avoid definition
>For if you Know Not
>You need not contain everything in separate partitions
>For Nuit needs not
>All-ways Division

Speech is a Power
Whether to curse or to bless –Fate's indemnity!
The Power of the Word Made Flesh
And so you shape your identity
But in Silence...

May you Know Not yourself

-from **"The Book of Going Back by Night'**
by Orryelle (Twilight Productions 2010, iNSPiRALink. 2013)

Each negative as well as positive power may be contemplated for their value, but as an example consider now how many people you know who have strong Will power but very little Will Not power!

Perhaps the inclusion of the final negative, 'To be Silent' in the existing axiom is a clue to the (non)existence of these negative (as in absence, not morally) powers. If so, it seems the timemit -if the transmission from Hrumachis is any indication- to break the silence about this and speak or at least write of them.

So Who is this **HruMachis**? S/He is the God of the Double Horizon in Ancient Egypt, the lion-form of solar Horus as the setting and rising sun, called in the Ancient Egyptian **'Book of Coming Forth by Day'** (translated by Wallis Budge under the less accurate title, 'The Egyptian Book of the Dead') Ra-Herakhty, whose hieroglyph is quite obviously the Sphinx (an alternate glyph for Hrumachis shows a sun disc breaking the horizon).

There is a theory that the Great Sphinx (monolith) at Giza is one of a pair, that the other which faced the opposite direction has long ago been buried or crumbled to dust. This makes sense to me as Hrumachis is traditionally the Lord of the Two Horizons, of the rising and the setting sun, and I wonder also if this second Sphinx was depicted as feminine, and the Greeks' apparent reassignment of the creature's gender resulted from a memory or secret encodement of this? For with all the other polarities the deity represented, male/female is likely to have been an effective way to symbolise this.

TimE, Fate and Spider Magic

Composite of Egyptian SphinX & Greek Sphinx collaged together from my 2 variant Strength/Lust Tarot cards. (see SilkMilk MagiZain s p o o (# 3)

Then again, perhaps this second Sphinx never existed on the physical plane, since She is an absence rather than a presence as the negative powers, a part of the unrecorded mystery that parallels in the akashic records the written his-story of mankind. This deity of absence will be considered further when we meet the shadowy Fourth Fate of the dark moon.

Another reason I consider there to be a dual and feminine aspect to the Egyptian as well as Greek Sphinx is due to its origin in the Egyptian Double Lion **Aker**, glyphed by two lion heads facing opposite directions on either side of the sun disc, and apparently joined (although in fairly abstracted form) at the waist or hips. This figure comes from two separate -yet still reflective/double- lions known as *Sef* and *Tuau*.

Here the common origin of the concepts of Time and of Fate becomes evident, for their names mean 'Yesterday' and 'Tomorrow'. Most translations and/or interpretations give them as Yesterday and Today, but I figure the former makes more sense in that they are looking to the far right and the far left (compare the Indian flag with this same image of two lions facing left and right, above a wheel, but with a third lion in the middle facing directly forwards). It seems the Egyptians related the spatial landscape of the two horizons to the concept of timemit, which makes sense considering that the sun and moon which rise and set there are indeed markers of cyclicity.

The Ancient Egyptian conception of Time was obviously quite different from ours anyway, as they had(/have/shall have) a Word **'Ink'** which means(/meant/shall mean) not only, 'is' but also 'was' and 'shall be'. This Word is beyond the usual confines of tense and was usually employed in reference to the Gods, who its seems had/have/shall have their places in eternity. That this grammatical ambiguity was also sometimes applied to pharaohs affirms the Ancient Egyptian belief that humankind can also aspire to immortality and divinity, that we are stars in the body of *Nuit* (Mother of the Universe), our potential which is guiding us towards our ultimate becoming.

The Ancient Egyptian hieroglyph for Eternity is three interwoven loops, like a combination of the lemniscate (infinity sign) and the serpentine caduceus.

Let us trace this double-lion imagery back even further to its very source in the first male and female deities of the entire Egyptian pantheon, **Tefnut** and **Shu**, who split from or were created by the herm-aphroditic **Atum** masturbating in the void. For Tefnut is usually depicted lion-headed, and Shu as Her polar twin has also been considered of leonine aspect in some versions of the diverse Egyptian mythological streams.

That timemit -later represented by the Lions of Yesterday and Tomorrow, then the double-lion Aker, then the Sphinx of the double horizon HruMachis- has its origins in the first male and female beings consolidates its intrinsic relationship with space (which was born from Tefnut and Shu as Nuit and Geb, the sky/space and the earth). For the creation of form from the splitting of the monad into duality (and further divisions therefrom) can only occur within the con-texte (from Latin: with weaving) of time's progression. The continuous cycles of birth and death (on a cosmic as well as microcosmic scale, i.e. change itself) are interwoven with form, as the warp and the weft of the tapestry of existence in the loom of Fate.

Tefnut is revealed in some Egyptian texts as another form or name of **Mayet**, the 'World Order', which is the earliest form of the Goddess **Maat**, the neter or principle of Truth and Measure. With Her twin Shu being a God of sky and air, we can see the most ancient source of the double current of Horus and Maat. That these energies are returning in our own Aeon/Age (as will be elaborated later) is perhaps an indication of reTurn to that source with the realignment of the Earth and our Sun's ecliptic with the galactic centre (peaking at the December Solstice 2012, but actively having effect for at least a few decades either side of this apex when viewed from an Aeonic perspective).

HruMachis is a form of **Horus**, Heru or Hru (Egyptian for 'day'), and I believe -as the name Hru-Ma-chis implies- also of Maat or Ma ('darkness') the dark, invisible or negative powers. The name Horus bears a marked resemblance to our English word hours, which as the Sun God travelling through the sky (the 'House of Hoor') is indeed a marker of such Measure or Maat, as we see Hoor's (the original name of Horus) eyes (the sun and the moon) rise on the Hoor-eyes-on.

The word hours also purportedly comes from the '*Horae*', from which we also garnered the word whore as they were the 'ladies of the night'. They were also the 'ladies of the hour' and Their dance (a wild cavorting ride akin to the sabbatic Wild Hunt of the Norse and Celtic) is the play of time, as aspects or segments of the Egyptian Goddess of pleasure and sexuality, **Hathor** or Het-Hoor, whose name means 'House of Horus' (and house of the hours?). The association with prostitution is most likely a later overlay from patriarchal views of liberated female sexuality as threatening.

Though Hathor -an ancient figure with origins in Syria- is quite well known, little is usually said or written of the *Seven Hathors*, who seem to be the Egyptian deification of Fate. Even as the singular Hathor was a Goddess of the Sky and the Stars, the seven represented the seven planets then known, and thus presided over the destiny of mortals. For the Ancient Egyptians believed that our fate was linked to the movements of the stars and the planets, an idea that has remained with us as Astrology. However the major difference (though one being bridged in some modern practises of soul-centred astrology with its more active rather than passive apprehension of destiny) is that the Egyptians believed the Stars were Gods, and that mortals could become Gods and/as stars in the firmament. So to them we were not just at the whim of fate or divinity, but could actively partake in its unveiling. Or as Aleister Crowley (who drew heavily from such Ancient Egyptian concepts) so succinctly stated, *'Every Man and Woman is a Star.'*

Re-Turning now to Her Wheel - the Greek Sphinx is also a figure of Fate, for Her primary appearance in Classical Greek mythology is as the beast who haunted the roads outside Thebes, asking riddles of passersby and devouring them if they failed to answer correctly.

As such She was a guardian of the Cross-roads, and a Gatekeeper b e t w e e n not only physical places but of the realms of life and death, a guardian of time. The Wheel trump is the X-roads of the tarot's major arcana when spread in a lemniscate (infinity symbol) pattern. Fate can indeed devour one, and this seems to be what ultimately happened to the tragic anti-hero **Oedipus** who apparently solved Her riddle, but certainly didn't escape a more abstracted Fate's clutches even if he did pass its physical representative.

The Sphinx's question was:

'What has one voice, yet walks on four legs in the morning, two in the afternoon and three in the evening?'

The answer Oedipus gave was, 'Man', who crawls in infancy, walks in adulthood and with the aid of a cane in old age. That this entire span of time was reduced to a single metaphorical day is interesting in relation to the original Egyptian Sphinx, whose setting and rising sun on the horizon were also referential to greater cycles they echoed in the fractal nature of time- of days and seasons and aeons.

So Oedipus unlike others before him managed to glimpse the bigger picture, and yet he failed to then apply this broader view back to the microcosm, as perhaps an even truer answer for him to give would have been, 'Myself'. Nevertheless, he ended up a victim of the rather tragic Fate that had been prophesied for him, and as a result ended up blind and thus ironically hobbling with a cane prematurely.

It was just after passing the Sphinx, who apparently leapt to Her death when he guessed Her riddle -though one does wonder about this method of suicide for a winged creature- that Oedipus met King Laius in his Chariot (another wheeled archetype from the Tarot) whom he killed without knowing it was his father, thus beginning to fulfil his prophesied fate. He met Laius at a place 'where three roads meet'. This is significant in that the triple crossroads is the traditional Greek sacred place of the Goddess Hekate, who was also a rather fateful deity and in Her triple aspect could be considered a composite form of the Moirae or Fates (whose three forms Her crossroads diverge into). She is also a guardian of the Underworld, to which Laius now crossed over.

So the Greek Sphinx is the harbinger of feminine mystery (represented with riddles), but also of free Will, for she is the guardian of the Crossroads which also presents choices, options of different paths or potentials to take along the strands of Her web...

Considering that our word 'Fate' comes from the Ancient Greeks, it is hardly surprising that we often have a negative view of the concept in the modern West, thus the tendency to view the idea as ancient superstition and something we are beyond even considering with the dominance of the rational mind.

The Ancient Greek view of Fate was often quite nihilistic. The great Tragedies of Fate their playwrights such as Sophocles wrote propagated not only an idea of it being unavoidable, but also that intense misfortune is often a part of this inevitability, whether you deserve it or not. Fate in such myths seems to have little moral inclination, but rather a pre-ordained sense of doom:

> 'The Power of fate is a wonder,
> dark, terrible wonder
> neither wealth nor armies
> towered walls nor ships
> black hulls lashed by the salt
> can save us from that force.'

- (Sophocles, **Antigone**, Robert Fagles translation, Penguin Classics).

The character of Oedipus is a particularly striking example, and one that continues to affect readers and theatre-goers to this day, for it portrays powerfully the classic struggle of 'Fate versus Free Will'. For the two concepts seem at first irreconcilable on some level: if there is some over-ruling power determining our circumstances, how can we ever really be free, and if we are free to exercise our will, how can there be pre-determined Fate beyond this?

And yet, there is a third possibility we will be exploring that reconciles this paradox in our co-weaving of our destiny...

Ancient Greece was very religious and this seems to relate intrinsically to their concept of Fate. Plays such as those by Sophocles and Euripides were seen by massive crowds in amphitheatres designed to seat 30,000 during festivals, and were the very ritualistic origin of theatre itself. They seem designed to remind the population of a city-state such as Athens that the Gods must be worshipped, that the divine powers must be acknowledged.

Lycurgus in Euripides' **'Bacchae'** is doomed because he fails to acknowledge the new God Dionysos. And yet even the Gods were ultimately at the whim of the Three Fates, who were considered even beyond Their ordinance as deifications of destiny, chance and even whim itself. Yet given even semi-abstract form in this way, chance becomes somehow more meaningful, as if there is a pattern or a soul (three souls?) behind even this caprice, an order inherent in chaos.

Although characters such as Oedipus seem to have done nothing 'wrong' in terms of intention, they suffer because it is their Fate to do so, they err tragically through ignorance. But this to me, is perhaps the whole point: That the key to co-weaving our fate is to recognise it, to tune into our destiny with enough conscious attention that we are aligning ourselves with universal will as our own True Will. So while Oedipus seems consciously unaware of what he has done (killed his father and married his mother), there are clues aplenty dropped. While these seem more for the audience -so that they grasp the inevitability of it all before he does and await his own dreadful unravellings- one does begin to wonder how much he is in self-denial. Many things he says, as well as being brilliant theatrical devices for the audience's sense of expectation, seem to indicate that on some deeper subconscious level Oedipus knows exactly what it going on. It gets to a point where he can no longer avoid the dread possibility he is confronted with, and so he deliberately sets out to unveil the mystery of his birth, and once doing so unravels it all quite quickly. When he has to admit he has indeed -despite his and his parents' attempts since his birth to avoid it- fulfilled the terrible prophecy given them by the Delphic Oracle, he blinds himself with the cloak-pins of his freshly-hung mother and lover Jocasta. He cries

out after this extreme act that he has already been blind for so long. Indeed, and now that he has finally become self-aware, he expresses his remorse in this powerful symbolic act which, as opposed to the suicide he first contemplates, seems to be his first true act of conscious free will:

> '...the hand that struck my eyes was mine, mine alone ⁄no one else⁄ I did it all myself!'
>
> -Sophocles, **Oedipus the King** (Robert Fagles translation, Penguin Classics)

Thus once he becomes conscious of his destiny, he has more control of its course- although a little late perhaps! What I wondered is whether if he had not tried to escape his predicted destiny, things would have worked out differently? For it was the very actions of trying to avoid his terrible fate that led him right into it, like some awful trap set by the Gods: his parents sent him away so he would not fulfil the omens of doom given by the Delphic Oracle, and so he knew not that they were his parents when he met them in later life. If he had, would he have still done these things, with the forewarning the prophecy offered? For what is the use of divination, if it gives us no opportunity to alter the paths of potential we are shown?

It is most fortunate, then, that no form of divination (e.g. Tarot, I Ching, astrology) I know of is as infallible and specific as the Delphic Oracle was reputed to be in the plays and myths of Ancient Greece! Such divinatory tools may show us the most likely possibilities, yes, and bring subconscious strata to conscious attention, but even the act of considering where we are going may alter it, and there are specific techniques for using such mediums to then consciously re-route these paths if we are dissatisfied with their predicted course. Such methods -particularly of using Tarot as a tool for Conjuration as well as for (and leading on from) Divination, I have explored in group workshops as well as privately, and will elucidate (with other such practical applications of the ideas seeded here) beyond **THE THIRD GATE**...

There are many paradoxes here inherent: If Oedipus or his parents had embraced his destiny rather than try to escape it, would it have been avoided? And if so, how would it have then been his destiny? -as the Delphic Oracle was purported to always be accurate. Perhaps the Gods or the very Fates knew he and his parents would react in this way to the oracle, otherwise they would have forecast via its medium differently? So it is almost as if Oedipus and his parents created his Fate by their very apprehension of it. That it is his very belief in Fate that drives him subconsciously to fulfil it.

So too may we apprehend fate -though in a more positive and less fearful manner than Oedipus and Jocasta- and thus align it with our Will. Before he realises it was his father, King Laius' killer (having met him as a stranger on the road, significantly at a place where three roads meet),

Oedipus cries curses upon the murderer of Laius. The audience know he is cursing himself (does he know also on some deeper level, already subconsciously guilty about his crime?) and cringe that he is bringing doom upon his own head. So even here, while it is a tragedy in his case, the mortal is co-weaving his own fate with the Gods.

While revising this book for the second edition (**iNSPiRALink. MultiMedia Press** 2006), I was also editing **Metamorphic Ritual Theatre Company**'s tarot ritual opera **'The Choronzon Machine'** (DVD from **iNSPiRALink. Multimedia Press** '06). Writing this new section of the book, in my simultaneous video editing I arrived at the scene where the Fool becomes the Magician and decides,

'I'm going to exert my Will, and Take Destiny into my own hands'.

As his natural reflective adversary (and literal contrary due to his physical posture) Choronzon as the Hanged Man hung upon the Tree of Life machine, retorts (yet thus affirms):

'Yes, it is your Destiny to do so.'

With all its paradoxes Fate is difficult to understand with the rational mind, which is why it is often in the realm of the Arts rather than science that it is delved into most deeply -science attempts to solve problems and give answers, where art, poetry and magick may just revel in the strange majesty of Mystery.

So it was that the concept of Fate was largely dismissed with the advent of scientific materialism and the Age of Reason. Humankind began to have a predisposition that all could (or at least should!) be solved and explained rationally, that the universe operated on specific scientific laws being progressively discovered, and that thus there are neither random patterns nor Gods or mystical forces that ordain our lives, only determinable natural laws. It is likely that the philosophical and progressive civilisation of the late Classical (patriarchal and rationalist) Ancient Greeks contained the first stirrings of this arrogant attitude, so that playwrights such as Sophocles were called to remind the populace of the prevalence of the Gods.

But now things seem to be coming full circle once more as we move into the realms of quantum physics and chaos science: for we find that even reason-able science is discovering the patterns of the universe are less predictable than the initial birth of the scientific revolution had us first believe. Some of the patterns unveiled in the very fabric of our reality seem to be devoid of order or intention, chaos and apparent randomness intrinsic in the universe.

And so, seeking new spiritual paths as well as reviving ancient pantheisms in an attempt to reinstil meaning into our divinity-divested existences, again we investigate the idea of Fate, of some outside force steering the course of our lives.

Now, however, we can look at things from the different paradigms we have collectively moved through, as well as through different socio-cultural lenses, to integrate these concepts into a more contemporary understanding that is simultaneously scientific and spiritual, material and mystical.

Psychological masters such as Carl Jung and Joseph Campbell have shown us that what the ancients saw as outside themselves can also be viewed as existing within our own psyches, that the Gods and myths are potent symbols for bringing vital strata from our deep minds to conscious attention. So we can look at it differently now in terms of divinity within as well as without. Yes, we may seem at times to be 'controlled' by external energies, by Gods or The Fates, yet we perhaps collectively co-created them with invested belief. We can embrace our own inherent divinity and recognise our own subconscious and superconscious ('higher self') part in weaving our destinies, not only with those others we co-exist with, but also with our perceptions and our beliefs. To bring this to awareness allows us to dance the warp and the weft of the weave of wyrd with relish, rather than slink in the shadow of an omnipotent and thus ominous fate of which we have no control.

Drawing his inspiration from Ancient Egyptian concepts of the God-self embodied, Aleister Crowley has reminded us that, *'Every Man and Woman is a Star'* and we may reclaim our divine heritage, remembering it is our own subconscious and super-conscious True Will -individually and collectively- that steers the course of our lives as reflected in the macrocosmic stellar web above, the arched and shimmering spangled vault of the body of our Lady Nuit.

Oedipus' act of blinding himself is symbolically significant. *'Blind Fate'* is a well-known term, but it is really only blind on the outer, i.e. conscious level. It is perhaps because of this that it is able to see more deeply in the mythic realms of the subconscious. Oedipus is expressing that he wants to see the truth within, to know his full being without distraction by the outer forms of the extant world. Earlier in Sophocles' play, he taunts **Tiresias** for his blindness when this blind Seer (note the significance of the title itself!) suggests Oedipus is himself the murderer he seeks. But Tiresias' inner sight proves accurate again and again, and Oedipus in the end realises he has been blinder with his two eyes than Tiresias with his 'blind' third-eye awareness in a dark world.

So the whole fable is ultimately an entreaty to 'know thyself' beyond just the outer tapestry of Maya ('illusion'), to turn the perceptions (symbolised here with vision, usually the dominant human perception-sense) in as well as out.

A separate yet entwined Greek myth (told in verse in Ovid's poignant, **'Metamorphoses'**) relates a significant earlier tale of Tiresias, from before he became blind. He came across a pair of

mating snakes, and struck them with his staff. As a result of this magical act he turned into a woman for seven (the number of Venus/Aphrodite) years, after which time he again came across coupling serpents, struck them and returned to masculine form. The reflective symbolism of this is clear, for the **Caduceus** staff of Greek Messenger God **Hermes** is entwined by serpents, who mirror each other in their symmetrical multiple crossing of the central staff, representing the convergence and separation of polarities in much the same way as the Hindus conceive of the male and female *Ida and Pingala* (solar and lunar) nadis or energy-channels of serpentine kundalini as crossing the spine (staff) in their ascent of the central sushumna channel. So striking the coupling serpents with his staff, Tiresias became a reflection of his former self - polarising his masculine form- then later 'crossed over' once more to return to his former form. Similarly Hermes Hirself, the bearer of the Caduceus staff as messenger between the worlds of mortals and of Gods (the passage from base to crown chakra of the kundalini?) -was often considered androgynous or of ambiguous gender.

A personal reflection of this tale (mirrors of mirrorsrorrim fo srorrim) reveals how ancient myths and archetypes may seep into our individual lives:

Many years ago I myself saw two large snakes mating -and they do indeed coil about each other spectacularly in much the same manner as upon the classic image of the Caduceus -which has been adopted as primary symbol by the medical fraternity as medicine and magic were once unseparated, even as the arts and sciences themselves were not so divided. The coupling serpents seemed initially unperturbed by the continuing observance of myself and a few others. However once I retrieved a camera (another, modern kind of mirror) and pointed it at the snakes they immediately split from each other and fled.

Around seven (I am not sure exactly which year I saw the coupling snakes) years later I took oestrogen (the primary female hormone) for nine moonths -in combination with mantra, invocation and intention- to womanifest my anima (woman within) in

HermAphroditic reification. It was only years after my resultant alchymic self-marriage that the significance even struck me (consciously) of the incident with the coupling snakes in relation to this progression and the tale of Tiresias.

In the last edition of this book, I expressed my intention to rewrite the divine play of **Oedipus**, with him somehow taking fate into his own hands and altering its course. Why? How could I have the sheer audacity to evenattempt to re-work one of the most powerful Tragedies ever in the history of theatre and literature!?

Well I did find it a most daunting prospect -the great work of satisfactorily altering an undoubted masterpiece- what with the sheer weight of the Ages I would be dealing with (and reshuffling) - But all the more reason to alter this classic and its huge impact on western perceptions. For the later Greek playwrights such as Sophocles were heralds of an encroaching patriarchy, and the Great Goddess of mystery and intuition, of deep knowing (rather than mere mental gymnastics) represented therein by the Sphinx, must be reinstalled upon Her pedestal. But how could I rewrite such a perfectly crafted tale without contrivance?

Because I had to! I felt it was my Destiny to do so...

I did not do so lightly, however, feeling a visit to the Delphic Oracle in Greece a vital part of the process. There is no embodied Pythia there anymore -the Pythia or Pythoness being the serpent-inspired (and serpent-wreathed in imagery of her) oracular priestess who sat on a three-legged stool over the fumes emitting from a c r ac k in the earth, transmitting the prophecies of Apollo. At least there wasn't until I went there with the aptly-name *Giselle Sybil*, co-writer of the Sphinx scene in my version of **Oedipus Tyrannos**- who became the Pythia for me in our ritual at Delphi, channelling the Oracle. In the main site we were harassed by a christian guard -it is an unfortunate and ironic aspect of modern Greece that the Church and State are entwined to the extent that such people caretake the temples of the Ancient Gods as if they were mere museums- who

wanted to call the police on us for burning laurel leaves at the Shrine of Ge/Gaia. This lies beneath the later Temple of Apollo, and bees buzzed out from cracks in the foundation stones. To evade the guard who began to tail us around the site, we ran off to the back of the site and exited a back way, thus emerging near the pure Castellian Spring where initiates once ritually bathed before consulting the oracle. This we also did, then continued to explore the territory behind it, entering a narrow passageway between walls of rock which were a beautiful dusty pink enhanced further by the encroaching hues of dusk. Intuitively we searched for the cra ck in the earth which the pythia/sybil's tripod had once straddled, having failed to find it in the main site. Finding a place where there seemed to be a lot of concrete filling in what may have once been a deep crevice, we then looked up and were stunned to see where the cliff-walls met above us -their shape now more evident as they became silhouetted agains the darkening sky- a labia-like aperture above. Perhaps we were actually in the cr ack the tripod once crossed?

And so we proceeded therein with our ritual, calling forth the Ancient Ones to aid us in our deepening gnosis.
As above, so below. Through honey-laced lips She uttered the sibilant ssounds to unravels Fate's changing tides.
Some of this was personal but I also invoked Oedipus within our rite, and from the oracle to him I found the first threads of how to re-weave his traditional tale for a new aeon...

Chorus:

Oedipus know
That you are the Pythia
Your own Oracle
Even as the Sphinx has mirrored you
So does the Pythonesss
It is not the voice of Apollo
That speaks through her
But the secret self

She is the deep mind projected
To be seen and apprehended
The soul's own inner wealth unveiled
What you know but do not know you know
So run not from your destiny
Become it wilfully

-From 'Oedipus Tyrannos' by Orryelle 2008.

I called my new version of the Greek Classic, 'Oedipus Tyrannos', reverting to the original Ancient Greek name rather than the Latin 'Oedipus Rex' theatre-goers are familiar with. The main reason for this is probably the same as why English versions of the play have usually preferred Rex: Tyrannos now suggests a tyrant, our word derived from Tyrannos, which originally just meant king or ruler (like Rex). But I wanted the implication of tyranny, since as one who loses self-knowledge while ordering others about, Oedipus indeed fulfilled this role.

Upon the idea of becoming one's own pythoness -in my own tapping into the serpentine and intuitive feminine aspect of being, activated more fully perhaps when I struck at coupling serpents with a single lens- I add another layer of mythic history or mystery:

Tiresias, the original serpent-striker, was later called to solve -with his knowledge from direct experience- a disagreement between Zeus and Hera over whether men or women receive more pleasure from sex. His opinion was women, and as a result of expressing this- which in turn was a result of his experience of the mirrorworldsdlrowrorrim- that Tiresias was cursed to physical blindness by a vengeful Hera, and then redeemed or compensated with 'second sight' (inner vision of prophecy) by Zeus.

Tiresias to Oedipus:

Though I answered truly from my own experience
-I of all people might know!-
Hera struck me blind for my insult by in-sight!
The truth hurts indeed, it seems –what a blow!
And jealous gods confer their pain to others

Yet Zeus blessed me with the gift of prophecy, inner Vision
And so I know still, I see still, I feel still
The serpents twined within
How they writhe and polarize
Betwixt the bones, beneath the skin

And so I see too, their reflection in you
Where the male snake is strong and resplendent
But the feminine serpent faint, untended
No balance, a staff of will,
With no chalice
For it to fill and fulfil

(Orryelle, Oedipus Tyrannos 2008)

It seems indeed that as he earlier advised to his Regent proud, Tiresias '..may be blind, but I can
See far more than thee, Oedipus'.

For Tyrannos was unaware of his subconscious and his intuition, so afraid to confront his own destiny and its awful implications that did naught but tighten the strands of fate from which he struggled to escape, just like an insect caught in a spider's web.

In my new version of the play, the actual events remain mostly the same- for Fate is truly the harsh and even capricious mistress of Circumstance, She is that which is inevitable. It is an at times seemingly unfortunate aspect of mortal existence that some things just seem to Happen, whether we like them or not. It is our perception and reaction to these prevailing circumstances, however, which allows the simultaneous exertion of our free Will, and thus our co-weaving of Destiny's intricate and never-shifting but ever-shimmering tapestry, where the play of light may make it appear different at different times though its weave remain essentially unchanged.

And so the first real change in my version of Oedipus Tyrannos is at the point where he actually physically blinded himself in the original play. I real-eyesed that this was symbolic of his awakened perception, the one thing that he did have control of. Over his mother-lover Jocasta's body, he goes to stab out his eyes as in Sophocles' version, but this time he stops at the last moment, and casts her cloak-pin away:

'...No! I Will stay my hand
It seems I had some bizarre subconscious need –some Will of Truth –or call it fate then!
to love my Mother in the flesh –so blind was I, only by this could I see
How I had failed to love my Greater Mother –Mystery Herself, Destiny
So when I slew the Sphinx I had to manifest this Terror to Wake me to realization.

But now that I have seen
At last how blind I've been
 –at least I don't have to do this literally!
I need not be as Tiresias,
the sacrifice is made already –he had no choice!
Why should I abuse mine?
Now that my inner eye has opened too
 ...I have seen my fate, and now I shall also
See it through!

> *For this is my Will now*
> *It is no circumstance that leads me to this act of despair*
> *Only to its possibility -I take this chance!*
> *I have control of my vision*
> *My perception is my only Will that is Truly free'*

How my new version of Oedipus Tyrannos turned out, and the startling and rather horrendous (but ultimately beneficial) effects its enactment as ritual theatre had on my own life and destiny, shall be expressed beyond **THE SECOND GATE**, as this first section maintains the intention of primarily delving into the past and HirStory of Time and Fate rather than current evolutions thereof. For such artifices may aid a writer -and more importantly you, dear readers- in organisation of the themes and memes expressed…

In the meantime (time being so mean in its Saturnian limitations), the blindness of Oedipus and Tiresias leads us (the Blind leading to the Blind) to another significant myth of Fate, that of the Norse God **Odin**, hung upon The **World Tree.** For He too sacrificed (voluntarily, with conscious Free Will) outer sight for inner vision, after His ordeal of hanging for Nine days and Nine nights upon the World Tree:

> *'I sacrifice outer sight for inner vision*
> *My view is inverted, I stare within*
> *Growing new eyes, under the skin*
> *For nine days and nine nights*
> *I have hung from the World Tree*
> *And I with my one eye I see*
> *The symbols woven in the webs*
> *In the Well above their secrets flow*
> *And ebb in the branches below'*

-from **'Le Pendu'** *by Orryelle with Metamorphic Ritual Theatre Co.*

Odin hangs upside down (the **Hanged Man** posture of the Tarot, being the trump of Sacrifice and inverted perspective) in the play, which echoes the inversion of his vision. Thus the well appears to him 'above' and the branches 'below', as if it is the tree rather than Himself that is inverted. Since our normal vision is actually the reverse of the way things really are, due to the reflective operation of our eye lens (which turn reality upside-down and back-to-front), this is actually if anything a shift back away from the World of Maya or phenomenonal (/perceptual) illusion to the inner reality of the shamanic realms.

The image of the inverted World Tree is reminiscent of the *Nightside of the Tree* in Hebrew Qabalah -a related model which we will reTurn to- and also the Hindu wish-fulfilling *Kalpavrishka Tree* of the Vedas which has roots for branches and branches for roots. Probably based on or inspired by the physical African Bao-bab tree, the pattern of this form resembles the human nervous system which branches out through the body with its 'roots' in the brain.

The only time I hung by one foot in the inverted Hanged Man posture for purely ritualistic purposes -rather than also for theatrical performance- I remained upside-down for a much longer period, wishing to gain full gnosis from the rite -for about 3 and a third hours, until the sun rose. I was hanging from a tree whose exposed branch-like roots extended over the undercut river-bank into the water I hung over. The still clear reflection therein of the night sky seemed after some timemit to be the starry expanse itself, and the sky 'below' my feet the river.

In our Hanged Man Metamorphic Ritual Theatre, Hugin the Raven of Thought sits in the branches of the Tree, and is reflected (visually
and aurally) by Munin the Raven of Memory in the Well of ReMembrance below. The relevance of this will become apparent...

TimE, Fate and Spider Magic

Norse God *Odin/Woden* hangs from the World Tree, *Yggdrasil*, co-weaving with the three Norns (Past, Present and Future) below Him the Rune of *Gebo/Gifu* - **X** - representing Sacrifice and the Gift.

This is also the X-roads of the Lemniscate (infinity symbol) through which the tarot trumps twist & turn.

The *Well of Mimir/reMembrance* below the Tree is formed by the coils of the World Serpent *Jormungandr*, whose body contains the runes or glyphs which Odin sees after his ordeal (9 days & 9 nights) upon the Tree, whose axis mundi trunk the great Dragon of Kundalini also winds up, caduceus-like.

Thus the *Well of Wyrd* (Fate) is also the *Wheel of Wyrd* -**ARCANA X** *(page   )*- seen from the other side of the Xroads - the Norns another angle on the three Fates (Spinner, Weaver and Cutter) who turn this **TARO/ROTA** Wheel, and Yggdrasil is the Tree of Life the Serpent climbs (winding through the paths or trumps of the Qabalah).

Hugin, raven of Thought sits above Odin in the branches of the Tree, and is reflected by *Munin*, raven of Memory in the Well below (where two-faced Hela also dwells).

Odin has dropped his eye into the Well, sacrificing outer sight for inner vision, to see the runes within the serpent's coils -the book of symbols- with His inverted perspective...

-(extract from the **Booklet of Kaos** accompanying the deck)

ATU XII - The HANGED MAN

(From **The BOOK of KAOS Tarot**)

The Norse analogue of the Greek Moirae or Three Fates - **The Three Norns** who weave their webs at the base of this World Tree - reveal the intrinsic relationship of Time and Fate -for as their names imply: -*Urd ('Necessity'), Verthandi ('Being')* and *Skuld ('Debt'* -though the Norse meaning is more complex than our word summarises) - they represent Past, Present and Future. Thus the Trinity are used as indicators for 'directional' phenomena through the web of time. The span of their cycle encompasses not just one lifetime but all time; they are the phases of existence -birth, life, death- on every level, deifications of Time itself, in its cyclic, circular, spiralling nature.

That the Norns weave their webs at the base of The World Tree Yggdrasil is significant in that Odin discovered the **Runes** (Norse Magical alphabet) while hanging from the Tree. For every rune exists in every spider's web, therefore it seems quite evident where he 'discovered' these symbols —so though He may have mentally formulated them into one of the most ancient of languages, the Runic Futharc —their actual creation was a feminine weaving.

These two different apprehensions of language —and the implications of fate and destiny involved due to the Norns' intrinsic role —is explored in this verse from my '𝔥𝔞𝔫𝔤𝔢𝔡 𝔐𝔞𝔫 𝔞𝔲𝔰 𝔡𝔢𝔯 𝔘𝔫𝔡𝔢𝔯𝔴𝔢𝔩𔱚' play:

ODIN:
'The Wind whispers to me their tunes,
The Runes, the Runes...
Yes, the Wind whispers to me their names,
As Yggdrasil's sap runs through my veins

I see the Symbols woven by the Norns,
Spun and sewn into and through their
Web of Fate
And so although I see the runes about me
strewn
I know I only co-create my Fate...
...My Destiny, as I sway upon the Tree...
For though it is He who discovers
Language,
and with the Logos exerts his Will,
It is She who weaves the threads by
which this Destiny is filled...'

The difference between a masculine 'His-story' and a feminine 'Mystery' is here implicit, and this *'Hirstory'* perhaps lies somewhere b e twi x t ...

But there is also another angle I have recently considered withOdin's discovery of the Runes while hanging upon the World Tree: For the 'Midgard Serpent' Jormungundr also encircles the Tree, and all the runes are writ upon the scales of His great body.

So could it have been there that He spied them, or are they there as a result of His discovery and announcement of what He found - for **Jormungundr** (like the Greek tail-biting **Oroboros**, encircles Midgard, the middle world or realm of mortal humans, whereas Odin was hanging betwixt the realms. Perhaps his decrying of the runes brought the symbols woven in the webs, into the realm of form via His Logos, such utterance by the Gods being the means of manifestation in many cultures.

A great serpent is also present on the Hebrew Tree of Life, though winding up rather than just encircling it, representing ascent on the Paths of the tarot trumps between the Sephiroth.

The association of the cosmic serpent with such mysteries is a common thread between different mythologies -as we have already touched upon with Tiresias' encounter- and in ancient Sumeria the myth of the feminine Chaos Serpent Tiamat demonstrates further the associations between language and the formation of time. She was divided in twain by the sword (the weapon of the air and the mind in western occultism) of the solar hero Marduk. In the ancient *Enuma Elish* Babylonian creation text, this division is related to the separation of the Earth and the Sky, in much the same way as Geb (the earth) and Nuit (the sky or space) were seperated by Shu (the air or atmosphere) in Egyptian mythology, allowing form to proliferate upon the planet. Tiamat's very name is reflective in the same way as earth and sky may be viewed as microcosm and macrocosm: Often pronounced TiamaiT or even TeyamayeT, its division reveals two reflective wor(l)ds, and the similarity to TimemiT is considerable. So Time begins or is emiT-ted with the division of the layers of reality and the beginning of form. Note also the presence of *Mayet* or *Maat* (depending on inflection) in the name TiaMat ('TeyaMaye/TiaMaatt'), suggesting again that originalduality of Shu and Tefnut/Mayet, significantly the parents or source of **Geb** and **Nuit**, the same sky and earth that TiaMaat was also split into. Simple wordplay perhaps, but the close physical proximity of these ancient cultures does validate speculation on common origins.

There are also two serpents entwining the Mayan Tree of Life, called Can and Nac or together, **CannaC** -another linguistically reflective name and indeed they are the serpents of light and shade. The Mayans were not close to the Ancient Egyptians in either era or geophysical location, yet the Egyptians also have a cosmic serpent called Nak, in addition to obvious cultural similarities such as pyramids and heiroglyphs.

Then we have the Vodoun deities **Odudua** and **Obatala** as the first man and woman in some African mythologies, and **Od** and **Ob** (reading as if reflective abbreviation sthereof) as two Hebrew magickal serpents. In India the Ida and Pingala energy nadis entwining the sushumna (central spinal nadi) are represented by a golden solar and a silver lunar serpent, even as the polar serpents entwine Hermes' ancient Caduceus staff.

The separation of the land and the sky and its mythic alliance with the origins of Time is not always serpentine in nature however- it is also demonstrated in the Ancient Greek story of **Ouranos** and **Gaia/Ge**. They are, again, the Sky and the Earth, and their child is **Chronos**, the Greek God of Time from whence comes 'chronology'. This errant son castrated His own father with an adamantine sickle, and threw His genitals into the sea, thus ending the continuous union of Gaia and Ouranos (Uranus to the Romans), and allowing things to exist between them (the act also had the fortunate side-effect of creating the love-Goddess **Aphrodite**, who subsequently rose from the seafoam).

Chronos with Rhea had many children (as one would expect from a God of Time) , but fearing their succession of His throne (ironic since He symbolizes succession itself- but I guess He must have been hyper-aware of it then!) Chronos began to devour his sons. This represents the destructive power of time, time that kills as well as births- because of time, things end.

Similarly the Hindu God of Time **Mahakala** is often seen as a devouring monster. One of Chronos' sons was Zeus, who escaped consumption when His mother fed Chronos a stone in a swaddling cloth instead. There are several variations on how Zeus was then reared. The one I find most significant is the one in which He was raised by a nymph named Adamanthea. Since Chronos ruled over the earth, the heavens, and the sea, she hid him by dangling him on a rope from a tree so he was suspended between earth, sea, and sky and thus, invisible to his father. Sound familiar? This is of course parallel with the Odin myth we have just been investigating, and not only by the physical state of suspension. Like Odin (whom Zeus shares several affinities with) in his ordeal hung upon the World Tree, Zeus is here b e twe e n the Worlds , neither here nor there. This shamanic state is further exemplified in this case by the fact that this made Zeus invisible to Chronos, the God of Time -for He was not only between places, but also beyond time.

Zeus grew up to give his dad an emetic, so that Father Time did emiT his children from his mouth. Interestingly enough some versions of the myth specify that they came back out in esrever order from that which they were swallowed.

It was *Prometheus* who helped Zeus eventually overthrow Chronos, and this is interesting in relation to the deed Prometheus is more known for- stealing fire from the Gods. That He also revolted against the Lord of Time is a symbolically similar act, for immortality is the main thing which separates Gods from mere mortals, and a practising Tantric knows that kundalini -the fire within- is the essence of this Divinity.

From the blood of Uranus' castration sprung three of Time's many sisters- the **Erinye** or Furies, who are similar to the Moirae but more consistently severe. It is particularly direful Fate which they preside over, for wrongdoers. They seem to thus deify the concept of karma, although only that of a vindictive nature. Nevertheless, it was believed their wrath could at least be avoided if one did not upset them, so they were called *'The Kindly Ones'* not for its accuracy (often anything but) but rather to placate them.

In Shakespeare's *'Macbeth'* the Three Fates seem to be conflated with yet another Greek feminine trinity, the **Graiae**, who pass a singular eyeball around between them. While this is probably poetic license as they seem to be a separate trinity from the Moirae in the original Greek myths from which the imagery was derived, the implications are relevant: that 'Fate is blind', yet shares a strange singular vision of its own.

If this symbolic imagery is applied to the Norse trinity of Fate and Time -the Norns- an interesting correlative arises: For while hung upon the World Tree, Odin dropped one of his eyes into the Well of Mimir ('Wisdom'), sacrificing outer sight for inner vision. So perhaps it is this eye which the Three pass between them, suggesting a co-created destiny woven by Odin and the Norns who use his inner eye? Thus he can now 'see' his Fate and tune into its patterns, having found his True Will in the Abyssal ordeal of hanging upon the Tree.

The Well is akin to the Sabbatic Cauldron, inwhich the Witching Triad scry, the Graiae or Wyrd Sisters (of 'Macbeth') who brew therein the Vinum Sabbati (The Wine of the Sabbat).

VINCULUM SABBATI

The Norns' weaving of the Web of Fate around the base of the Tree is reflected and refracted therein. In various mythic and magickal systems, the eye is traditionally a symbol of the vagina, even as is the Well or Cauldron itself...

Comparing to the Norse World Tree aXis mundi the Jewish Tree of Life (Qabalah) we find the reflective 'Nightside of the Tree' accessed via Arcana 23 leading into and through the Abyss from the hidden ('non-')sephira *Daath*, which is both inverted and reversed from the dayside system.

Applying the idea vertically as well as horizontally (although such configurations are only really relevant when looking in from the logical Dayside, the Nightside being ultimately beyond reason itself and its Euclidian 3-dimensional geometries), I discovered a mirror world below the Tree also, a realm I call *Phos Nia* -for this is a linguistic reflection of the realm of limitless light above the Tree - the *Ain Soph*.

That Ain Soph spell-ed backwords is Phos Nia is significant in that Phos is a Latin term for light (the root of our word 'phosphorescent') and Nia is the 'Eye of the Daughter' and associated with darkness in the Thelemic and Maatian mysteries (also a Naiad is also a water nymph in Ancient Greek mythology).

So **Phos Nia** is the 'black light' below *Malkuth*, the physical realm and traditional sphere of the Daughter, of Earth. The strange Underworld realms beneath the Tree are reminiscent also of Celtic Faery lore, and The Eye of Night Below suggests again Odin's Eye plummeting down into the dark depths of the Well of ReMembrance, the deep shamanic dreaming which reflects the world of form above...

The Eye in Sorcery (especially in A.O.Spare's *Zos Kia Kultus* and its predecessors) is a primary symbol of the Kteis/Yoni, so if the Well is seen as the gateway from noumenal to phenomenal worlds, it becomes the vaginal portal of vision (the Imaginal realm bridging them) through which form is birthed.

As Kenneth Grant (author of *The Typhonian Trilogies, Starfire publishing*) has pointed out, both Mayet ('The World Order', an early name of Maat the Egyptian Goddess of Truth and thus ultimately Noumenal) and Kali ('Blackness') equal 61 by Gematria, and the numerical reflection of this is 16, the number of kalas (rays of time, secretions or lunations) which emiT from Kali's yoni (in this metaphor the Well)...

You should be glimpsing now the reflective power of the Well as a portal between dimensions. While the fluidity and rippling surface of water is particularly conducive, a simple glass mirror (preferably circular like the moon whose astral light can also be caught therein to enhance receptivity) will suffice for ritual purposes, and is thus the witch's traditional scrying tool.

Pranayama (breathing exercises), dancing, and/or chanting ('*ReMEMber, ReMEMber, reMEMber...*' is one simple suggestion) can induce the trance needed to be receptive to reflective scrying.

Evidence of the potential effectiveness of mirror scrying is the vision of a fellow member of the global *Horus-Maat Lodge*, who during a new moon ritual saw therein a man with right eye open and left eye closed; while in a synchronous linked theatrical rite which he was consciously unaware of, I hung inverted as Odin from the World Tree with my left eye open and right eye shut above another round mirror which we were using to represent the Well of ReMembrance.

We were at the time of this astral contact in opposite hemispheres of the world (he in New Orleans, USA, I in Victoria, Australia). Further left-eyed synchronicities ensued with someone being astrally initiated to the ChAOrder that same night, whose magickal name is a metatheses of Iannu, the Winged Eye...

Tracing the erratic intricate weave of the eye-globe's journey
With delicate quill through strange lands
(The Scribe) Thoth's Will is to seek out the Eye
And return it to the Hand
The Word made Flesh'

-Orryelle, **Liber Pennae-Ultim-Atum**, II-41
(www.horusmaat.com/LPUC.htm)

The name of the Norse World Tree in Midgard (the realm of Humans) is *Yggdrasil*, which translates as 'Ygg's Steed', Ygg being one of the many names of Odin/Woden. Elsewhere Odin's steed is called *Slepnir*. Although depicted as a horse in modern translation, I always wondered about Slepnir's eight legs in relation to Arachnean magicks. When my friend Ra'en pointed out that in most of the older

Norse texts it is referred to only as 'Odin's steed' (and noted how specific the Norse usually were with their language) we set to speculating upon whether Slepnir was originally actually a horse or a spider?! Strange as riding a spider may sound, such imagery is not uncommon in shamanic traditions and it is certainly no stranger than an eight-legged horse, and relates interestingly to the Norns weaving webs at the base of his other 'steed' (or perhaps another name and form of the same?) Yggdrasil. The World Tree reaches out to all the Nine Worlds of the Norse mythoscape, like a cosmic spider's web spanning and connecting dimensions.

Also relevant here is the myth of Odin riding across the night sky chased by a horde of giants or demons. Faster and faster he drove Slepnir onwards to escape them, until flecks of foam fell from His steed's mouth. Where these drops hit the earth below, fly agaric mushrooms sprung up from the ground, the flecks of foam becoming the white spots upon these bright red faery fungi. If Slepnir were a venomous spider rather than a horse, this would make more sense given the poisonous nature of these mushrooms, and also the web-like perceptions of Fate induced by their ingestion. Fly agarics also only grow at the base of certain Trees (pines, cypress...), having a symbiotic relationship with them -the relation of the two steeds again suggested...

The name of the first of the Norns -and possibly originally of them all as a singular composite- was **Urth** or **Urd**. This is the root of our word 'weird', which comes from the Scottish *'Wyrd'*.

While the Scottish accent blunted the name Urd into its current English form, the German tongue softened it into Urth, from whence our word Earth probably also derived. The point (besides demonstrating that Words/wyrds themselves are Wyrd/weird) of this etymological tangent is that 'Wyrd' was originally a term for Fate, or more specifically The Fates or *'Wyrd Sisters'* (called this in Shakespeare's 'Macbeth') so the web they weave is the Web of Wyrd, woven from the warp of time and the weft of space. The Crossroads where we meet Hekate are thus the Cross-stitches in this tapestry. That 'Weird' has since come to mean 'strange' makes sense if you think about it, for is not weirdness that sensation we have when a strange synchronicity occurs, as if pre-ordained - that eerie feeling of connection with our Destiny. Fate is Wyrd.

Our Word 'Word' also possibly stems from wyrd, even as the Word Text comes from Latin *'Texte'* meaning 'to weave' (cf. textile) - something which will be explored thoroughly in my subsequent interpretation of *The Book of the Spider* beyond **THE SECOND GATE**, and graphically/heiroglyphically in the wyrd word webs here:

```
Black and w      Day and n      Dark and l                                g
        h                i              i                                 n
        i                g              g                                 o
        t                h              h                                 r
        e                t              t and heavy     right and w
                                                                  a
                                                                  n
warp and w       Length by b    Strength & d            left d
        e                r              e
        f                e              p
        t                a              t
                         d              h
                         t
                         h

Warp and w      To adapt be a   Thedaft&thed
    e b b               d             . e
    w o l f             e               f
        t               p               t
                        t

Warp and w       Death and b    Living and d    Needle and t
    b b e               r              e                h
      f l o w           e              a                r
        t               a              d                e
                        t                               a             E
                        h                               d             b
Sew and w        Sow and r      Reap and s      Suck and b     Come and g    b and f
        e                e              o              l              o              l
        a                a              w              o                             o
        v                p                             w                             w
        e

Heart and h      Think and k
        e                n
        a                o
        d                w
```

TimE, Fate and Spider Magic

```
The waaarrrrppp and the      The corpse and the        The waarrp and the
              weft                      cleft                    weft
```

and the left   The right

```
        and over              and over              and over
Under                   Under                 Under
```

```
    and overtones           and overtones            and overtones
Undertones              Undertones              Undertones
```

```
Where and when    There and then    Near and how    Here and now
```

The Loom of Maya is the central matrix/ source of the wyrd web. Its warp and its weft (horizontal and vertical stitches) are the inhalations and exhalations of Fate, as She sits at her loom, drawing together the threads of individual destiny into the grand tapestry of illusion. The weird words of the web are woven together in this logos-matrix....

```
         Time and space    Time and place    Rhyme and pace
                                                        crotchets
         How and why    When and which    oitsss
```

```
Son and daughter    Fire and water    Staff and cupboard    Dopp UdwnanD    Earth & sky    Slither any
                                                                                                        ykl
```

The Sanskrit term *'Tantra'* also means 'to weave' or 'in the loom' andthe Tantras were also texts, sacred scriptures whose name was laterapplied more generally to the spiritual philosophy (and subsequent evolutions thereof) they espoused. The primary tantric Goddess Kali is the void from which time dothhtod emit, and Her necklace is the garland of fifty letters of the Sanskrit alphabet.

The Warp of the Wyrd is the Loom of Maya. It is the tapestry of time and space woven by Lachesis - the Weaver of the Three Fates- who oversee the Labyrinth of incarnate existence. The different threads which initiates bring into the Labyrinth, spun by Clotho -the Spinner- when they enter the Labyrinth (birth), are woven together into the great Web of Wyrd (Fate). The way these different lifelines are woven together forms the intricate web of inter-relationship between all beings, the etheric (rather than virtual) inter-net.

Once thoroughly woven in, the threads are cut by Atropos -the Cutter- when you die. But that's not the end, as shall we seen as we introduce the enigmatic *Fourth Fate..*

The Wyrd sisters or Fates are usually considered to be Three- Spinner Weaver and Cutter of life's thread- yet the Hidden connection between Cutter and Spinner is the key to this cycle's continuance. Nothing truly ends, it just changes form.

This change is often hidden, for in terms of the lunar cycles the mythic Three Fates or Moirae (Greek)/ Parceae (Roman)/ Nornir

(Norse)/ Morrigan (Celtic) reflect and oft represent, the dark phase of the moon is unmentioned.

As an absence rather than a presence, this mystery is not given name or form in most of the ancient mythologies of the lunar Goddess who generally appears in triple aspects. Now we know that the moon does not truly vanish from the skies once a moonth, it merely becomes invisible to the naked eye; and that it is not truly a 'new' moon that subsequently appears, other than nominally, but the same astronomical body in the next phase of its cycle.

The dark phase of the moon is thus a ' c r a c k ' between the worlds, a potent time -or perhaps even a space beyond time- for seeding new realities at the end of a cycle and the beginning of a new one.

Since the Horus-Maat Lodge's inception on a new moon, this time has continued to be one of ritual working and pan-global astral and magical communion for its members worldwide. (Note: I am referring by 'new moon' here to the peak of the dark moon, i.e. the turning into the new lunar cycle rather than first visible crescent).

Regardless of such global activity or the aeonic inclinations of the magical practitioner however, the new moon is a powerful time for any inner work - it is the seeding of new possibilities which will then often bear fruition on the following full moon, that being a time more of outer work and celebration.

Suggestions by Fraters *Alexander Blok* and *Alobar Greywalker* that there is a 'Fourth Fate' prompted a discussion and exploration within the Horus-Maat Lodge of this hidden dark face of the moon, and the results are contained in the Dark Moon verse of my **'Liber Qoph vel Hekate'** and Commentary – see **APPENDIX C**.

(I recommend daily usage of this lunar adoration for anyone wishing to tuneinto the cycles of the moon, as a preliminary and continuing adjunct to the other practices andrites suggested within the Third Gate of this book.)

We realised that the Fourth Fate is the one who s p l i c e s the thread -cut by the cutter to end one life- back to the spinner for the next round of the Wheel, the next layer in the spiral. Time is continuous... ... ...

Hail Nought, Not, Nuit, Maat,
Yours the dark and secret art
While crone's scythe cuts breath and with death
The thread of life appears to dwindle
From No-thing you craft another mask
And re-splice it back, on another track
To Clotho's spindle

*-from **Liber Qoph vel Hekate** (Appendix C)*

This secret connective thread is perhaps akin to the Norse magical ribbon called *Gleipnir*, which was created by the dwarves to shackle the chaos wolf Fenris, who had previously broken every chain the Gods had put upon him to prevent apocalypse in the form of him devouring the sun.

According to the ancient *Poetic Edda* and *Prose Edda*, Gleipnir was made of six wondrous ingredients: the sound of a cat's footfall, the beard of a woman, the roots of a mountain, a bear's sinews (meaning nerves, sensibility), fish's breath and bird's spittle. The creation of Gleipnir is said to be the reason why none of these things exist.

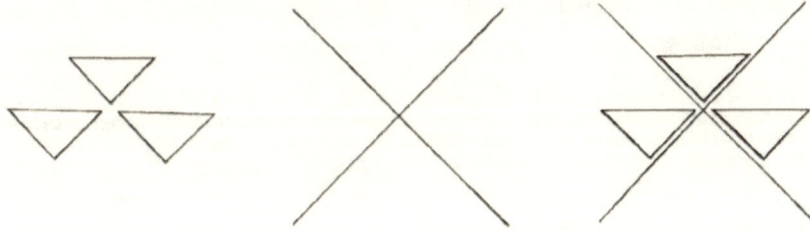

By merging two existing symbols, I have discovered a simple diagram *(above)* which visually demonstrates this 'absent' yet existent aspect of the lunar cycle. A composite symbol, its components then complete form are shown above.

The three triangles (left) are a traditional symbol for The Three Fates or Triple Goddess (I am unsure of its origin), and the X (centre) is a basic glyph for the Crossroads/X-roads. As three-faced Hekate is in Greek lore a Goddess of the Crossroads, where She is usually met (it being a crossroads betwixt the Worlds as much as the meeting of 3 or 4 directions), it seemed natural to place the Moirae symbol over the Crossroads glyph, and I was astounded at the simple yet powerful result (right) —the three triangles of the visibly-present phases fill 3 of the quarters, while the 4th quarter is empty, yet it is very much there as framed and defined by the crossbars —the dark Fourth Fate, invisible yet implicate.

The fourth fate is already implicit in the initial symbol of the Crossroads alone however, for it is only usually in modern contexts

that it is shown with four arms or paths. The Ancient tradition in
Greece was that Hekate or other deities of Fate would be met at a
triple crossroads, a place where three roads meet. This seems to
represent the triplicity of the lunar Goddess again, or of the Three
more obvious Fates. Yet in the Sabbatic tradition there is an inner
teaching of the fourth path from this crossroads, the dark or crooked
path to lands of fae, on which Hekate may take you down into the
Underworld.

There is a fourth face, though unseen
There is a fourth path, whom few know
A fourth Fate, who awaits
In shadow

-(*Liber Qoph vel Hekate*)

Again I am reminded of the Pythoness at Delphi, whose three-legged stool perhaps represented the Three Fates who informed her oracles. And yet, these three legs perched over a great crack in the earth, and it was from deep within this dark crack that the noxious fumes emitted which inspired the priestess's prophetic trance; even as the dark crack twixt waxing and waning lunar cycles above is the time when most mortal women in reflection emit that most potent kala, the menstrual moon-blood which will often open in their own psyches a crack to the underworld of deep knowing; the oracular subconscious realms of intuitive power.

There are names for this hidden dark phase of the Moon, but in their mythic contexts they are usually offered as more general deities or archetypes rather than specifically relating to the dark phase of the moon, this being more implicit. A possible exception is Nephthys, the dark of the moon in the Ancient Egyptian pantheon, although She also represents darkness and night in general, not only the shadowed moon therein; Even as both Hekate and (/as?) The

Moirae are the daughters of **Nix**, the Greek deification of the Night.

In the Italian Witchcraft tradition the dark lunar phase is acknowledged as 'Umbrea' (the Shadow) along with her sisters Diana (ancient Roman name applied to the waxing phase), Losna (full) and Manea (waning) (-*'Hereditary Witchcraft'* by *Raven Grimassi, Llewellyn 99).*

Other names which could be applied to the dark phase are also the names of composite forms of all the phases. This makes sense as the hidden Fourth Fate or 'Splicer' is the continuity of thewhole, the ever-present yet physically-absent essence which binds together the parts thereof. The Greek name for the Three Fates collectively is 'The Moirae', a plural name for the Three -but there is also a less known composite thereof known singularly as **'Moira'** *('The Greek Magical Papyri in Translation',* ed.*Dieter Betz, University of Chicago Press, 1986.),* and She is the archetype we find in the Justice trump of the tarot -a woman with scales and a sword, equilibrating the polar aspects of existence.

This archetype is a Greek form of the Egyptian Maat, lady of the Scales of Justice and Neter (principle) of Truth and Balance. Both of these attributes in the lunar context we are here examining are primarily applicable to the dark phase of the moon -as Balance She mediates between the waning (death) and waxing (birth) p

hases; and as Truth she is ultimately invisible, as 'No-thing is True' when we go beyond the masks and veils of apparent or manifest perception-realities, rending the tapestry of Maya (Sanskrit/Hindu term for the physical realm as 'Illusion') to reveal the intangible essence beyond.

Yet the more apparent realities of Her other forms and phases also have their own Truth when perceived, and are thus a part of the whole which is Maat/Moira/Maya.As Goddess or Neter of Measure, Maat determines the whole cycle, becoming as much Her masks (while adopting them) or tapestry as the elusive spirit behind them...

The Justice archetype of **Maat** as Goddess of Truth, is ultimately faceless. S/he is an intangible essence, as Nothing is True, in terms of Absolutes. From this source-void come the different masks crafted by our perceptions and experiences, either collectively or alone. Depicted here are different cultural and mythical masks and forms of Maat.

The Egyptians represented Maat with the Hieroglyph of the Feather, here doubled to represent the positive and negative permutations of duality as No-thing manifests into form. The symmetry of the image is indicative of the Balance and Equilibrium which Maat represents. Implied too is Norse *Hel/Hela/Holla*, who is also a Goddess of Judgement and Justice and is depicted half-black and half-white, both decaying crone and blossoming maiden.
The two-edged Sword (symbol of the Hebrew letter of this card, *Zayin*) of Division shown is an extension of this, the mind's perception cleaving the essence into pattern, the tapestry of Maya (Illusion).
The hilt of the sword is engraven with Ibises, the totem of **Thoth**, Scribe-God of Records and Measure and consort of Maat, and from it hang the Scales of Justice, on which Maat weighs the Heart of the deceased against Her feather of Truth, as in Egyptian mythology.
The Serpent of the Ages coils in a Lemniscate (infinity symbol) of Eternity around this Sword, which as its axis forms a sigil of the Word of Maat, **IPSOS** *('By the Same Mouth')*

ATU XI - ADJUSTMENT / JUSTICE

from **The BOOK of KAOS Tarot**

The other primary Name and Form which can be applied to the Dark phase of the Moon -and is also a name of the entire cycle deified- is that of **Kali** (seen as one of the masks in my Adjustment/Justice trump). Dark Hindu Creator/Destroyer, Her name means 'Blackness' yet also She is a Goddess relating to Time itself.

In the same way as in the ancient Egyptian (and contemporary Thelemic) pantheon Maat is both the Absence and the masks which it wears to form presence, so too is Kali the Blackness from which the Kalas emiT -the forms which manifest from the void. Both Kali and Maat represent this process itself - Measure of cycles, Destruction-Creation and the Spa c e s I n Be twe e n .

The Sanskrit term *'kala'* is a complex one. Primarily it means rays of time, but in Tantric texts it is also an oblique reference to the emissions from the yoni of the Goddess. These are of course allied in terms of lunations, an intricate system of correlation between the greater cycle and the personal feminine one. There are 15 kalas of the Goddess as Kali - these are of the waning moon, and 15 of Lalita as the waxing moon. Both relate to the *Nityas* of each, a complex system of yantras, mantras and forms (which can be visualised during different daily meditations over a moonth). As two Goddesses who are really different aspects of the one Goddess, they overlap on the full moon (the 15th kala as the totality of its components), thus forming the 28-day lunar cycle.

Yet there is also considered to be a mysterious '16th Kala'. But from Whom doth this Great Kala emit?

The Word Emit itself is a linguistic reflection of the Word Time, just as form is created from the colour spectrum refracted from White, which mirrors and is birthed from its polarity of Black -the void.

This brings us to an important point about Kali in relation to Time. It is a common conception -especially in the West- that Kali is the Goddess of Time. Well, sort of, but when you really lookinto the Hindu Tantric mysteries, She is more the void from which Time is birthed. As the Mother of Time She is obviously concerned with its creation, but is ultimately the noumenon beyond time and form, from which the phenomenal world springs, and thus also akin to Maat's ultimate (non)form as No-Thing -for there is no absolute Truth, only the individual truth-masks which individuals, collectives and cultures project with belief.

The more direct and lesser-known Hindu deification of Time itself is a God known as **MahaKala** -'Great Blackness', Kala being a masculine word for blackness in Sanskrit even as Kali is feminine blackness, although the word kala in the multi-layered Sanskrit language also means Time itself. He is a dark form of the more well-known Hindu God Shiva, Whom we shall meet in depth further along the spiral...

So MahaKala is the Great or ultimate Kala, who as Time itself doth emiT from the yoni of Maha Kali-Ma(at), The Great Black Mother. Yet He also to this womb reTurns, as He is both Her son and Her lover, in a symbolic sense. So His seed which re-impregnates Her in eternal cyclicity is also itself perhaps the Maha (Great) Kala...

That Kali is depicted with eight limbs, and is feared and revered for destroying or consuming Her mates, brings us back to that other great and ancient archetype of time and fate - the spider.

The Hindus have a concept of the forms of the manifest world being woven as a great tapestry -the web of Maya, 'Illusion'. That this name is similar to the earliest known name of

Maat, that of 'Mayet' meaning 'The World Order' is no coincidence (unless of course one considers 'co-incidence' as merely the extant pattern of synchronicity which it truly is).

This is a web of form and thus space, but Time is the loom, Kali's black womb, on which/from which Maya is woven.

The Magickal Kalas
The coloured web
The ebb and flow
Waves which Come and Go
As Kalas from their clefts
Weaving the warp and the weft
Of the web of Fate
Which they Ate
As it seeped forth from them
O net of jewels
Spindled, spooled With rolling tongues
And spun out into etheric strands
Of lust warp-woven Through supple hands
Spindlefingered play of tension
Sends feathery ripples Into Morphic pools
The Orphic lilting Of petals folding out
From lips of crimson enfolding
The Black Goddess within
From Kali Come Kalas, pale and translucent
Veils of intent, latent shall
Be Secreted from the
Realms of infinite
Potential

The tapestry of time (Kali) and space (Maya) are interwoven in the tantra/loom, in the wombs of creation, the double halls of Manifestation.

Time, Fate and Spider Magic

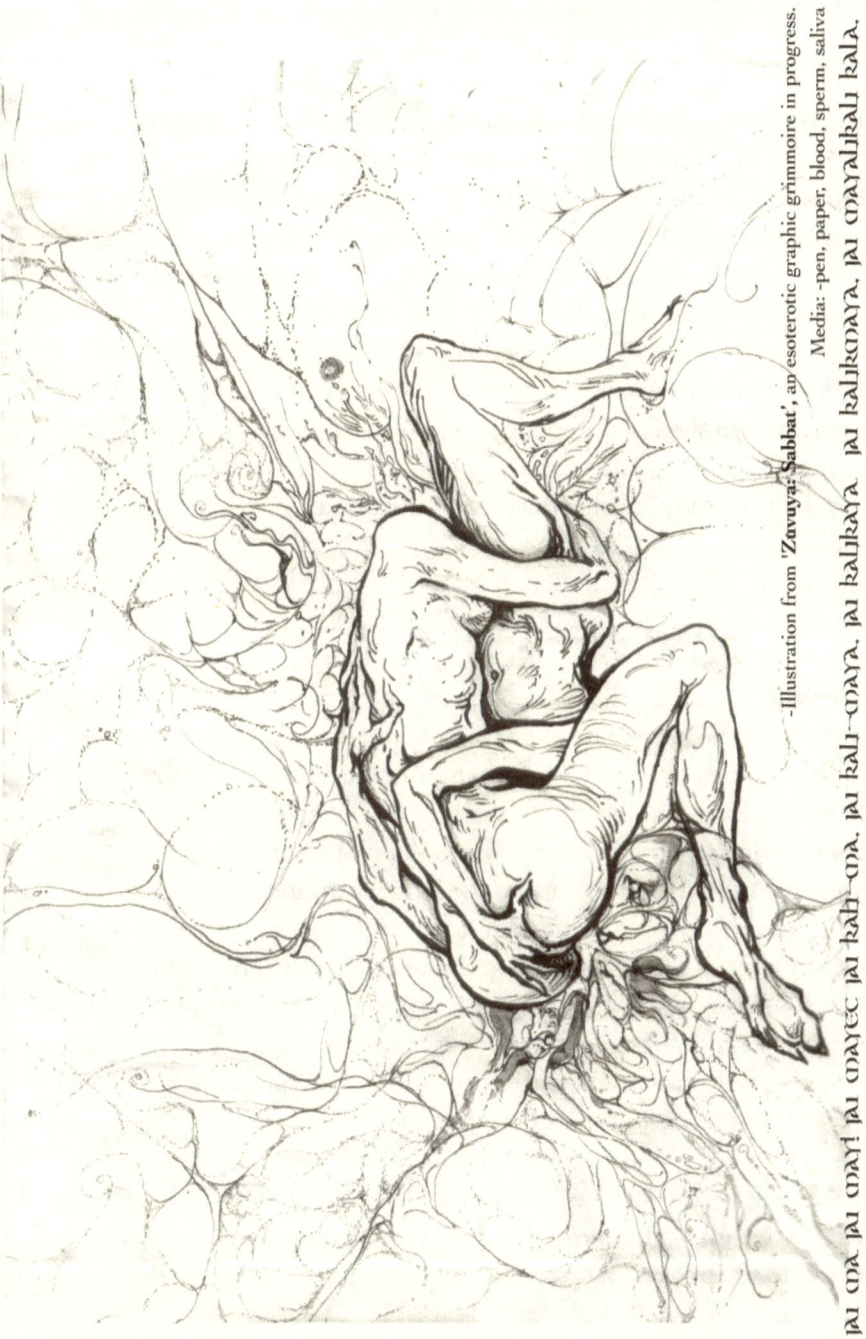

—Illustration from 'Zuvuya-Sabbat', an esoteric graphic grimmoire in progress.
Media: -pen, paper, blood, sperm, saliva
jai ma jai may! jai mayec jai kali-ma, jai kali-maya, jai kalikoaya, jai kalikaya, jai kalikali kala.

In Ancient Greek mythology Ge (/Gaia) the Earth Goddess and Ouranos (/Uranos) the Sky God were locked in eternal union. So great and incessant was Ouranos' passion that the Children who would otherwise have been born from Their union could not get out of Ge's vagina, as it was always occupied by Ouranos' phallus. Many **Titans**, the primordial first beings, were thus trapped within Her womb. Here the Hundred-handed Giants, the *Hecatochiron*, trying to escape, can be seen reaching out their fingers from within Her belly, causing rocky crags on the Earths' surface.

Parallel is the Ancient Egyptian tale of Nuit and Geb- the Sky Goddess and the Earth God in eternal union so that form could not exist. The genders are switched, but the symbolism the same - in a state of utmost unity, there can be no form, no change, no life -only undifferentiated totality. As with Geb and Nuit being separated by the air-God Shu (the transparent layer of breathable atmosphere between them), Ge and Ouranos had to also be divided for the proliferation of Life on Earth.

In the Greek myth the separation is more severe: So that His brothers could escape from the womb, their own son **Khronos** -the God of Time- castrated His father, bringing a dramatic end to their incessant love-making. In this image He is shown in this act of division, and from it forms are immediately springing into being: the sweeping motion of His lunar sickle with which the act is perpetrated is the moon's orbit around Her body and cyclical phases thereof, Khronos' own head is the ringed planet Saturn (His name to the Romans) and the very seeds which erupt from the severed genitals become stars spattered across the night sky of Ouranos's dark body.

So this is destruction for the purpose of creation. It is Time which allows form to exist, for without birth and death, growth and decay (on myriad levels and layers) there can be no change. And so the new space which has formed between Ge and Ouranos is in the shape of an hour-glass, that other ancient symbol along with the sickle or scythe for Khronos/Saturn.

Illustration originally from Orryelle's black book SOLVE *(Fulgur Limited 2012)*

Time, Fate and Spider Magic

Some scholars contend that Greek *Chronos* the God of Time is a different being to the earlier *Chronus* or *K(h)ronos* the Titan who castrated His father Ouranos, but I disagree. They may have been differentiated in later times, but as the Titan Kronos is the wielder of the sickle and associated by the Romans with their time-God Saturn, a common origin seems obvious.

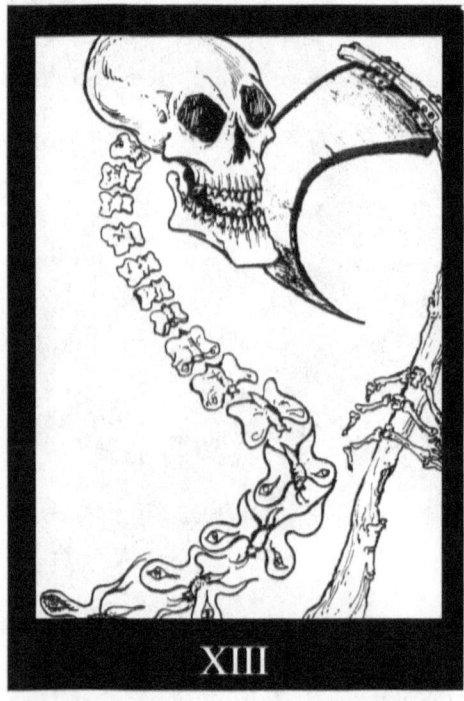

XIII

One of our outermost planets is of course named after the Roman time-God Saturn, thus this planet's astrological correspondence with restriction, heaviness and blackness.

He is the archetype from which the 'Grim Reaper' is derived- cowled Old Man Time, bearing a scythe, which was once the sickle of Chronos. The sickle was a tool originally for harvesting crops rather than souls, for Chronos was once an Agricultural God. Knowing when to reap and sow the crops was of course intimately related to seasonal cycles and thus time, thus His evolution into this more general figure of time and death.

In western astrology Saturn usually represents restriction, burdens and constriction -but we may befriend Time, He may be an ally if we cease to struggle with Him and instead flow with His course, knowing His organisational function within reality.

In Vedic astrology, the Saturnian planetary spirit **Shani** is perceived similarly. His altars and statuary are always covered with a thick black oily substance, and lamps on them are always kept burning, and on His day Saturday (Saturn-day) many Indian temples have extra visitors coming to His tarry altar. He is always paid the utmost respect, but it seems that much of this comes from fear rather than adoration. For Shani is a God of Karma, perhaps the eastern equivalent of Fate, although there are subtle differences of perspective between the two concepts.

In the west we tend to simplify the idea of karma to simply being a kind of moral cause and effect, where we get what we deserve from our actions. But since there is no absolute good or evil- such moral codes differ according to the social and cultural mores of different times and places, and also personal inclinations- it is hard to imagine any 'higher powers' that can effectively judicial this. Karma does seem to be about cause and effect, but its intricate patterns are subtle beyond the scope of our normal perception. Hindus believe it spans more than one incarnation, so the 'karmic debts' of a soul can already be considerable even as soon as it is (re)born into the World, thus neatly explaining the apparently undeserved unfortunate circumstances some beings find themselves in. But it is not all about morality, or even underlying intention.

The popular contemporary 'Chaos Science' example of the butterfly flapping its wings and causing -through a long line of unprecedented cause and effect- an earthquake elsewhere -gives some idea of the intricacies of Karma.

Fate, as the Greeks originally conceived it- seems to also contain a chaotic or random element to it. Although the concept as with karma is intimately linked with the Gods, characters such as Oedipus still don't seem to deserve their allotted destiny. Yet there does seem to be some kind of pattern behind both Fate and Karma, though one rarely knowable to the mortal who struggles with them. It is our goal in this work to tune into this fine weave, intuitively rather than with our reason, for we may never fully understand its complexities from a logical viewpoint.

There is a hymn from the *Martandabhairava Tantra* which identifies Shani with Mahakala, so the planet Saturn is directly related to Time in both the East and West. Significantly, this tantra also relates Mahakali and Shani to **Mrityunjaya**, which is Shiva as conqueror of death. So He has only Himself to overcome, it seems. One can only move beyond Time by mastering it, by becoming it fully enough to understand and so transcend its caprice- to pierce the veil of illusion.

However on the Tree of Life the planet Saturn is attributed to Binah, and this is the primary feminine sephira (although above the Abyss, opposites are equable), the sphere of the Great Black Mother. The true source of time is revealed -Kali-Ma.

Om Adya Kali Devata Svaha!

TimEmiT is ultimately the domain of the feminine- the destroyer and creator of cycles of life, the Great Mother from whence all sprang...

The name C(h)ronos probably has the same roots as 'crone' and 'crow'. Saturn is usually seen with one of these majestically morbid black birds, and Odin is always accompanied by two; but originally they were the emmisaries of Hekate, the eternal crone (wisewoman) of time, She who spins, w e a v e s , cuts ...and splices...

CRONOSLOGOS

Crono-logy is the logos of Cronos (Saturn, Time)
Logos is what you say
Saturn (time) is not a line
What you Say-turns and Sa'turn re-turns
This is the re-currence of the current current
Cronos is the Crow
And the Crone is the Crow
The Crow is Hekate, primal goddess of Fate

Before Grandfather Time there was the Grandmother clock
Tock tick, tick tock,
After Grandfather Time was Grandmother Clock,
Grandmother Time, Grandmother Fate,
Grandmother spider, who ate time at 8 o'clock and the ticks and the tocks
wriggledabout inside Her;
She the diviner, the holy divider of cycles;
She circles the clock-face, she measures the tock-pace
She measures the threads; cuts them, you're dead.

Time to die, time to be born,
This is the whim of the Norns
Cronos and the Crow, crows circle home,
Grandfather Time and Grandmother Rhyme exist at the same time
They are the same time
Same place, different face
The she-turn-all
He-turn-all
'E-tern-al
Here and Now

In the Hindu Vedic cosmology, our current period is the **Kali Yuga** or final Age when chaos reigns -certainly seems to be the case- although thankfully this segues eventually back into a new Golden Age according to their beliefs. Inevitable I suppose, although I suspect a lot more death and destruction will need to occur before we can see this glorious new dawn.

The Hindu conception of time's cycles is incredibly vast. A single yuga is considered to span 24,000 years or so - a full cycle of equinoctial precession- and all this is but the blink of Shiva's eye. When His third eye opens, apparently, the phenomenal world will all disappear back into the great void -Kali's cosmic yoni, the Mayan *'Womb of the Great Mother'*, the Dark Rift of the Milky Way?

But let us move now from the vast sweep of time which the Indians call Yugas to a perhaps more easily apprehensible model of the Ages which in the west we call Aeons. An Aeon is the western concept of an Age or a long period of time, usually considered to be around 2000 years. This century has seen numerous speculations on the significance of this aeon. Various aeonic formulae and models have been projected to not only map out the progression of the aeons so far, but also from the patterns of the past to speculate on the future of our planet and our species in aeons to come.

As the encroaching second millennium rose its foreboding head, followed in close succession by the 2012 'paradigm shift', theories abounded as to the future of humanity. Both these aeonic apexes have now passed without catastrophe -at least not on the actual prophesied dates (2000 and 2012), but several 'natural' disasters occurred in the short period between these milestones of global anxiety and hope: a spate of earthquakes and tsunamis which were likely at least partially repercussions of human interference with earthly cycles and rhythms rather than just expressions of such. The Fukushima disaster in Japan definitely highlighted the tenuousness of some of our civilisations' infrastructure, when the initial 'natural disaster' of earthquake and following tsunami were soon dwarfed by the radiation threat from uranium power-plants they devastated. While this woke a few million people up to the reality of such obvious dangers and Japan ceased its use of nuclear power, the US Govt merely responded that their nuclear plants are 'safe' (even the ones built on fault-lines in California) and after a few months of people fearing it was the beginning of the end, life went back to normal for most.

Will we still suffer apocalypse of biblical proportions, our ecosphere collapsing as we rapidly consume the Earth's dwindling resources, or can this same advancing technology which has brought us to the brink of self-destruction save us, or at least allow our escape to another planet/ solar system/ dimension? Or does our salvation lie in rapid spiritual evolution? I think only a combination thereof can avert disaster for humanity, as it is our technological advances outracing our spiritual advancement which has caused most of the problems.

At this time of accelerating change and impending potential disaster, various paradigms are being presented.

One of these paradigms is the emergence of the *'Quantum Age'*. This theory -that there are many different realities created by many different perspectives- explains the proliferation of different aeonic theories itself. In this 'Aeon of aeonics', however, there are threads of relation and a strange underlying consistency of vision, if one looks beyond the outer apparent differences of viewpoint.

Rather than just present another personal eclectic vision, I intend then in the following few pages to show how the different Aeonic formulae of various individuals, sects and cultures weave together; to form an overall collective vision of where we've been, where we are and where we're headed.

We live in a time of cultural diversity, and yet global unification. This has been called the *'Information Age'*. Never before has such a vast range of information been available to so many as now via modern telecommunications networks. We have access to all cultures, all races, all places. While the depth and subtleties of direct contact may often be lost through such long-distance or virtual connections and the 'browse' mode they usually induce from information-overload, they do allow a general overview of different cultural and sub-cultural paradigms as never before. Combined with the increased means of physical travel across the planet, these new communication technologies allow the intermingling and cross-pollination of different cultures. While unfortunately the western materialist consumer mass-production monoculture mindset is dominant, there is beneath it an emerging global multi-culture. This is increasingly evident in the youth of today, who seem to be making a gradual shift from the hedonistic mindlessness of 'Generation X' into an acceptance and integration of a multitude of different cultural aspects.

There is a Hopi Indian prophecy which relates to this emerging Planetary culture. Amidst various other prophecies which have been

evidently fulfilled -such as 'iron horses' and the 'cobwebs which stretch across the sky' of the above-mentioned technologies- is this passage:

'When the Earth is sick and the animals have disappeared, there shall come a new tribe formed from all cultures and all races, to heal the earth. This tribe shall be called the 'Warriors of the Rainbow'.

This prophecy was proudly embraced by the counterculture of the sixties and seventies, the beatniks and hippies and flower-children in their colourful garb who were in some ways the beginnings of the modern ecology movement. As the ecological situation becomes more urgent, more mainstream defenders of the environment also begin to increase, while new hybrid subcultures also proliferate with continuing alternatives to consumer greed and mass-marketing.

The hippies were followed rapidly by the punks, reacting against the idealism and 'turn the other cheek' peace and love vibes with a more realistic, gritty and reactionary aggression to help break down the structures of social and political control.

The youthful enthusiasm and rebellion of such movements epitomise Crowley's concept of this being the **'Aeon of Horus'** - for Horus/Heru is the 'Lord of Force and Fire' and a child-God. But this somewhat punk attitude if left unchecked and unbalanced can ultimately only diffuse into entropic chaos or merely replace the Father with a Son who grows up to make the same mistakes and cause the same patriarchal problems.

Enter Maat: the Goddess of Justice, Her symbol the scales of balance, She is the equilibrating force we need to evoke, and Her relationship with Horus to form a double-current in our Aeon will be examined shortly...

It is vitally important that the Hopi prophecy of the Rainbow Warriors be maintained as what it originally meant -Unity in Diversity, and acceptance thereof. There are certain individuals and groups who would like to think they are the Rainbow People and some of these have actually become quite closed-minded, unable to accept those who don't embrace their New Age dogmas or who offer fresh alternative perspectives.

Some of this 'Rainbow movement' has been demonstrating that it is still possible to live in harmony with the Earth and with each other. Rainbow Gatherings around the world continue to occur, removed from 'normal' society and living in an idealistic and yet effective tribal 'total consensus' democracy. However we need to expand to establish more long-term, self-sustainable communities.

This Hopi prophecy is also called the 'Thirteenth Tribe', being the new global tribe which emerges from the union of the 'Twelve Tribes' or source races of humanity. These 'twelve tribes' also exist in the Bible, whose prophecies bear a strange affinity with many of the Hopi prophecies. While the bible makes no references to a thirteenth tribe -and indeed the patriarchal christian religion is responsible for the branding of thirteen as an 'unlucky' number because of its relation to lunar/ feminine cycles - it is interesting to note that with his twelve disciples Jesus becomes the thirteenth.

I had an intense vision for a group chakra weaving relating to the idea of the Thirteenth Tribe, which symbolically unites many of the cultural paradigms and aeonic currents discussed here. It was manifested as the **13-Tribe Weaving** -see **APPENDIX D**.

The 'no electric power' rule at most 'Rainbow Gatherings' makes a refreshing break from the gadget-orientated society most of us live in; but long-term alternatives must also be sought -new 'clean' technologies which work with rather than against the Earth's biosphere. This is beginning to happen. Digital technology is a lot more refined and ecologically friendly than the clumsy smoke-churning monsters of the industrial age, and electronic information distribution reduces the need for paper from trees.

It is too late to go backwards to an age without modern technology. While learning to live simply off the land, un-reliant on gadgetry, is a vital process -especially for if our technological society does collapse or self-destruct -we need to also move forward into

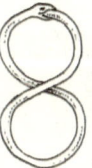

technological harmony with our environment. It is the attitudes of humans, greed and exploitation, rather than their tools which endanger us. We need to think more about what we do, and create accordingly, rather than just rushing forth with blind and linear short-term ambition.

In *'The Mayan Factor'(Bear and Co., 1987)* Jose Arguelles writes about going 'beyond technology', claiming quite accurately that *"20th Century technological comfort...is a closing off of the sense fields and a narrowing of the perceptions...akin to a caged animal suffocating on its own waste products."*

Technology is also doing many wonderful things for us and our planet; offering incredible developments in medical science and global communications. Recent discoveries in genetic bioengineering and nanotechnology, suggesting these fields will advance in the next ten years at the rate computer technology has advanced in the last ten years or perhaps even faster, offer the possibility that science may allow us to reshape our very flesh and forms sooner than we deemed possible. I believe that we can potentially move through technology into new paradigms, our technology developing until we can create practically any physical reality we desire. As we begin to realise this infinite potential, more and more people will become aware of our inherent divinity and realise we don't actually need tools to do this: 'Technology' will become obsolete as we transcend the scientific-materialist paradigm via it ultra-manifestation enmeshed with our very DNA bringing us back around to that DNA's own latent (and largely unused 'junk DNA/Dark Matter') power.

The only real offset and stumbling block to this potential is the abuse of technology, as its development seems currently focused around short-term profit from producing unnecessary 'creature-comforts' to insulate us from rather than deal with the problems facing our world and culture. The shift involves increased awareness of the web of life, of the subtle and delicate interconnectedness of all beings -humans as animals, other animals, plants and minerals.

Arguelles also talks of the use of global computer networks and radiosonic temples of harmonic sound (the ancient all night trance dance revived through 'techno' festivals -even some of the mainstream gatherings have a vague sense of ritualism about them) - some of the prophecies since 'The Mayan Factor' was published which have actually manifested.

While some of Arguelles' personal interpretations and projections are perhaps over-optimistic and inaccurate, his basic premises seem quite sound. He saw the Mayan culture for the incredibly advanced civilisation they were, charting astronomical movements and cycles of time with a precision equal to that provided by our modern instruments. Their calendrics went beyond mere mapping of the physical machinations of the solar system however, showing also how information travels from **Hunab Ku**, the galactic core, to us via our sun.

As modern Mayan priest *Hunbatz Men* asserts in his book *'The Maya: Science/Religion'* to the Ancient Mayan culture there was no difference between science/technology and magic/religion. Myths are maths, each number being an important metaphorical symbol rather than just a means of calculation. Similarly in the Western Esoteric Tradition of the Qabalah, numbers have significance beyond their capacity as mere measuring devices. The symbolic values of the sephiroth are in fact remarkably similar to the Mayan numerology from 1-13 as described in Arguelles' book.

It is the division between science and magic, beginning with the 'age of reason' when industry and 'rationality' began their assault, that has been largely responsible for the current planetary crisis. Material practicality has sacrificed aesthetics and mythology in the quest for mundane comfort and conformity. But gradually this duality is being transcended. 'Science' is beginning to acknowledge possibilities that have long been known in the world of magick.

Quantum physics, chaos theory and the like allow the random factors and perspective leaps that have long been confined to the realms of mysticism. Similarly, magic has been becoming more 'scientific', refining its methodology, embracing the chaos/quantum

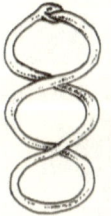

paradigm, and employing modern technology as another magical tool. From our current state of lingering division it is difficult to fully appreciate this synthesis. Perhaps our technology will develop to an extent where we can manipulate matter almost instantly with our minds -magic.

"Any sufficiently advanced technology is indistinguishable from magic"
-Arthur C. Clarke

What is technology? Basically- tools, extensions of the human body with which we manipulate our environment. From stone axes to microchips, it's all technology at various degrees of advancement. What is 'natural'? Are we, as animals, separate from nature? Does our use of tools differentiate us that much? There is often talk of humankind 'destroying nature' as if we are separate from it. I'm not of course advocating wanton abuse of earthly resources. I'm sure our realisation and reformation of the abuse already perpetrated is also part of the 'natural' process. Or perhaps it's natural for us to wipe ourselves out and the rest of the earth and its denizens carry on without us?

According to the Mayan Long Count calendar, the final baktun, Baktun 13 from 1992-2012 finished on the solstice of 2012, December 21st. Rather than anything with a sense of finality, reality seems to be carrying on at its usual pace, which is quite breakneck in the modern west. There is no '14th Baktun' so presumably from a Mayan perspective we are now in some kind of infinite '13 o'clock' of the 13th Baktun, i.e. the Dreamtime.

The Mayans, of course, never said anything about solstice 2012 being the 'end of the world' -that was all the fear-mongers, movie-makers and New Age fruitloops who misinterpreted the calendar end, or simply exploited it for commercial purposes in the guise of spirituality. The Mayans themselves heralded it as the time for *'The Return of Kukulkan'*. Called **Quetzalcoatl** by the Aztecs, **Kukulkan** is a major deity of the Ancient Mayan civilisation. This time is not the 2012 December Solstice as an isolated instant, but the whole period of rapid change around that aeonic cusp, continuing to unwind its iridescent scales.

Kukulcan/Quetzalcoatl means 'feathered serpent', an obvious metaphor for the kundalini energy. Kundalini is the 'serpent power' which resides in our nervous systems, rising up the spine to provide inspiration and illumination (the wings unfold at the crown of the head). It exists in almost every ancient culture. The Caduceus, snake-entwined winged staff of the Greek Messenger of the Gods, Hermes, has been appropriated by western medicine. It has always been a symbol of Magic and healing.

In Hindu and Vedic traditions, the male and female serpents Ida and Pingala entwine the central 'sushumna' axis of our spine, weaving between the 'spinning wheels' of our chakras. In his book Hunbatz Men gives evidence of ancient Mayan clay figurines with four dots at the base of the spine, six at the navel, etc. -the numbers of dots at each of these 'power centres' corresponding with the amount of 'petals' on each chakra in the Hindu system!

The return of Quetzalcoatl, Hunbatz claims, is a metaphor for the activation of the chakras and the rising of the Kundalini. The biblical flood when Noah apparently built his ark was a proven historical event. The next 'apocalypse' is supposed to be by fire. Won't it be nice if this is metaphysical kundalini 'fire' rather than literal ecological cataclysm?

What does this 'return of Kukulcan?' imply? Kundalini rising in many? i.e. awakening of the collective consciousness and mass enlightenment?

The rise of the microcosmic serpents in our spines, and of the great serpents of the Earth? In many ancient cultures the rise of the great serpent signifies the 'end of the World' or the 'end of time', i.e. big changes. To the Australian Aborigines the rise of the **Rainbow Serpent** signifies the end of the World. The Norse (who also apparently prophesied the coming of 'rainbow warriors', although I

have yet to find evidence of this) told of *Ragnarok*, the battle of the Gods at the end of the World, when the chaos wolf Fenris consumes the sun and the Midgard Serpent, the great snake encircling the World Tree (Yggdrasil), rises.

This tail-biting serpent was called Oroboros by the Ancient Greeks and Tiamat by the Babylonians. In the bible it is Leviathan, and the Beast of the Apocalypse has the number 666. In Jewish Kabbalah 6 is the number of the Sun, suggesting as the Norse myth does that our sun may be destroyed or destroy us (depletion of the ozone layer?).

The final (13th) baktun in the Mayan long-count calendar was the baktun of AHAU, which represents solar consciousness- a solar age, when we began tuning in more to the galactic core, via messages to our solar plexus chakras through our own Sun or Kin.

Robert Coon - one of the people who mapped out the global chakra centres where the *Silver Dusk* performed the **Global Chakra Workings** - prefers the Aztec calendar, which he claims replaced the Mayan 'dead' calendar, and thus charts 2039 as the 'return of Quetzalcoatl'.

But what is any 'ending' anyway but another beginning? It is most likely a return to the primal shamanic D r e a m t i m e when matter and spirit were undifferentiated. Flipping through the lemniscate:

Here we are again at the Gates of Dawn, where the Piper plays his pipes. He draws down the moon with his tune and the Gates they Open. Osiris rises. O Sire rise again. Thus the procession began, the progression of the aeons...

Let us now examine each age from the beginning until now, and various interpretations thereof...

The Beginning has been called variously the *Dreamtime, The Shamanic Aeon* and the *Nameless Aeon*. It is not really the beginning of time as such but a prologue to it, as time was as yet unrecorded and not even necessarily acknowledged. It is too long ago for us to know. Like the future, it blurs into myth and speculation. 'History' as the recording of sequential events, had certainly not begun.

To the Aboriginals of Australia this is called the Dreamtime. It is the time of myth, when the Ancestor Spirits created the World. One of these ancient being is of course the timeless Rainbow Serpent, **Almudj.**

Another archetype of the Shamanic Aeon is **Pan**. As representative of the primal and ancient atavistic animal in man, the Horned God/dess was 'all' in this aeon. Thus came the Greek word Pan, meaning 'All'.

Aion tells of this Nameless Aeon and the Pan Current in his **Book of Gate called Pan**, the core text of *'The Book of the Horned One' (Concrescent Press 2012)* ascribing Qabalistic and other occult symbologies to this primal entity. Pan is 'the beast' within humankind, dominant before civilisation began. Thus the end-times with their 'Beast of the Apocalypse' again link back to the beginning.

But this 'Nameless Aeon' is all-ways present, thus the recurrent symbology/mythology of the Horned God/dess. It is the central core or axis of the aeonic caduceus/lemniscate, the sushumna through which the other aeons weave and cross. Just as the beast - our underlying animal/instinctual natures- is always inherent within us despite the veneer of civilisation, so too is the central dreaming always there, submerged as it may be under some rationalist or materialist paradigm. And to it we shall ever re-turn…

In Qabalah, the underlying esoteric tradition behind what became the biblical exoteric Jewish religion of Christianity, there is a formula called *Tetragrammaton*. This is a four-lettered (tetra=four) word for God in the ancient Hebrew Alphabet: **YHVH** -but it is also a magickal formulae for four successive aeons. It relates to the four extant elements, and even as the Qabalah apparently has its roots in

Ancient Egyptian Lore, these aeons each bear an Egyptian deity as their symbolic 'figurehead' or title. The first letter, Yod, represents Osiris, the 'He(h)' Isis, the 'Vau' Horus and the final 'He' Maat: The father, the mother, the son and the daughter.

This is a very western view of time-periods and certainly doesn't apply to all of the world historically or even her-storycally, but if recognised as such a limited perspective it still offers some interesting insights to the parts of the world to which it applies.

The Aeon of Isis, the Matriarchy, actually preceded that of Osiris despite the apparently contradictory order of the letters YHVH, which is ordered according to the idea of the male seed (the Y or Yod of the formula) initiating the process of conception rather than as a reflection of aeonic progression. The Aeon of Isis was the first actual 'aeon' of history, or more accurately at this point, 'herstory'. Not much was recorded yet, but civilisation had definitely begun. The Mother, Goddess of Fertility, reigned as agriculture started. The moon and the Earth were worshipped and venerated as sacred Goddesses, basic pagan culture flourished.

Then gradually the Patriarchy came in. The advent of the solar calendar brought in the Aeon of Osiris, the father. Solar pagan cults flourished. Organised religion began. Christianity started to spread across the world, becoming eventually the dominant paradigm as it displaced the old world mythologies and pantheons with its monotheistic dogma of 'one (male) God'. Simultaneously we saw the rise of materialistic scientific rationalism and the advent of industrialisation. Technology began to progress at an accelerating rate, and art became submerged beneath this onslaught of practicality.

Magic became esoteric, occult, hidden. Ritual, the dance of the common people with the elements during the matriarchy, became the cloistered province of the patriarchal priesthood. Those few who continued the ancient ways did so in secret, fearing the wrath of the fundamentalist church and its inquisitions.

Nevertheless magic and paganism did continue in the shadows, and as science became ever more dominant, *Aleister Crowley* emerged as a figurehead of an occult revival. By this time practically anyone who dabbled in magic was branded evil, so rather than try to refute this Crowley exploited a sinister image as 'the wickedest man in the world', playing the adversary and attracting many who were frustrated with the mediocrity of the Church and State.

Crowley's practises actually introduced an element of 'science' to magick like never before, introducing more precise methodologies while still revelling in the poetry of ceremony and ritual.

Enter the Hawk: In 1904 Crowley inaugurated the **'Aeon of Horus'**, the Crowned and Conquering Child with his receipt of the Book of the Law, *'Liber AL vel Legis'*

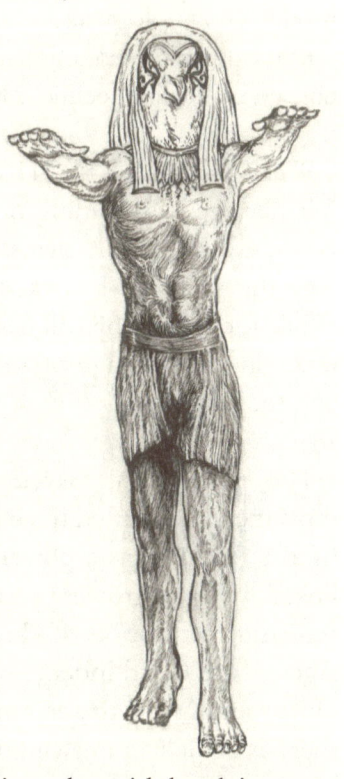

The aeon of the Son or Child was born with the purge of the first World War, which Crowley saw as the cleansing of the rubble of the Old Aeon. Horus is the hawk-headed warrior lord, son of Isis the mother and Osiris the father, whose throne he inherits in the ancient formula of Tetragrammaton.

The influence of Crowley and his work on the occult world is vast, stretching to many dimly-lit corners of various sects and orders. The independent receipt of similar information, also with hawk imagery, by others such as psychic Uri Geller, psychologist and psychedelic revolutionary Timothy Leary, quantum philosopher/author Robert Anton Wilson, and Damanhur ('City of Horus') Federation's founder Falco, fuels Crowley's claims of transmissions from extraterrestrial sources, apparently through the binary Sirius stars; or at the least

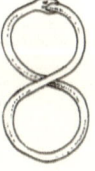

confirms the seeds in our collective consciousness planted by the ancient Egyptians (a culture very similar in architecture and astronomical interests to the Mayans) who worshipped Sirius as Sothis.

On the outer, the aeon of the Child also indeed seems to be manifesting. Since the nineteen-fifties a new spirit of youthful rebellion has emerged from the conservative values of the patriarchy, from the advent of rock music to the hippy flower power movement to the reactionism of punk to the current synthesis of all of these subcultures (and more) into a new breed which often embraces both modern technology and old world spirituality. Pagan, pa
ntheistic and even animistic attitudes re-emerge and the christian church begins its decline into stagnation.

When I first read that Horus had a twin, Maat, and that Crowley felt her age was coming next, in another 2000 years or so, I was confused: If they are twins, surely their aeons would be concurrent? And this seems to be exactly what is happening in modern society. While the patriarchy still has some dwindling hold on things, we are emerging into an age of sexual equality, an Aeon of both the son and the daughter.

The reactionary extremism of some of the early Feminist movement has shifted the balance and opened the way for the return of the feminine as a powerful political and spiritual force. This is linked with the growing ecological movement, with a long-overdue return to veneration of the Earth as a living entity, Gaia. It is the Age of the Child indeed, but that of the Son *and* the Daughter - Horus and Maat. It was a relief and confirmation to discover that there is actually a growing magickal current along these lines -the Magick of Maat, Goddess of Truth and Justice. This Egyptian deity, who traditionally weighs one's heart against a feather at death, represents truth and balance, and this is indeed Her role in our Aeon.

While it seems Horus and Maat are not literally twins in the usual familial sense (though in Ancient Egyptian mythology everyone seems related somehow), they certainly seem to be twinned currents.

As explored in my *'Book of Going Back by Night'* *(TwiLight Productions 2011, 2013)* this twinned energy seems to be a return to the source, as the very first male and female deity to the Egyptians are leonine Shu and Tefnut, who is another name of Mayet the World Order, earliest form of Maat.

Crowley's Magickal Child, *Frater Achad* (Achad is Hebrew for 'Unity'- numbering 13 in Qabalah) or Charles Stanfield Jones, inaugurated the 'Aeon of Maat' in 1948 but was largely ignored and rebuked by Crowley for this action as Aleister had only just inaugurated the Aeon of Horus.

In 1974 Priestess Nema recieved a transmission from Maat, *'Liber Pennae Praenumbra'*, during a time-travel working. Working within the Thelemic paradigm established by Crowley, her angle on the 'double current' of Horus and Maat is that the Maat current is coming backwards from a future aeon (thus the Maat current reflects the atavistic resurgence of Spare's Zos Kia Kultus) when time is perceived differently, manifesting now through those open enough to receive the information, the 'mutants' who are the avatars of the coming race of *'homo veritas'*.

Thus the advent of the Maat current in our present aeon does not contradict Crowley's ideas of Aeonic progression as it would at first seem, rather it indicates that time is not so linear and predictable as we previously perceived (and thus created) it -that in our aeon it begins to warp and bend as we realise the potential of its wo/manipulation.

> *'I am the unconfined. Who is there to say me nay, to say, "Thy time is yet to come," when Time itself is my chief serving-maid...'*
>
> -*Maat speaking in Nema's* **'Liber Pennae Praenumbra'**
> *(www.horusmaat.com/liberPP.htm).*

The Maat current thus comes back from the future even as the Horus current goes forth. NOW is the intersection of these polarities which occurs in the present, in the *PanDaemonAeon*-ic (Carroll's term for our new aeon) uniting eternal moment of the

sacred HermAphrodite.

The aim of Maat Magick now is primarily to awaken the collective consciousness of humanity, linking us all in universal empathy. It is hoped that this can be achieved in time to save our planet.

Magickal writer *Kenneth Grant* elucidated on the nature of this backwards-flowing current in his book, *'Outside the Circles of Time'* *(Frederick Muller Limited, 1980)*. He draws threads between Maat and the Arachnean re-turn of lunar worship (witchcraft and the neo-pagan movement), while also establishing the relationship between Maat and Horus. Achad called the aeon of Maat the **'Ma-nifestat-Ion'** for which he employed the symbol of a 3-fold 13-pointed Star with the letters of this word around its points. For as the daughter of the Tetragrammaton formula she manifests and completes the work through the element of earth.

In this current age Quantum Physics and Chaos Theory embrace and unify both science and magic. Peter Carroll's *'Liber Null and Psychonaut'* *(Samuel Weiser)* established the idea of 'Chaos Magick', a new outlook on magical practises embracing multi-culturalism and multi-belief-systems, more scientific in approach even than Crowley's. The term he derived from both the topical 'chaos theory' emerging in science and mathematics, and the work of artist and sorceror *Austin Osman Spare* (1888-1956), who introduced many of the ideas forwarded by Carroll of personalised magical symbology based more on innovation than tradition. This attitude of Spare's was an extension of his contemporary Crowley's own experimentation, while also a rejection of the pomp and trappings of ceremonial magic for a more grass-roots and pragmatic approach. While much more of a traditionalist than Spare, Crowley did freely adapt the traditional magical systems and symbols he used to his own ends. A part of this was his mutation of the Qabalah.

As eloquently put forth by Frater -0+ in his essay on *'Quantum Qabbala'*, we must in this age continue to update such ancient models and formulae to avoid becoming stuck in the ruts of the patriarchal tradition which has employed them for so long.

To upgrade the fourfold Qabalistic formula of Tetragrammaton to a model which accommodates the Nameless & Wordless Aeons (as Nema and Aion 131 call them) or the Shamanic and PanDaemonAeon (Carroll's term) we can employ the fivefold formula of **Pentagrammaton** as an Aeonic formula.

In the tetragrammaton the letters of the father, mother, son and daughter also each represent one of the classic elements -Fire, Water, Air and Earth respectively. As usual, the etheric fifth element of spirit, the quintessence which underlies and imbibes the other four, has been largely ignored. After being independently inspired by the concept of a Pentagrammaton (see my *'Liber Pentagrammaton'* www.crossroads.wild.net.au/liberp.htm), I discovered that there is actually an ancient esoteric doctrine reflecting it -the formula **YHShVH**. This is a name of Jesus the Redeemer, Yeheshua, just as the YHVH is the name of his father Yehovah.

As I had surmised, the fifth letter is Shin ('Sh'), the triple fire-tongue which represents both spirit and fire. Interestingly, this letter is placed in the middle, just as spirit resides in the middle of the traditional elemental medicine wheels of most pagan and tribal cultures, as well as modern witchcraft and ceremonial magick. Again, this is the sushumna or axis of the aeonic caduceus/lemniscate. It has all-ways been there, and to it we shall re-turn. That is why only one extra letter is needed to adjust the formula to accommodate these systems -I believe the 'beginning' (Nameless or Shamanic Aeon) and the 'end' (Wordless or PanDaemonAeon) are one and the same, the DreamTime Axis of manifest TimEmiT.

(My transmission 'Liber Pentagrammaton' reveals the new angles on the formula. It was released with a two-part trans-global *Pentagrammaton Ritual* - www.crosssroads.wild.net.au/pent.htm- in October 98, which laid the foundations for the **Global Chakra Workings** - see **APPENDIX D**).

Just as the pentagram is as valid an elemental model as the medicine wheel, the letter Shin can alternatively be placed at the beginning or end of the formula: YHVHS with its plural form suggests there is 'more than one God' i.e. pagan animistic pantheons are implied, or the S suggests the feminine, i.e. God/dess.

And as Nema has pointed out, ShYHVH spells Shiva. Shiva in earliest known forms (Pashupati and Shiva-An) is basically the Horned One of the eastern traditions, and as Alan Danielou has explored thoroughly in his wonderful *'Gods of Love and Ecstasy: The Traditions of Shiva and Dionysos' (Inner Traditions, 1992),* bears a marked resemblance to the ecstatic intoxicated God of the Thracians (and later the Greeks), whose cultus was similarly represented by the phallus/lingam and the bull. Even as Yeheshua is the Son of Jehovah, **Dionysos** was reborn from the thigh of Zeus (another lightning-wielding angry jealous bearded guy in the sky) in classical Greek myth. Another symbol of Dionysos is the black goat, whose head we find on Baphomet and in the Pentagram.

Thus my conception of the archetype for this extra letter applied to the aeonic formula is in contrast (yet ultimately com-plementary) with that of Jesus -it is **Baphomet**, the Hermaphroditic Horned God/dess. Both Creator and Destroyer, S/He is Kali-Shiva.

The image of this primal being has returned to us in modern magick through the *Knights Templar* and Eliphas Levi. Crowley, and Peter Carroll's *Illuminati of Thanateros* have also used this entity as a figurehead.

(It has unfortunately also fallen into the hands of silly 'satanic' cults who can't seem to separate the ancient Horned God from the 'Devil' created in his image by the Christian Church they purport to despise while embracing the flip side of the same moral dualism.)

Baphomet basically represents the primal instinctual nature of humanity and the rest of the animal kingdom, and as such it seems natural for it to be neither male nor female or better yet both, and thus most accurately represented (being an entity of the earth-force and therefore sexual) as hermaphroditic. While there is no historical evidence of the use of the name before the Knights Templar, Qabalistic gematria suggests 'Baphomet' (=131=Pan) is actually an ancient formula. Could this hermaphroditic form of the Horned One been the original vision, and the masculinisation of Pan/Cernunnos a part of patriarchal his-story? There are ancient Hindu texts describing Shiva as also being hermaphroditic (as **Ardhanarishvara**), as was the original creator Atum in the earliest versions of Egyptian mythology, and Dionysos was considered at least of a bisexual and effeminate nature.

In Iberian Craft, the magical tradition of the region where the Knights Templar undertook Moorish crusades, the goat's-head super-imposed over the pentagram, with horns, ears and goatee-beard forming the points, is a major symbolic key of initiation and has come to be associated with Baphomet. Leonardo da Vinci overlaid the human figure on the pentagram/pentacle, and this has become a symbol of man aspiring to the heavens or divinity, the goats-head of the inverse pentagram thus becoming a symbol of man bound to carnality and manifest existence.

This is a dualistic Christian perspective however. Although Baphomet is both God/dess and Demon/ness, S/He is ultimately beyond these moral distinctions created by 'civilisation', and herein lies the key of the syncretic image of horned and winged HermAphroditic Baphomet: There is truly no such distinction between human and beast, for we too are animals of this earth and a part of a greater ecosystem which we are more wont to befoul if we think of ourselves as separate from it. And from a pantheistic perspective everything living thing is imbued with spirit and divinity, not just 'man'.

Baphomet is thus perfectly represented by the Hebrew fire/spirit letter *Shin* in the Pentagrammaton formla. Hirs is the sexual passion and animal instinct of fire, but also the pure spirit of the Hermaphrodite, a traditional symbol of the alchemical marriage. The solar (masculine) and lunar (feminine) currents are united within the self to produce a balanced soul -not so different from Yeheshua, (whose 'second coming' is sometimes related to the return of Quetzalcoatl) after all, at least not from the essential spirit of Jesus and his teachings rather than the distorted recensions thereof through several millennia of patriarchal control.

Thus, the hermaphrodite is a symbol of the central dreaming axis through-which the male (Osiris/Horus) and female (Isis/Maat) serpent currents of the aeonic lemniscate (infinity symbol/ figure 8) caduceus cross:

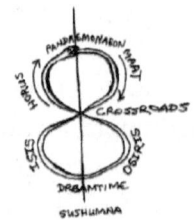

In his *'Book of Gate Called Pan'* (central text of his 'Book of the Horned One', Concrescent Press 2012) *Aion 131* calls this axis the Nameless Aeon -as a primal essence it is ultimately beyond titles and symbols. Peter Carroll, in his chapter on 'Aeonics' in 'Liber Kaos' *(Samuel Weiser)* calls it 'The Shamanic Aeon' in the beginning, and projects at the end of his study of the ages that we are now going into the 'Pandemonaeon'. I prefer taking this name to its Greek roots and spell-ing it 'Pandæmonaeon' -suggesting both our current age of ChAos (undoubtedly as we fragment into a trillion different quantum perspective-realities) and also translating into 'All(Pan)-Spirit(daemon)-Aeon', suggesting a re-turn to the central dreaming axis. So perhaps the Nameless Aeon has All-ways had a name?

The pentagram or five-pointed star is a symbol and tool of the element of earth in paganism, but is also a symbol of Nuit, the Goddess of the Universe to the Ancient Egyptians, who depicted Her arched body filled with five-pointed stars. Thus the symbol, for all its animal earthiness, takes us beyond this little blue planet to the entirety of manifest existence. Thus it is the most common symbol of magick, the means by which we can bring our hopes and dreams to earth, into manifestation. It is a star, and it is the human figure.

Crowley emphasised this: *'Every man and woman is a star'*. There is a large element of 'star magic' within the Maatian Current also, including feathered masks which I relate as much to the 'return of the Bird Tribes' prophesied by American Indians as to their alchemical origins.

We seem to be approaching or even already crossing a major Cross-Roads, as first 2000 then 2012 pass and still we sit poised on the brink of destruction or breakthrough into a new way of being. The Mayans called the alignment of our planet and sun's ecliptic with the centre of our Galaxy the 'Crossroads' of their Sacred Tree. The apex of this was Solstice 2012 -but a blink of the Gods- but the new patterns continue to emerge from this point in these centuries of rapid change…

If this is applied to the YHVH Aeonic model above, it seems that Crowley's inauguration of the Aeon of Horus was somewhat premature. Astrologically, we didn't move into the Age of Aquarius, which is also considered the Age of the Child, until 2008.

When it is considered that 'aeons' usually refer to periods of at least a couple of thousand years, it puts things into perspective: that this is actually only the beginning of the great transition, the Crossroads flip into the next great arc of the wheel. As usual, esoteric theories precede their exoteric manifestations - beings such as Crowley, Achad and Nema are prophets of the continuing paradigm shift, into the Aeon of the Immortal Child. Osiris and Isis merge at the Crossroads into the hermaphrodite, then birthing/splitting again to form the Twins, Horus and Maat.

The galactic core our sun's ecliptic has aligned with is visible as a dark cleft in the middle of the Milky Way. The Mayans called this Crossroads the 'Path to the Underworld' or the 'Dark Path', and it was considered to be the 'Womb of the Great Mother' from which the universe was born; thus it is the means of rebirth through death and relates to Star-mother-goddesses such as Nuit or Isis, from whom the new aeonic child (ren) shall be spawned...

This is a great crossroads of all paradigms. Time itself is beginning to be perceived/manipulated differently. Our full potential as Homo Veritas will be eventually realised as we all link minds and ultimately, souls, not with consumer monoculture but as a fully-potentiated Unity in Diversity.

Thus we re-turn to the Dreamtime where we began, as the great serpent of time, Tiamait/Orobororos, swallows hir own tail, in what the Mayans call 'Zuvuya' -the circuit by which everything returns to it's source. This is the end result or ultimate Truth of the backwards-flowing current of Maat. In Qabalah Truth ('Maat') =131= Pan ('All') = Baphomet.

Maat's symbol is the feather of truth. According to Kenneth Grant, TzITz is a fabulous bird of Jewish legend and also means 'to be feathered' or 'fledged'. Its number, 190, is also the number of QTz, which means 'the end' or 'the appointed time.' Being more specialised in Qabalah and Thelema than Mayan mythology, Grant didn't seem to notice the full cross-cultural significance of this: QTz suggests to me Quetzalcoatl, the 'feathered serpent'!

The Mayan language has both backwards and forwards words, and those which read both ways are, like the mirror figure 131, words of ultimate Truth. Thus the number 13, sacred to both the moon (lunar cycles) and the sun (Mayan 13th baktun -solar consciousness), are mirrored and united in this Qabalistic key.

The international chaos magic group IOT has as its axiom *'Nothing is True. Everything is permitted'*. There are no rules -this is neither matriarchy nor patriarchy, it is just an-archy!

Maat as the 'absolute truth' whose form is only suggested by the varied truths of many cultures.
 -from Orryelle's red book '*Conjunctio*' *(Fulgur 2008)*

But 'in the future' and by the same mouth of paradox, 'Everything is True. And No-thing IS permitted', for the future is Maat ('Truth'), and there is No absolute Truth. Think about this for a while, it may help you understand the backwards and forwards-flowing nature of emiTime...   The Axis has all-ways been t/here.

Several mainstream monotheist religions share the eschatological image of a **'Beast'** of the Apocalypse:

The biblical Book of Revelations describe it with seven heads and ten horns, ridden by our lady **Babalon**, the holy harlot whom Crowley has promulgated as a more positive figure and Jack Parsons (a student of Crowley and a NASA rocket scientist) saw as the 'H' final or daughter of the YHVH aeonic formula earthed by his *'Book of Babalon'*. I see Babalon as an aspect or mask of Maat (see my 'The Book of Going Back by Night', iNSPiRALink. 2013).

In Islam, the 'Beast of the Earth' of the end-times is described even more bizarrely by Ibn al-Zubayr :

"Its head is like the head of a bull, its eyes are like the eyes of a pig, its ears are like the ears of an elephant, its horns are like the horns of a stag, its neck is like the neck of an ostrich, its chest is like the chest of a lion, its color is like the colour of a tiger, its haunches are like the haunches of a cat, its tail is like the tail of a ram, and its legs are like the legs of a camel.'

(Tadhkirah by al-Qurtubi)

Another common thread in *Eschatology* (the study of the end-times) is the coming of a heroic avatar on a White Horse: in Islam the prophet *Madhi*, in Vedic Hinduism the tenth avatar of Vishnu, *Kalki*. Kalki shares the attribute of a 'sword flaming like a comet' with the Christian and Jewish *St Michael* who is proposed to slay the Beast in a cosmic battle at the end of time.

I hardly see this as a likely solution, more as a symptom of why we are actually facing such potential 'end times'. Dualistic notions of good and evil are not going to save us, rather we need to transcend such moralities and their inherent judgementalism and recognise and accept our cultural and personal differences, and to heal the body-mind-spirit split such concepts foster.

The only 'messiah' we can count on saving us is Ourselves, in collective recognition of Unity not in monoculture but in co-operative diversity. The Beast truly lies without as much as within our own labyrinthine minds, for it is our own bodies (and our greater body, the Earth), and we must unite with rather than slay it.

The Archangel Who once slew the Beast
And trod Him Underfoot
Is now seduced, A Feast for the Senses
The Beast deduced a choice twixt
Love and War
Is not so hard to make

And so in passion's throes, instead of blood
Sweet seeds the angel shed
The Beast he fed, a feast illumined
Until the hosts a-summoned come
Unto His hungry Maw
The starry horde a-shudder 'neath
His clenching paw
The drum upon the Cauldron
Beauty and the Beast
BeCome One
A feather-fledged,
Serpentine Conundrum

-*St Michael and the Beast,*
song lyrics by Orryelle 2012.

In his study of Aeonics in *'Liber Kaos'*, Peter Carroll ends with wondering whether in this current aeon we will end up scrabbling over tinned food in the post-apocalyptic rubble, or flying through the stars.

This seems to be the question everyone's asking, but ultimately, either way -no matter how far we advance or extend ourselves into the multiverse of possibilities, we'll still look within and find only ourselves -an animal housing the quintessence of spirit.

We have looked back at Time's spiralling course from several different angles and through varied cultural lenses now, in terms of its mystery or mythic hirstory. Now we may look at where this accumulation of symbols and archetypes from the past has brought us, as we pass through...

TimE, Fate and Spider Magic

TimE, Fate and Spider Magic

The Second Gate

TimE, Fate and Spider Magic

Spiels of thread, Threads of spells
All weaved into the wondrous webs
All a part of the flow and ebb
The hoops and wheels Spun and reeled
The loops and spools Strung and spieled
Into the Web of Fate
For She is the guardian of the Second Gate
Mother, And the Cutter awaits

Soft webs, gossamer webs, webs of finest silken strands
Wound and bound with the Weaver's hands
Wind-blown webs, wind-swept webs,
Lines of Life, Cords of Power
Fasten together in this quickening hour
Threads of tales, tales of threads
All weaved into the wondrous web
Into the Web of Fate
For She is the Weaver and the Cutter awaits
You have passed the Second Gate
The threads are drawn together
A matrix matted of matter and ether
Spun from threads of tales and tricks,
From twists and turns of Fate in-which
Different lifelines converge
Mesh and merge
Binding, winding, dividing, divining
...In the Web of Fate

Delicate webs, in-tric-ate webs; Binding webs, Bonding webs, warm webs, wet webs, gentle lapping sticky webs...

(-lyrics by Orryelle, from *The Loom of Maya* track of Mutation Parlour's **LABYRINTH CD**.)

Terence and Dennis McKenna's *'Timewave Zero'* software tracks the Spiral of time. As explained in their, *'The Invisible Landscape'* (Harper Collins '93) this model was derived from experiments with Ayahuasca -a shamanic concoction of psychotropic plants of South America- and the hexagrams of the ancient Chinese oracle, the I Ching, which although at least 5000 years old is notably resonant (in its oldest format, the 'Fu His') with relatively recent scientific discoveries about our DNA genetic code.

The date they arrived at for the centre of their spiral map of time -as apex of 'the concrescence of novelty'- was December Solstice 2012, the date the ancient Mayan 'Long Count' calendar was to end. Because the McKennas had no conscious knowledge of this at the time, its discovery made a 'point' about the significance of the Mayan end-date for many -myself included- beyond the initial wild speculations of Jose Arguelles on Mayan calendrics. Of course it is also likely that the McKennas tapped into the psychic field of the land where they began the experiment- Mexico, home of the Mayans who probably used the same entheogens as they were on at the time. Nevertheless, the 'synchronicity' is a significant one, regardless of its channels of reception.

While it would be easy to now dismiss the McKennas' theories as drug-addled nonsense since nothing much actually 'happened' (at least on an extant level) on 21/12/2012, I think there is certainly something interesting about their perception of time as a spiral, one that resonates deeply with my own perceptions of time and of fate in relation to its mythic herstory.

So if the centre of the spiral really was Solstice 2012, are we then now spiralling back out? Or are we shifting subtlely into another frequency of time-perception altogether, from this central dreamtime 'axis'? It is important to remember that even a year is the blink of an eye in an aeonic sense, and to expect significant immediate change on a single solstice day is a somewhat myopic viewpoint. In the bigger picture, things are definitely changing quite rapidly, and the amount of people (even including all the deluded newage fruitbats with at least mostly positive agendas) who performed synchronised ritual worldwide on the December Solstice 2012 is likely to have an effect that is less than immediate in its gradual unfoldment.

Personally I have also had some strange and profound insights into the nature of time on Ayahuasca (while in Peru) and on its Australian analogue (made from acacia bark -significant in that 'acacia' is Latin for akasha, and the extracted tryptamines of acacia do seem to facilitate deep memories of the Akashic records stored in our cellular DNA or genetic memories). However my greatest realisations about time's spiralling properties have been while on fly agaric (amanita muscaria) mushrooms, those white-spotted bright red magic mushrooms so often seen in the vicinity of toads or gnomes in faery tales, purportedly (according to the researches and theories of Gordon Wasson and others) the ancient magickal 'Soma' of the Indian Rig Veda manuscripts (though others suggest a vine - banisteriopsis or an Indian equivalent, containing the active ingredients of ayahuasca?).

During intense journeys with these sacred fungi (which must be dried before consumption) I have become hyper-aware of the spirals of time, and of the webs of fate woven therefrom. Every moment seemed pre-ordained, yet somehow simultaneously and inevitably self-determined, and I could feel the next word, action or event coming around in its cycle, like a wave seen on the horizon in the ocean of time, gradually coming closer until it inevitably and predictably rolls over the self.

On my first fly agaric journey, the 3 witches with me (who had only partaken of a single bite of the mushrooms, which was quite apparently enough to tune into my larger dose trip) and I began to speak sentences together, each of us uttering a single word around in a circle that formed cohesive passages which we all apparently knew.

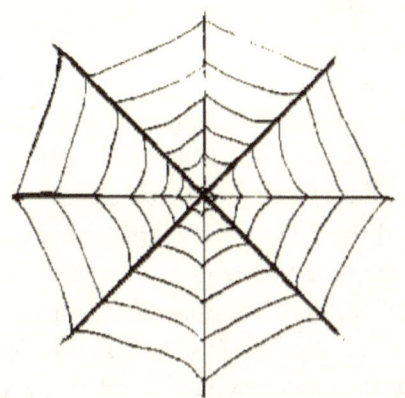

Manifest existence is a vast weaving, intricate and complex.

Time can be mapped magically on the spatial plane with a simple diagram of a spider's web: the spiral of time with intersecting rays.

Within The HermAphroditic ChAOrder of the Silver Dusk (www.crossroads.wild.net.au/order.htm) we use a composite symbol based upon this web pattern called The **ChaOrder Wo/Mandala** for astral travel through time and space.

It is the traditional basic spider-web form of eight rays intersecting a spiral; but these rays are here also the eight black outwards-pointing arrows of the ChaoStar (*illustrated below*).

The ChaoStar symbol, originally from the fiction of Michael Moorcock, was popularised in the Chaos Magic movement by Peter Carroll and his successors. It has been effectively introduced as a meme so that almost anyone may now recognise it as a symbol of chaos. Thus it has been adopted by various death metal bands and

generally given a negative edge; Unsurprising given its one-way and thus unbalanced nature. The ChAOrder star, as you will see, takes its meaning further...

Eight is an appropriate number for many reasons: it is the number of a spider's legs, and thus as Her web an extension thereof; it is the neo-pagan Wheel of the Year -the eight Sabbats (Summer Solstice,

Lughnasad, Autumn Equinox, Samhain, Winter Solstice, Imbolc, Spring Equinox, Beltaine) of modern Witchcraft. In earlier traditions from which the system is derived the solstices and equinoxes were probably celebrated in different parts of the world to the other four according to climactic seasonality; it is unlikely any ancient culture celebrated all eight. Nevertheless in neopaganism this eightfold system is prevalent and thus Eight represents the seasonal quarters and cross-quarters of the year as calendrical markers. Eight is also the (often corresponded) directional quarters (North East South and West) used in most ritual circle-castings, at which the elements or elementals are traditionally evoked; and the cross-quarters (NW, NE, SW, SE) or spaces i n   b e t w e e n.

Eight-spoked wheel or star motifs are evident in many Islamic carpet weavings -from the middle-east to Kashmir in India- representing Fate or Fortune's wheel. In Qabalah Eight is the number of *Hod*, the Mercurial Sephira of intellect, of communications, maps models and systems -again, webs or networks.

The 8-rayed ChaoStar (or it's 3-dimensional form as the ChaoSphere —see the centre of the Wheel in my **ARCANA X** illustration, p.) also implies the 'eight colours of magick'. A system derived from the fiction of *Terry Pratchett*, Peter Carrol has applied it to this model where eight colours are corresponded with the eight arrows of the chaostar and represent eight different basic types of magick, e.g. yellow as ego magick, black as death magick, silver as sex magick, green as love magic, etc. This is the usual chakra spectrum of seven plus 'Octarine' which is defined as the particular specific hue the individual mage finds pertinent to his practices.

Anton Channing in his article 'The Kaosphere and New Aeon Alchemy' in Chaos International magazine #25 *(BCM Sorcery, 2002)*, presents a revised and I believe refined development of this chaosphere colour system —or devise your own personal one…

In the **ChaOrder Wo/Mandala** (*above*) the spiral which the eight outward-pointing arrows intersect forms an additional eight arrows pointing inwards, created by the negative space b e t w e e n the outwards-pointing arrows. These represent Order as the counterpoint to Chaos.

This mud-map is a representation of the dance of polarities: outwards, inwards; black, white; yin, yang; expansion, contraction; order, chaos. The animated version of it which appears on The Silver Dusk wwwebsight (www.crossroads.wild.net.au/order.htm) seems to actually pulsate, as if it is inhaling and exhaling -indeed this is what the wo/mandala is about. Chaos is essentially E x p a n s i o n -the outwards movement of energy in random patterns of flux. Chaos is creative and opening outwards, so the chaostar is indeed an appropriate symbol for it. Order, on the other hand, is Contraction -it is drawing things inwards and together into a net of structure and systemisation, containing the infinite potential in a set form or mode of apprehension. This is of course as necessary as chaos, it is the way we make the universe manageable and comprehensible with our finite (and therefore contractive) perceptions. Just as too much order and control can limit our perspective (something which chaos magic seemed to initially rebelling against, ie. hidebound and outdated specific magical systems), continuous chaos and expansion leads to entropy, and often results in unearthed magick, as everything is so constantly in flux that it cannot be grounded.

Of course both chaos and order are all a matter of perception ultimately, and lead to the same point either via the centre or the rim of the Great Wheel, the axis/axle or the infinite outer expanses of the mandala. This is the transcendence of duality, including the apparently polar concepts of 'chaos' and 'order' themselves.

However to exist/perceive in the world of form requires our immediate re-turn back into the realms of division and manifestation; which is why the *'Gods are always Going' (-Crowley)*, and Hadit (the Thelemic name for the Point of Manifestation) is ever in motion.

So the ChaOrder WoMandala (which has also appropriately become a part of the logo for **iNSPiRALink.Multimedia Press** of which the first edition of this book was the first publication) inhales and exhales, contracts and expands, as it doth emit time. Time emiT flows in as well as out. We are inspir(al)ed, and we expire -birth and death, of ideas or of forms which coagulate there-from.

The eight outward-pointing positive arrows combined with the eight inward-pointing negative space arrows form the traditional Sixteen Kalas of Kali, the emissions of the Great Black Mother of Time.

Thus this model is akin to the Hindu and Tibetan *KalaChakra Wheel*, as will be further explored...

These kalas or emanations from the womb of Kali are the different phases in the female cycle, the different secret-ions at different times of the moonth, but on an energetic-etheric as well as physiological level. That the kalas flow inwards as well as outwards in the ChaOrder WoMandala is indicative of the two-way flow of timemit.

Time-emiT flows andna sbbe sdrawkcab as well as forwards, and the future can affect the past as much as the past affects the future - it's all a matter of perspective. Even as the negative-space inwards-pointing arrows in the ChAOrder WoMandala are far less obvious to most than the outwards-pointing ones, it is a bit more difficult to perceive the reverse flow of time than the forwards cause-and-effect linear timeline which we are much more accustomed to perceiving.

Sensations of Deja-vu and future memories are phenomenal indications of points of potential to follow into noitpecrep esrever. There are techniques of reverse speech which can help one tap into the reverse flow of time, as I will explore a little further into this time-twisting tome...

Crowley's *'Liber Brasyt vel Thisarb'* (http://mysteria.com/liber/L_913.txt) also suggests helpful techniques along similar linesenil.

Looking at forms of prophecy and divination in a different manner from the usual are also basic steps towards this perception shift: Divination is as much conjuration from a reverse-time perspective as apparent conjuration is also reverse-time divination. When one truly engages with this perceptual shift the apparent difference between conjuration and divination begins to blur.

This backwards flow of time is especially evident in the Maat current of Magick. Most people I know who have come into contact with the Maat current have had some kind of omen, feeling or indication towards its energies before and leading up to their direct contact via other practitioners or resources with the confirming information which follows. Perhaps this is actually the effect of their 'later' contact with the current, its gnilppir-sdrawkcab morphic resonances.

As a generalisation (and any metaphor or model can ultimately be naught but generalisation), feminine or negative (in terms of electrical currents rather than any moral connotations) energy flows inwards (receptive) while masculine or positive energy flows outwards (active), so -as demonstrated graphically in the ChaOrder WoMandala- it is unsurprising that in the 'Double Current' of our aeon, that of Horus and Maat, it is the energies of Maat that move 'backwards'. For the key is in the spiral -there is no real 'backwards' or 'forwards' in time, for time is not linear. There is only inwards to the centre of the spiral, i.e. moonwise or absorbent/contractive, or outwards from the centre of the spiral, i.e. sunwise or radiant/expansive.

The ancient Vedas, Sanskrit scriptures which predate the Tantras, do not actually mention *'Kundalini'* -not at least under that name. Their equivalent seems to be **'Kala Agni'** -which translates as 'Time Fire'. This energy of time is said to rise, in much the same way as the tantras speak of Kundalini rising. The fascinating aspect of the Vedic version for me is that this rising fire is said to reverse the flow of time: time is perceived to flow backwards from the future rather than just forwards from the past, so that the Time-God MahaKala - a form of Shiva- is no longer seen as just a devouring monster but a creative being. Kala Agni rises, and resultantly Soma- the other meta concept present with Agni throughout the Vedas- rains down, affecting the consciousness. The Soma here is presumably akin to the Amrita or nectar of immortality accessible via Khechari mudra and other potent yogas or extended meditation trances, for its descent upon Kala Agni's ascent produces euphoria.

Thus with the rise of Kala Agni and the reversal of the 'arrow of time' we may become a *'Kala Purusha'* -a prophetic being of time who senses future and thus aligns Fate with True Will.

This is so remarkably consistent with my own experiences and resultant concepts of reverse timemit esrever , that when I discovered its presence in these ancient scriptures while in India in 2005, it was strangely self-referential for me: this was confirmation of my own prophetic sense of the reverse flow of timemit attained from kundalini gnosis, so that finding out about Kala Agni after already sensing it coming was a profound example of itself!

Although they didn't call it kundalini in the vedas, the metaphor of the rising serpent is incredibly congruent with the idea and the concept of time as a spiral. For the kundalini traditionally sits coiled (3 and a half times) around the base of the spine, but once activated spirals upwards -thus we see our usual restricted sense of time rising up on the arrow of Kala Agni to a transcendent sense of Eternity.

There is a popular conception in India of **MahaKala** as consuming and monstrous. Even the more common blue (rather than black) form of Shiva is the Destroyer of the prime trinity of Hindu Gods (with Brahma the Creator and Vishnu the Preserver).

Chronos-MahaKala from Orryelle's **SOLVE** *(Fulgur 2012)*

Indeed time kills people, animals and plants, collapses buildings and temples. Whole civilisations crumble and fall, all swallowed into His great maw in the relentless and inexorable forwards flow of time.

But the rising of time fire and the blissful descent of soma puts all this in a different perspective, even as Chronos was made to regurgitate his children. An entropic force becomes a creative one -

Shiva as pure Consciousness, accessed by Shakti (pranic energy) ascending the spine.

And ultimately somatic states may take us to the great void beyond time (regardless of its perceived direction), as MahaKala is Himself consumed, by Maha Kali...

... only to emit once again from Her great Yoni *(as in the illustration on the previous page)*, with a renewed appreciation of the wonderment of form.

A point of relevance to the difference in male and female apprehension of timemit is suggested by the nature of different sexual orgasms. This came to my attention when first talking to a genetic male who had experimented with estrogen intake for an extended period. After 6 moonths or so of taking the female hormones oestrogen and also progesterone daily he found that when he orgasmed he no longer ejaculated. Any male who has worked with Tantric or Taoist techniques of more deliberate non-ejaculatory orgasm knows this is often a feeling of implosion, which when properly practised can be as intense as or often even more intense than the more explosive outer-orientated ejaculatory orgasm; but in his case it was not practised or intended, rather a result of taking female estrogen over an extended period of time.

This suggested to me that female orgasm is perhaps more implosive, and thus moves emit ni sdrawkcab as a normal male orgasm moves forwards in time. Most of the feedback from my presentation of the idea (primarily for the purpose of such feedback from women) through several magical and tantric communications wwwebs supported the theory, but while many women indeed felt their orgasms to be inward or backwards moving there were some who did not, so it is by no means conclusive and I am interested to hear more from genetic females -especially practising tantrikas or taoists- upon the subject.

Regardless of the validity of this theory, the practise of non-ejaculatory orgasm by genetic males is potentially a means of be-coming more hermaphroditic in nature, and perceiving the timeflow differently. Indeed, those who continue such practises do generally seem more given to intuitive (generally considered a more feminine trait) inspiration and are less linear, forwards-striving and over-ambitious. Personally I find that with sexual magick the forwards or sdrawkcab movement of phenomena through timemit is usually somewhat relevant to the explosive or implosive nature of orgasm.

The spiral reveals the inner nature of Time. It appears to be linear but only because we perceive such a tiny amount of it at once that we cannot notice its vast curve; just as we cannot notice the curve of the spherical earth which we inhabit. It took a long time for scientists to establish that this planet is not flat, and even now the spiral nature of time is not a universally accepted paradigm.

There are however recent theories in modern physics which postulate time as a spiral. In my case it is more a deep feeling, a glimpse into an innate knowing of time and fate's nature from my work with the Great Spider Goddess.

Of course I do not expect anyone to take this on faith, but I do suggest thinking about and even working with the model (using the methods presented beyond the Third Gate, or/and your own) and see if it resonates with you experientially. And consider this: Time is obviously cyclic - it is crafted by the orbits of sun, moon, planets, etc., through which weave the life cycles of birth and death; these are the patterns of constant change. Cycles are the play of recurring phenomenon, but they are not merely circular, for when we come around to the same point again -say for example the full moon- things will be different from how they were on the previous full moon. We are not at the same point in a circle, but at the corresponding point on the next loop of the spiral...

Of course all of this is metaphorical -it is time mapped onto a spatial plain, and it is important to remember that the map is not the territory, and in this case even the 'territory' is not even really that, since that word itself has spatial implications!

Nevertheless the time spiderweb is useful as a map, and one may use it to navigate time ritually.

For is not Ritual itself a map, being a reflection of macrocosmic events within the microcosm of the Magician's circle, whereby H/She may effect change on a personal level in such a way that it may potentially reflect back into the macrocosm?

So if we consider the spiral of the spider's web as 'normal' time, appearing as linear only from the limited perspective of the evident 'now' in much the same way as the world looks flat from our tiny point upon its vast surface, what then are the Rays of this great spider's web?

Well a spider uses the rays upon which to travel. Insects get caught in the sticky strands of the spiral, while s/he travels freely on the frictionless rays between its coils.

This provides an interesting metaphor for our perception and apprehension of Fate, the spider being the prime zoomorphic archetype of this -She who spins, weaves and cuts the threads of our destiny. We can be insects caught in Her web -pawns of Fate, helpless and trapped in the sticky spiral of our own pre-determined destiny. Or we can 'take Fate into our own hands', so to speak, and become akin to spiders ourselves, moving freely on webs of our own making.

Red Spider, Black Spider
Spirals outside and inside Her
Collide Kaleidoscopic scope
Hide your psychotropic hope
Of Release
You are bound by belief, Oh well fed
But free to disbelieve
And Retrieve
Yourself from your own Web

-Lyrics from **Red Spider, Black Spider** song by Orryelle

To illustrate, I will refer now at length to some verse (to follow) I 'received' one strange dawn; and the whole matter of what this 'channeling' portends illustrates the issue of destiny further, as I will eventually demonstrate.

Many moonths before the receipt of this work I had tried for the first time the 'MexicanDreaming Herb' *Alea Zachitechichi*. After a strong tea and consecutive smoke of the dried plant, traditionally one is supposed to ask a question of it before retiring to sleep, anticipating then a divine answer or guidance from within the world of Dreams.

Unfortunately I remembered little of my dreaming that night, and what I could vaguely recall (which did have an unusual yet indefinable quality about it) seemed largely irrelevant to my magickal request, which was 'to find the Book of the Spider'. This is an 'astral grimoire' which resides -according to Kenneth Grant in his brilliantly non-linear epic, *'Outside the Circles of Time'* (Frederick Muller, 1980) - in the tunnel of **Qulielfi**, the Nightside reflex of the path of The Moon (ATU/Arcana XVIII, Path XXIX upon the Dayside of the Tree of Life).

It seemed at the time my request had been ignored or at best forgotten by my waking mind, but even on the dayside the Moon trump represents subconscious strata - the corresponding Hebrew letter *Qoph* is symbolised by the Back of the Head where resides the Cerebellum or subconscious of the brain. So the tunnel of Qulielfi on the more atavistic Nightside of the Tree is buried even deeper, it is therefore little wonder that it took so long for any of *The Book of the Spider* to begin to emerge into the light of day and conscious consideration.

When moonths later I wrote the first half of this book (*Hekate edition, 2000*) it occurred to me that this was perhaps the Book of the Spider?; or at least related. I had expected a more poetic, inspired and even channelled work, yet it was almost with a sense of relief that I found myself constructing a piece of writing expressing these concepts in straightforward terms that could readily be comprehended by the 'layperson', being at the time rather tired of the thick veneer of impenetrable symbolism and esoteric lingo which often enshrouds such texts.

Then later, when I had left this writing for some time unsure quite how to proceed further, a poetic and esoteric '*Book of the Spider*' (or at least some verses thereof) came through after all, and reminded me of the actual value and purpose of such works: The Twi l i g h t La n gua g e or Crepuscular Vernacular of such inspired verse may elude even the recipient for a while, thereby allowing a gradual unveiling via progressive interpretation (that of the self and others) which often reveals inherent content beyond the usual reaches and constructs of the recipient's conscious mind.

Thus the work is truly 'channelled' in that it appears to come from somewhere 'else', though whether this 'other' source is truly external and alien or the deeper strata of the subconscious and even unconscious mind (and whether there is ultimately any difference between these) remains debatable. Suffice it to say that I was not consciously aware of the full meaning or implications of these verses upon receipt.

The verses came through after a long night of magickal conversations culminating in an auto-sexual rite upon retiring at dawn. This book you are reading and its considerations were obviously an influencing factor on the reception, much of the writing presented before **THE SECOND GATE** having been written not long before it. The verses, in poetic format, took the premises I had already offered further, my subconscious -or was it something 'other'; Fate Herself?- providing keys to further delineation.

I have no desire to abandon the straightforward explanations of the concepts whose delineation I have embarked upon either however, so this book will continue to explain the theories of spiderweb timetravel in a direct manner henceforth, using the following verses from the '*Book of the Spider*' only as further demonstrative material for this expression, rather than obfuscating its clarity (despite the paradoxical convolutions of this ironically explicative sentence!). The following part of this book thus becomes somewhat of a commentary on the verses, elucidating the symbolism therein for the layperson but also, ultimately, demonstrating various methodologies of application in practical terms.

After writing the above introduction to my own verses of *The Book of the Spider*, I read Kenneth Grant's then recent book, *'Beyond the Mauve Zone'* (Starfire, 1999), and was surprised to discover in Chapter 8 (page 179) that Grant had himself found/received 'The Book of the Spider' which he calls also *Liber 29, 'The Book of Okbish'* and planned to publish it with 'an elaborate commentary' in the impending final volume (*'The Ninth Arch'*) of his series of Three Typhonian Trilogies. This dumbfounded me, as I wondered for a while whether I should still call my transmission *The Book of the Spider*?

I decided it was a general enough title to share (especially as Grant's has a more specific title also, 'Liber Okbish'), as I was unaware of Grant's intentions when initially inspired to present this related material myself (certainly I mean no discredit to Mr Grant but rather acknowledge a shared current with a great appreciation of his own work); and that if as I suspected these verses were indeed received from a similar source, how they relate or correlate (or Not) with Grant's own transmissions from the tunnel of Qulielfi would be most interesting to discover when he published them.

I wrote to Mr Grant with some of my own Book of the Spider before releasing it and his reply confirmed no antagonism about my independent apprehension of this astral grimoire or parts thereof; rather interest in its possibly congruent premises:

> '...It is clear from your 'Extract' that you intuit some of these Mysteries and I shall therefore be an avid reader of your forthcoming book, which I hope will meet with every success, although there may be very few 'out there' who will follow the drift of your researches.'
>
> -*Private correspondence with Kenneth Grant, 11 Oct '02*

TimE, Fate and Spider Magic

Just before the publication of the initial *'Hekate edition'* (limited to 100 signed copies) of this book (then titled the more obscure, *'Emit fo yrotsreH feirB A'*) Grant published his *'The Ninth Arch'* opus, and although I have not plumbed its convoluted depths thoroughly (this could take years!) I now see what Grant meant when he said,

> 'I think you have no reason to suspect that your work covers ground similar to that of OKBISh, as OKBISh is founded on altogether 'other' principles, which will be evident to you when 'The Ninth Arch' appears a few weeks from now '

(-private correspondence, 11 Oct '02).

His epic is esoteric and obscure beyond even his earlier works. While I greatly appreciate Grant's continuous blurring of the lines b e t w e e n 'fact' and 'fiction' in a phantasmagoric and surreal magickal praxis of constant Becoming (indeed, I aspire with my own work to consider poetry and aesthesis at least the equal of scholarship and clarity), I feel his final volume has perhaps gone a little too far into his own (and those members of his 'Nu Isis Lodge' whose work aided the receipt of the transmission) personal Magickal Universe for the work to be accessible to many. But as he also said in his letter to me,

> 'What will also be evident is that various elements from Q, and related Tunnels, defy comprehension by the Day -or the Night-Mind, although by direct apperception they may perhaps be sensed. It is a difficult field to analyse and I think you already appreciate the nature of some, at least, of the difficulties involvd in the way of interpretation.'

So in contrast the verses of *The Book of the Spider* transmitted to my self seem a lot more accessible, and I hope that along with my commentary thereon they may form a bridge b e t w i x t more obscure and deeply 'Nightside' works such as that of Grant's, even as Grant himself in earlier (and more readily comprehensible) works has written of the Spider as weaving Her webs across the vast chasm b e twe e n the Dayside and Nightside of the Tree of Life, as metaphor for the bridge between the conscious and the subconscious mind, physiologically the pons brain-bridge between the cerebrum (forebrain) and the cerebellum (backbrain). This bridge is *Daath*, and leads to or through the Abyss, so it is dangerous yet vital territory.

I consider magic in general to be concerned with this relationship and its spanning, one of the reasons I consider all magic to be ultimately arachnean in application (as it concerns weaving strands between one thing and another) if not necessarily in aesthetic. And I have no doubt from his other work that Mr Grant's recent apparent plunge directly into the abyss of the unconscious with 'The Ninth Arch' was not without deliberation.

It is especially fascinating to me that from his comments at the end of 'Beyond the Mauve Zone' Kenneth Grant is suggesting an Arachnean direction for the magics of this aeon, as Spider Magics have always been prevalent in my work and that of my magical clan. Certainly they seem energies pertinent to the concept of the current 'Information Age' of global telecommunications (as reflected in the Hopi Indian prophecy that, *'The land shall be criss-crossed by a giant spider's web' (-White Feather, Bear Clan)* -and World travel, and the congruent Hindu concept of the Kali Yuga or Age of Chaos in which, *'All information of All Peoples will be available to everyone.'*

In regard to the propensity of these different versions or perhaps sections of *The Book of the Spider*, see also the commentary on the first stanza.

Since the publication of the first *('Hecate')* edition of this book, I received several more verses of *The Book of the Spider*, without any specified intent to do so. These followed an extended ritual-which though originally intended to take just one night took three consecutive nights to successfullycomplete- in 2004 inwhich I and a magical partner (who wishes to remain anonymous) invoked Arachne progressively with mantras and tantric sexual practises. Part of the intended practical result of this ritual was the audio recording -while in an appropriate state of sexual tension- of some lines of the existing Book of the Spider (verse 3 following) - for addition to a recording of the verses (with music/soundscapes) begun in London the year before.

(The complete audio of *The Book of the Spider* is on the DVD accompanying the hardback edition of this book, or available separately via www.crossroads.wild.net.au/inspiral2.htm)

This was eventually achieved along with the other (more complex) intentions of the rite, so it was a fascinating unexpected additional (yet integral) result that more verses came through in writing immediately after the ritual's completion -as if the previous verses had to be fully woven into the web and re-corded for more to be spun...

And again in 2011 while exploring each Nightside tunnel progressively for a large drawing for my Black Book **Solve** *(Fulgur Limited 2012)*, I unexpectedly received a few more verses of The Book of the Spider, perhaps not surprisingly in the *Tunnel of Qulielfi* again.

I will go further into this secondary and tertiary receipt of verses and the rituals which inspired them after exploring
the initial 2002 transmission. But first, the uninterrupted Verses of the Book in its entirety (thus far) before a breakdown with further Commentary... :

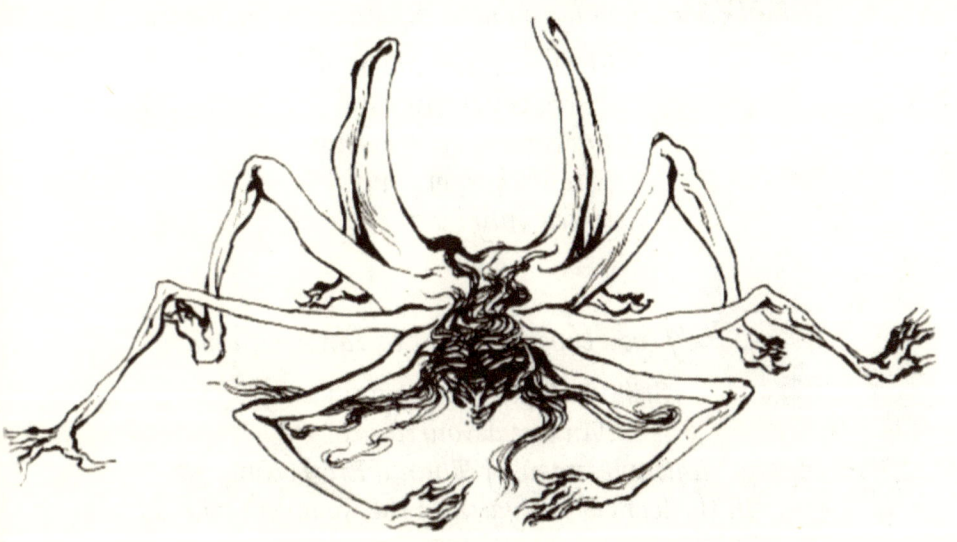

The Book of the Spider

1.) I weave the interstices t w i x t the Rotas,
And spin the paths that unite and divide
Yet I dwell in the S p a c e s I n B e t w e e n,
And the tunnels behind.
I am the funnelweb spider
And my lair is my tome, spiralling
Qulielfi copper mindfire

2.) Only the *finest astral silk* is spun from my chasm
And though its geometries may be unbearable to some
In their alien joining of dimensions otherwise askew
The strands are delicate fibres, soft underfoot
And only in traversing them is there danger.

TimE, Fate and Spider Magic

3.) Unless you have found resonance of frequency
With these alternate angles
Invade not my rays
Unless thou art thus kin
Else stick to my spiral
Released only by my venom

4.) If you choose instead to dance with me
Still you may become my mate
And be devoured yet
But in ecstasy, of ThanatEros' boon
In the loom of Maya, Into the womb of Gaia

5.) That is why I come through the sticky strands of sex
I live and grow strong in the moments Just Before
(but you may only feel my subtle vibrations along the
web if the moment is prolonged)
And in the moments Just After
(but then also you may not notice or remember me if
oblivion of consciousness is complete)
When I come to Feast

6.) But the smell of Blood is my greatest attractor
Especially that from the Triple Chamber
Of my own Labyrinth
As incarnated in the flesh
A tunnel of ingress as much as the webs of the Nine

7.} *I* come through the g a p s , when the expected is averted.
For I am Fate, Beyond the intent of the Magician
At least, oft Beyond hir conscious will,
Yet aligned with hir True Will.

8.} *If* the Magician be nimble and True,
He can twist and dance with Fate's strike,
And see the Greater stakes
Beyond the expected extant course

9.} *For* my apparent cruelty
Is but the mask of the Mother
Who knows the best for Her children
Beyond the immediate

10.} *Focus* not on a single strand
Failing to see the whole weave
For She whom doth from TimemiT
Knows its full course
And the Pattern of the Greater Web

11.} *If* you lament too long
Upon what is Lost
You will miss the opportunity
That void invites to fill itself

12.) When the intended does not occur
Fill the gap it leaves
With a new and unexpected ecstasy
Adapt to be adept
For the Will of Truth is greater than the self
And all Spells work -it's just a Matter of Time

13.) MahaKala and Ghuede are two masks of one essence
For Time cannot exist without Death
And Death cannot exist without Time
He holds us in the grip of Sex
Knowing our urge to procreate and to beCome
Is our impulse also towards our own dissolution
Shiva, surrender, even as you dance!

14.) Liminal Rites are my Twi-Lights
Love and Lust are my learnings
Truth and Trust are my twin torches
My path is twisted, ever-turning
My twi-fires are ever burning
Guide of Longing, Light of yearning
Queen of Night

COMMENTARIES:

The initial six verses of *The Book of the Spider* (or this particular Scribe's part thereof) came to me quite non-laterally. After completion of a dawn rite I began to drift off to sleep, quite tired after a night of magickal discourse and formulation.

On the edge of my awareness I sensed a being, part human and part arachnid, multi-armed like a Hindu Goddess. She was not quite there, and yet not quite absent, seemingly in some crack b e t w e e n the worlds. I did not 'see' Her as such even in my mind's eye, rather I just kind of sensed She was there, with some kind of message for me. She began to tell me (without a voice) words which I felt compelled to write down, so I semi-rose enough to scrawl the information on a bedside scrap of paper which I had used recently to capture dream fragments.

Thinking the transmission completed, I once again retired and began to drift into sleep. Again She beckoned me from some obscure between-space, back to pen and paper. Thrice this occurred before I was allowed full slumber.

1.) I weave the interstices t w i x t the Rotas,
And spin the paths that unite and divide
Yet I dwell in the S p a c e s I n B e t w e e n ,
And the tunnels behind.
I am the funnelweb spider
And my lair is my tome, spiralling
Qulielfi copper mindfire

'*Rotas*' are Wheels. In terms of the Tree of Life -which the transmitting entity seemed to use as a model to translate its locale (or perhaps its just one of my own methods of translation/interpetration?)- I suppose these wheels would be the Sephiroth or spinning spheres or planets thereon. But Rota is also an anagram of Taro, so the tarot trumps are implicit too -almost explicit as 'the paths that unite and divide' bet w i x t these spheres- and the 'interstices' their points of conjunction; Angles or corners between the paths and spheres, points of meeting with no specific properties of their own, from which to spin the paths.

So She is responsible for the weaving of the systems -maps and models such as the Tree- rather than having a set position thereon - She is free to move anywhere on the web.

My initial interpretation of these first lines was Qabalistic, but more recently I have considered it also in relation to the Three Fates -Rota as the Wheel of Fate (anagram of Taro as hand of Fate?) and the 'paths that unite and divide' as those of a Crossroads, where arachnean Hekate is traditionally met. Uniting and Dividing could be considered paths of birth and death, as She is the psychopomp betwixt upper and underworlds.

In the last line of the first stanza the communicating entity reveals that She is indeed from the tunnel of Qulielfi, the Nightside Tunnel which is the reflex of the Moon Path. Copper is a metal with peculiarly psychic qualities as a receptor (used in the cables of telephones as well as other more esoteric communication devices) thus the Mindfire mentioned and the relevance to this intuitive rather than logical zonule:

The Moon path (Tarot trump XVIII) already concerns psychic receptivity, so its reflex on the Nightside of the Tree -Qulielfi- delves even deeper into subconscious strata -such as that which has been brought to conscious attention via the receipt of this book.

It is perhaps relevant here -while on the subject of psychic receptivity- to note that Maeve, a small child living in my house at the time of receiving the transmission- gave me a picture of a 9-legged spider in an 11-rayed web the following evening. She said she drew it that morning just after rising, which was around the time that I received the transmission just before going to sleep. See also the final line of Verse 6.

The tunnel itself is the Qulielfi Spider's web, as it is a funnelweb spider, i.e. its web is a three-dimensional coiling rather than flat spiral. 'My lair is my Tome' suggests that theWeb itself is the True '*Book of the Spider*', and that any texts elucidating its Use are but interpretations thereof, maps and models.

Almost every *Rune* (a Norse and Celtic pictographic magical language) is discernible in the angles and interstices of every spider's web, it is itself a complex weaving of symbols. The Word of words and their weaving, 'Text' comes from the Latin root Texte which means to weave, as in 'textiles' (the craft of fabric weaving) and texture (the fabric or form created by this art or craft -in modern usage usually as perceived by the sensation of touch). Text itself cannot be 'textural' in the modern sense of the word, but it can certainly create the illusion thereof - a metaphorical texture, since writing -the weaving of text- is itself a craft of metaphor itself, of representation, re-cording and illusion. Yet if the word texture itself comes from the same root (of the same Tree?) as text, the implication is that the weaving of Words can create form as much as they re-present it.

Thus, 'In the beginning was the Word...' but, '...And the Word was God' could be read as the Word (language itself) being God, the creative source, or as 'God' being the particular Word at the beginning. Then again, the Word is 'in the Beginning', so presumably there might have already been some Beginning in which to contain it? Self-referentially, this demonstrates the flexibility of Words but also of their interpretation, suggesting that the reader or listener is as much the God as the writer, speaker or weaver -an important point in relation to the Fate vs Free Will dichotomy presented by following verses: we co-create our fate by our very perception of it.

Which came first, the weaver or the web? (...which weaver (witch weaver)? which web??)

Since the publication of the first edition of this book I discovered a fascinatingly relevant fact in arachnean anatomy: Spiders have what is known as 'book lungs' -strange membranous sheets in their abdomens. They inspire and expire through these 'pages' and this

gives them the life to weave their text-ures from the same abdomen which contains these inspir-ational folds. A spider's web with its
   pictographic angles and interstices is akin to a book ('*My lair is My Tome, spiralling*') as a powerful microcosmic symbol-structure of larger patterns of geomantic or even stellar interconnectivity. So the
   further microcosm of a spider's body itself containing book lungs within the centre of this text-ured web creates a pattern of vast fractal complexitiy...

Thus any '*Book of the Spider*' is but a chapter of a greater Tome, a strand of a greater starry Web.

Indeed, this seems to be quite directly the case, in terms of receipt of inspired texts with inter-woven material, even under the title, '*The Book of the Spider*': My own warp and weft here; Kenneth Grant's 'Liber Okbish' -also called The Book of the Spider or Liber 29, 29 being the number via Gematria of Qulielfi.

(Curiously I also found in a secondhand bookshop Paul Hillyard's *'The Book of the Spider' (Harper Perennial 98)* while doing the revision and expansion of this web for the new (third) edition. It is primarily scientific in approach, but proved an interesting reference for biological facts about various species and their habits, with a dash of arachnean folklore).

After the three-day tantric invocation which resulted in the unexpected receipt of a second transmission of verses a year or so after the initial nine, a return to communications with the outside world brought (through the electronic wwweb) the synchronous wonderment of a simultaneous set of spider verses received by a fellow member of The Silver Dusk -*Justin Patrick Moore*- without being consciously aware of our activities, posted upon their completion. So this fragment too will be presented further on. These are all then The

Book of the Spider, and yet none of them are. The true tome, as She tells us, is her lair or spiralling funnel web.

2.) **Only the** *finest astral silk* **is spun from my chasm**
And though its geometries may be unbearable to some
In their alien joining of dimensions otherwise askew
The strands are delicate fibres, soft underfoot
And only in traversing them is there danger.

The '*finest astral silk*' which begins the weaving of the second stanza suggests the astral nature of this transmission. It is through the lunar dreaming portals of *Yesod* (lunar 'Foundation' sephira on the Tree of Life, representing the astral plane) and the path of the Moon that the webs become evident, though their source is beyond these outer spheres and paths. For they come from the 'Chasm' of Daath / the Abyss, which due to the inversion of the Nightside Tree, connects with the dayside portal of Yesod as a point of ingress for Nightside denizens into our dreaming. '*My Chasm*' also seems to refer to the spider's web-spinning duct, or the yoni of Kali from-which the kalas are spun.

The spider weaves b e t w e e n dimensions. Because these realities are 'otherwise askew' -i.e. They do not connect in direct linear reality or 'normal time'- the logic of the waking human brain may find them overwhelmingly incomprehensible or frighteningly alien:
'*...its geometries may be unbearable to some*'.
The strands connect the realms/dimensions of dreaming and waking; and the related dayside and nightside of the Tree of Life, cerebrum (conscious mind) and cerebellum (subconscious mind) of the brain.
The connections are tenuous, oblique, and 'delicate' as expressed. To traverse them is to bring the depths of the sub and even unconscious mind -including primal atavisms- into the light of reason, a potentially dangerous practise, for such forces can be powerful enough to overwhelm the flimsy reasoning faculties of the conscious and 'civilized' self and throw one's very conception of reality into question.

3.) Unless you have found resonance of frequency
With these alternate angles
Invade not my rays
Unless thou art thus kin
Else stick to my spiral
Released only by my venom

4.) If you choose instead to dance with me
Still you may become my mate
And be devoured yet
But in ecstasy, of ThanatEros' boon
In the loom of Maya, Into the womb of Gaia'

Now the crux of the verses is revealed, in its direct relation to and exposition of the use of the Spiderweb model I am presenting:

It is the rays of the web which this spider is traversing to communicate the information. It moves between the spirals of the regular time-space continuum, its presence thus seeming tenuous. It is only because of the gnosis of my rite (as expressed in the comment upon the next stanzas) that I was able to perceive its subtle presence.

These rays are the strands which connect otherwise unaligned strata. Their geometries are thus non- Euclidean in terms of the way we usually perceive time-space, even though they appear as straight and direct 'rays' or lines of transit upon our spiderweb map, which is after all only a 2-dimensional model of a multi-dimensional reality.

To find the stated *'resonance of frequency'* with these rays Be t w e e n, one must find one's True Will.

In this way we become the masters of our own Fate, rather than the helpless victims of Fate. Rather than insects caught in the web, which literally stick to Her spiral, we can become like spiders or co-weavers of Destiny ourselves, and thus 'kin' to Fate Herself, as represented here by the Spider Goddess of Time's web.

And yet, spiders eat their own mates, so one may yet be destroyed by our kin (*'And be devoured yet'*).

Death and thus transformation are inevitable, but there is a vast difference here in the process: as the spider's food we are unaware and merely semi-comatose prey, whereas as the spider's mate we die in the ecstasy of love-making, dancing with our Fate and even wielding it as a ray of True Will or Arrow of Art. The intricate nature of True Will in relation to Fate will be examined at length later in this book.

The nature of the '*venom*' is more layered than I first realised. Obviously many spiders release venom to stun or kill their prey, but most poisons used in the right proportions and context can also have medicinal properties, something that has been known and used by herbalists, physicians and other healers from ancient times into the present through homeopathy. So again a dual nature is suggested, according to one's apprehension. This is exemplified by **Serket/Selket**, the Ancient Egyptian scorpion (another arachnid) Goddess. She is the protectress against venoms and stings of snakes, spiders and scorpions, though of course potentially venomous Herself.

I recently discovered the word ATOR relates etymologically to both Spiders and their venoms, and to poisons more generally, including their medicinal qualities.

This links back to the first line of the Book of the Spider, for ATOR is the palindromic mirrororrim of ROTA, the Wheel/s which begin this Tome spinning.

How this palindrome relates to Magic Squares (and Magic Wheels) -and the relevant etymology of ATOR- will be further explicated later in the weft...

There is a fascinating rite in Salento (southern Italy) which involves the venom of the spider creating something akin to a possession state in the 'victim', purportedly to expel the poison via physical exertion. The bitten dances in a circular motion (ROTA to expel the ATOR!), and this is the origin of the dance called the

Tarantella and associated musical form called the Taranta. As *Francesco Dimitri* explores in his wonderful essay on the subject, 'Saint Spider' in *Abraxas Journal #3 (Fulgur Limited 2013)*, the 'performance' seems more like a ritual of possession and exorcism than simply a physiological folk healing practise.

There is an obvious phonetic correlation of Tarantella with the genus of spiders called Tarantulas, though according to Paul Hillyard's factual *'The Book of the Spider' (Harper Perennial 98)* the real culprit was later discovered to likely be the *Latrodectus Tredecimguttatus* (Mediterranean Black Widow) species rather than the *'Lycosa Tarantula'* (actually a wolf-spider, and not very poisonous) as originally thought.

But to me it is even more intriguing that both of these words also bear marked similarities to *Tantra*- a Sanskrit term for a series of Holy Books (our modern western use of the term in relation to sacred sexuality is derived from this). For a more literal meaning of the word Tantra is 'in the loom', suggesting an interconnection via Indo-European roots in the very fabric of our language.

Also as the Tantras are also sacred scriptures, consider again 'My lair is my tome' in the first verse.

Thanat£ros is a composite of the Gods of Death (Thanatos) and Love (Eros) in the Ancient Greek pantheon, belonging thus to the same mythology as the Three Fates or Moirae. The ecstasy which is His boon is that of death in orgasm, the continuance of life via the conception and birth of a child.

As a psychological metaphor, this is the knowing that death, whether big or the 'little death' of human orgasm, is but change; and the acceptance and enjoyment thereof.

Perhaps it is because arachnids weave connections between different realms or perspectives including microcosm and macrocosm, that their 'little death' (orgasm) is often combined (or even analogous) with a bigger death?!

Spiders sense their prey via the vibrations along their web when an insect lands in it. Following this they locate and stun the victim and cocoon it to be devoured later when the spider becomes hungry.

Similarly the male spider plucks the strands of the web like harp-strings as a part of its mating ritual, and the female spider knows the subtle difference in these varying vibrations between mate and prey.

The difference is in conscious intent:

Those who have found or realised True Will may dance and mate with Fate, while those who have not may often dread it and feel trapped thereby. Either way one is ultimately consumed by it, but the perception and thus the experience of this consumption is as vastly opposed as love and fear.

Here we reach the really bizarre strands of multicultural linguistic correlations in this texte:

In the exorcism rituals of the Tarantella in southern Italy, those who have been bitten by the spider are called *'Pizzicato'*.

This seems to be part of a dialect specific to Salento and these rites, yet the term as used in western musical scoring (which employs Latin-based terminology for expressions of mood and tone) refers to the plucking of the strings of a musical instrument that is normally bowed!

The mating ritual of the male spider who plucks the strands of the web to signal his intention is inherent. This then is further evidence of the sexuality (otherwise quite suppressed in Salento's strict catholic culture) which Francesco proposes in his essay is intrinsic in the rite. The 'bitten' (usually female) has indeed had her strings plucked…

Maya is the Hindu Goddess of Illusion, a deification of the idea that all is transitory and therefore ultimately unreal or illusory. Maya's loom is thus what the Web of Fate is spun upon, and when we realise this we may play with fate and form, unhindered by attachments. Like the Latin root 'texte', the Hindu/Sanskrit term 'tantra' means 'to weave' or 'in the loom', so a suggestion is made here of means to access the rays of the web, as explicated in the following stanza.

The *'womb of Gaia'* is the result of the weaving, i.e. The manifest World of form or creatrix of birth into the material plane.

It is revealed here how the Spider being communicating this transmission visited me -on one of these rays which connect *'dimensions otherwise askew'*, i.e. joining different loops of the spiral of 'normal time'.

In the next stanza the method of gnosis which allowed me to perceive Her and receive this information is suggested...

5.) 'That is why I come through the sticky strands of sex
I live and grow strong in the moment Just Before
(but you may only feel my subtle vibrations along the
web if the moment is prolonged)
And in the moments Just After
(but then also you may not notice or remember me if
oblivion of consciousness is complete)
When I come to Feast

6.) But the smell of Blood is my greatest attractor
Especially that from the Triple Chamber
Of my own Labyrinth
As incarnated in the flesh
A tunnel of ingress as much as the webs of the Nine

Here we begin to touch upon some practical methods to access and use the Web. The means of Gnosis in this case was sexuality, specifically the prolonging and extending of the moment just before orgasm. The rite which preceded this reception was auto-sexual, but of course the same effect may be created through copulation -the only potential difficulty there being that the energies have a natural tendency to drift into idle communion between the partners in the post-orgasmic state. Auto-sexual rites are more easily focused unless the participants in duo or multi-sexual rites share a common intent for focused reception.

The prolonging of the state before orgasm is usually called in western sex magick '*Karezza*' (though the original concept expressed by Mr.Karezza was quite different from what it has usually come to mean). The energy builds but all activity is slowed down when climax is felt approaching. With care and discipline the pre-orgasmic state can be maintained (allowing it to subside and rise again if loss of control feels imminent) to the point that it verges on overwhelming (and sometimes almost ceases to become pleasurable). An intense gnosis cannot be achieved immediately, it requires prolonging of this state until a certain h y p e r t e n s i o n is achieved, and even beyond the advent of this.

Extended deep breathing is essential to circulate the prana/energy -up the spine to the crown for gnosis and also around the entire body- and to maintain balance on the precipice of orgasm without slipping over. This then is a cra ck through-which magickal phenomena may be glimpsed.

This practise should be pushed constantly beyond its previous limits, so that the period of hyper tens ion is progressively e x t e n d e d both in duration and correspondingly also in intensity, as the etheric body strengthens in accord and allows us to go further.

When really s t r e t c h i n g the possibilities of this technique, one's perceptions -particularly of time- may begin to warp considerably, which is I guess why such practises are a part of 'Tantra' -as we begin to weave the energies on a more subtle level we become aware of the illusory (i.e. perception-based) nature of the strands of time and space 'in the loom of Maya' ...

The state of post-orgasmic ('the moments Just After') bliss is also good for magical contacts with other realms and their denizens. There are various things which may prevent one from perceiving these potentials however, as expressed in the verses. Oblivion may occur, the conscious individuated being obliterated in the moment of orgasm. Particularly if this state leads into sleep, it is unlikely that one will remember or even perceive any potential trans-dimensional communications.

One way of avoiding this for men is non-ejaculatory orgasm. If properly learned (for which I recommen the various books on Taoist sexual techniques by Mantak Chia) and practised, this can feel as intense or even more intense than ejaculatory orgasm, while more energy is retained, and therefore usually a thread of conscious awareness with it.

On the other hand, I have personally found full ejaculatory orgasm (on the rare occasions that I indulge in it) to sometimes be more potent -if that thread of awareness can still be maintained- for trans-dimensional contacts and visions in the aftermath, but only when the energy has been built up with non-ejaculatory sex over a period of a moonth or so, so that the release and subsequent gnosis is thus deepened. For near-total obliteration of consciousness is the aim, allowing the gates to open to realms of unreason which the conscious mind might otherwise censor -and yet the slightest thread of awareness must be maintained to allow comprehension or at least recollection of the contact.

To create an audio re-cording of this stanza in the appropriate space, the same technique of extending this brink state was employed in a sexual rite with a partner almost a year later. The result was not only an appropriate state for the recording, but also the receipt of further verses (*7) - 13)*) due to the gnosis achieved.

And finally Blood is revealed as the prime attractant of the Other, **'*Especially that of the Triple Chamber*'**. This is a reference to the womb, the vagina and the labia as three chambers of the Arachnean Moirae's Labyrinth - that of Spinner, Weaver and Cutter - '*as incarnated in the flesh*' i.e. in the body of the Priestess. Menstrual blood is therefore suggested as the most attractive substance to the Spider of Qulielfi, carrying as it does a charge of psychic resonance which can be potentiated through ritual use of the sacrament.

This potent Kala is associated with the waning or dark moon, in the microcosm of the Priestess's cycles even if these are not fully synchronised with the macrocosmic lunations; so it is particularly pertinent to invocation of Kali or Maat.

However regular blood from the veins is also an attractor, to a lesser degree, of the Other, and one directly available for magickal use to the solo Priest as well as Priestess. For those not averse to such physical extractions, penile blood is particularly potent for the priest. This is a tradition evident in the ancient cults of Egypt (Ra 'mutilating his penis' in *'The Book of Coming Forth by Day'*), Central America (The Mayan/Aztec Kukulcan/Quetzalcoatl performing phallic bloodletting, a myth I discovered soon after performing a similar rite atop His pyramid at Chichen Itza) and Sumeria (Enki) - new Godlings being wrought from the blood thereof in each case.

The first time I performed a major blood-letting from my phallus, severing the sphincter within the urethra just below the glans, I was greeted by the Spider-Goddess. The bleeding was profuse as I had aroused myself to counter the pain and enhance the gnosis, so my visions were quite vivid :

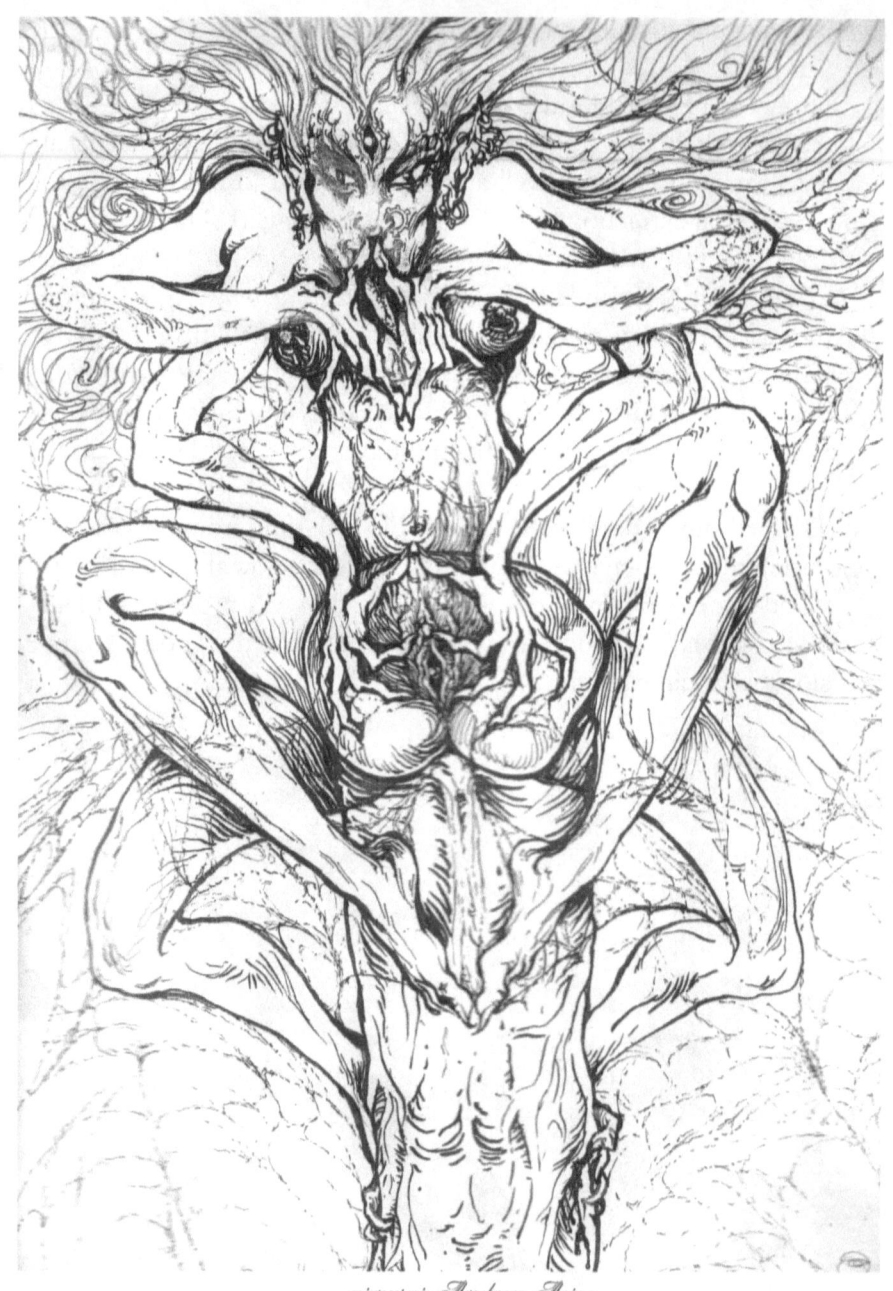

microcosmic Arachnean Anima

She came in several forms, lurking in multiplicity in the periphery of my vision, multi-limbed and arachnean, the central form having tongue dangling in Kali-esque bloodlust. They Who are She seemed obviously attracted to the blood, but perhaps especially so because I had previously consecrated my urethra in a self-tattooing rite (see my **Liber TTT part II** in **SilKMilK MagiZain s p o o l # 2**, iNSPiRALink.'05) as the vagina of my anima, so this was the magical equivalent of my first period. The combination of pleasure and pain, and the ultimate transcendence of this duality by convergence of extremes, is another gnosis here suggested.

In stanza *6.)* the triple chambered womb is presented as a means of ingress for the Spider Goddess- She comes through the blood and other Kalas emitted there-from. To taste these various secretions is about the most direct congress with the cyclic nature of the Great Goddess one can have; But note that not all are necessarily to be experienced in sexual rites alone, for some of the most subtle yet intense kalas can only be created by the priestess raising her kundalini to the crown chakra, and to effectively do so may require sexual abstinence combined with etheric (via suggestion, ceremony and implication) rather than actual physical stimulation.

The incarnate womb of the priestess is presented as one means of direct ingress for the eight-limbed one, and contrasted with Her other primary means of access, '*The Webs of the Nine*'.

My initial interpretation (the only one given in the earlier edition of this book) was that this refers to the sephira of Yesod, sphere nine upon the Tree of Life: the astral plane. It is through dreams and visions that She may visit us, and yet the body of the priestess is a very tangible presence of the Goddess also, in that She, assuming Her inherent divinity fully within the context of magical ritual, is the Triple One incarnate in the realm of Malkuth (the physical plane).

Nine is Three by Three, and Three is the Supreme Essence of the Great Black Goddess in the Mother Sphere of Binah (attributed to Saturn, the planetary body named after the Greco-Roman God of Time).

Sephira Three as the triple Goddess and origin of Cyclicity- is refracted through the Webs of the Nine in Yesod.

It is also significant that Binah —which as the Black Sea, the Mother and the beginnings of TimemiT is the obvious home of Kali upon the Tree of Life- is in Jewish tradition the home of the *'Neshamah'* which is the higher self, and therefore represents Fate as an aspect of the Guardian Angel.

There are also the Nine Worlds in the Norse traditions, all connected by the Norns' webs to the central axis mundi World Tree (the 9-legged spider steed Maeve drew while I was receiving these verses?) where Odin hung for 'nine days and nine nights' to discover the rune-symbols created by their interstices.

The keeper of the Rainbow Bridge *Bifrost* between the realms of Gods and that of mortals, Heimdall, was said (in the Icelandic Edda scripture) to have 'Nine Mothers' -probably meaning the Norns or theTriple Goddess in the over-world, underworld and middle-world. But the impression is given in the Norse mythos that 'Nine' as well as being a specific number seems to sometimes be used as a more general term suggesting 'forever' (Odin's ordeal?) or a nigh-infinite number of things. It is also a sacred number in Hindu traditions, where 'nun-Durga' is the nine forms of Durga, the Mother Goddess also celebrated for three days each in Her threefold forms of Sarasvati, Laxshmi and Kali.

And now we move to the second transmission of verses, received over a year later in 2004. As mentioned these followed a 3-night powerful tantric invocation of Arachne, but receipt of these verses was not a part of the intended outcome of the working. Rather, we were charging magical threads in an interpersonal weaving and cutting of physical (symbolic) as well as etheric strands.

This -along with an audio recording of stanza 7 of The Book of the Spider (as already presented)- was eventually achieved, then the following additional verses came through immediately after closing circle, a vital overspill of the intense gnosis attained:

7.} I come through the g a p s , when the expected is averted.
For I am Fate, Beyond the intent of the Magician
At least, oft Beyond hir conscious will,
Yet aligned with hir True Will.

8.} If the Magician be nimble and True,
He can twist and dance with Fate's strike,
And see the Greater stakes
Beyond the expected extant course

9.} For my apparent cruelty
Is but the mask of the Mother
Who knows the best for Her children
Beyond the immediate

10.} Focus not on a single strand
Failing to see the whole weave
For She whom doth from TimemiT
Knows its full course
And the Pattern of the Greater Web

Again the g a p s or s p a c e s i n b e t w e e n are referenced as a point of ingress for the Spider Goddess, as She resumes communications. These verses especially align Her with the concept of Fate, since the g a p s mentioned here are those 'when the expected is averted' - when disappointment is experienced. For disappointment occurs when an appointment fails to be met, i.e. certain expectations or goals fail to be fulfilled within a specified (appointed) timeframe.

This occurs when there is an apparent incongruence between Fate and Will; they seem at odds as the Will or Desire of the Magician (or even layperson in simple practical matters) is thwarted -as if Fate/Destiny (/the Spirit/s of theUniverse/Chance/Chaos or the Gods, depending on your paradigm/s) has other plans.

True Will is often, however, another matter entirely. What we really want -or perhaps need- is often way beyond our conscious desires. When our more immediate ambitions (and disappointment is usually to do with immediacy -we may get what we want later, but we want it now) are thwarted, we may discover later that a situation is actually more complex than we realised, and it becomes evident why we seemed to suffer earlier, as we begin to discover longer-term effects.

Here the part of us that can see beyond the immediate, the subconscious or deep mind which knows what is best for us in the bigger picture, is treated as a separate entity, as Fate -for it may seem very separate when we are in the grip of lust for more immediate results. But our Destiny -the higher (or deeper?) self that knows our True Will beyond such conscious desires, knows more than we think (since true knowing is essentially beyond conscious or surface thinking).

Sometimes the failure of our plans or desires may seem harsh. Fate can be cruel, but it is often the cruelty of the Mother Who knows more than Her child of what is really best for them. For example a small child in innocence and ignorance may want to play with a box of matches. The mother who removes them from the child's grasp may seem mean to the child, stopping the child's play, and it is only (perhaps years) later that the child will understand what matches do and may realise that the Mother was actually preventing possible burns because she knew more than it did of the inherent dangers.

So it is on a more cosmic scale also, as Fate, Ma Kali or Grandmother Spider may have more idea than us about the bigger (or longer) picture, for '*She whom doth from TimemiT Knows its full course, And the Pattern of the Greater Web*'. But this is of course only one example and even as a metaphor should not be taken too far: Fate or Time may seem at times to burn us as much as to prevent burns, yet even the most severe lessons may later assume their place as their function clarifies. And so Kali Ma -the Black

Goddess of birth and death- may appear severe, Her outer image armed and with blood dripping from Her lolling tongue, fangs gleaming, adorned with a belt of human hands and a garland of skulls. And yet when one comes to know Her -if not deterred by such outer vestments, if facing our fear and penetrating beyond the carnal image- Kali is the most loving and benevolent essence, even Her most destructive apparent actions often lead to longer-term positive Change.

We must learn to accept even apparent misfortune, to 'twist and dance with Fate's strike', for it is only our struggle which generates greater difficulties, pain and further karmas. I am not advocating passive surrender of course, merely acceptance when it becomes apparent that something is beyond our control.

When ordeals are experienced the pain felt often needs to be expressed; in which case we should, powerfully and without restraint, then allow ourselves to move on.

The essence of this missive to me is the potent reminder that we cannot always consciously see the larger weave of our destiny, so instead of dwelling in lamentation when things appear to go wrong, grieve, accept the situation and allow the greater course to unfold. The knowing that there may be a greater reason beyond our immediate concerns may aid this process.

Some of these lines from *The Book of the Spider* were later incorporated into my rewrite of the Ancient Greek tragedy, **Oedipus Tyrannos** (as introduced before **THE SECOND GATE**), as it deals also with Fate and its apprehension. In it they were spoken by Hekate Moirae to the protagonist Oedipus when he met Her where 'Crossed Roads Three', a recurring motif throughout the play:

> *'My apparent cruelty*
> *Is but the mask of the Mother*
> *Who knows the best for her Children*
> *Beyond the Immediate'*

These sacred words, received in trance from the Spider Goddess, helped me live through and even love through the hardest of lessons, giving me the courage to keep going and stay (semi)sane even when it seemed the Fates had only great suffering to offer in the short term. For as often seems to happen in ritual theatre, the spill-over into my personal life while re-working the Oedipus myth was intensely challenging, and in this case traumatic.

So I will here tangent to demonstrate how such ideas can be applied by a personal (and relatively recent) example:

In my new version of the play (2008) I attempted to turn the fatalistic Classic into a demonstration that Fate and free Will are not mutually exclusive. With a strong personal belief in Fate and Her powers I did not change the circumstances in the traditional story – for circumstances are often beyond our control- instead I changed the way the characters perceive, relate and react to these circumstances.

So basically my new version was about making the most of bad or difficult circumstances, and this being ritual theatre the Gods of course tested my own (as writer director performer) capacity to do this to the utmost, rather relentlessly during the 3-moonth period of preparation for the performances. My life situation at the time was dramatically overhauled, causing me to question and doubt some personal values and intrinsic ideals I had maintained strongly throughout my life.

Central to the emotional triggers and painful adjustments in the shattering of my ego at this time was the breakdown of a three-year relationship. One of the bitterest ironies was that the woman in question was going to play the role of *Hekate-Moirae* –representing the very embodiment of Oedipus' (played by myself) tragic Fate in the dramatic reflection. Several times I wanted to throw in the whole production, but there was too much and too many (13 performers) involved already, and this would be giving up on the very integral ideas I was wishing to express with the play- that we can triumph through the most difficult of circumstances. ('Can you just?' Countered the Gods, 'Well lets see about that…')

She —a priestess of Kali who dallied sometimes too with Hekate- pulled out of the production in the pain and difficulty of our breakup, which made it all both easier and harder. After years as lovers, yet independent artists this would have been our first major creative work together —a potential unfortunately never realised.

By the time her decision was definite it was too late to find someone else to take the part, but she agreed to perform it for the camera. Interactive video projections were already a part of the production so this sufficed.

Several things got me through this period of intense grief and adjustment—of which what I have touched upon only scratches the surface of what I had to deal with during this period: One was intensive energetic and physical practices, energising my system for more rapid processing- I was doing regular Butoh dance classes and added a Suzuki physical theatre intensive to these for one very intense week during the peak of my crisis. Each day our instructor would push us beyond our supposed energetic limits for three hours. This exacerbated my already tenuous state, and yet allowed me to reassess my capacities on an emotional level also, allowing a rapid transformation by fire.

The other thing which —or rather witch- got me through was Hekate Herself, and Her eastern twin Kali. The two were related in the ritual theatre also, and the reflections therein for me abounded in a way that went far beyond any artifice of 'acting'.

There is a scene in my 'Oedipus Tyrannos' in which Hekate-Moirae transforms into Kali-Moirae, the six arms of spinner weaver and cutter uniting into a different form now of the dark Goddess rather than Hekate Triformis. The devouring aspect of inevitable Fate looms over Oedipus, and begins a deadly dance. He cringes in terror and tries to escape, but every time he runs to one edge of the stage he is stopped as if by some invisible net. These etheric cords tighten the more he tries to escape —just like an insect caught in a spider's web, whose every shudder causes the strands to tighten about him. The space he can move within grows ever smaller, his movements become ever more constricted until he is but a trembling taut bound form before Her slowly lowering blade, whimpering in terror.

The first time I 'rehearsed' this scene it felt very real. Afterwards I still felt trapped, confined by awful yet inevitable circumstances and reflectively, physically constrained, my muscles still locked up from my struggle.

Fortunately there is a redeeming scene later in the play: Kali-Moirae again appears, and performs exactly the same dance. Video projections were used to make it especially obvious to the audience that it was identical footage. However this time Oedipus –having transformed through his progressive realisations up to that point in the drama- perceives Her dance differently, and reacts so differently that the entire scene unfolds remarkably differently. So to the audience also, Kali's dance appears different in such an altered context, though Her actual movements are identical.

Oedipus no longer struggles with his Fate- instead he dances with Her. His dance, rather than fearful or antagonistic, now becomes increasingly more ecstatic. Reflectively, Kali's own extreme and undulating movements now appear more sensual than threatening, and their joyous dance together becomes more akin to love-making than to a struggle.

The dance ends with Oedipus lying down before Her in surrender, and when She brings downs Her blade at the scene's end, he shudders in ecstasy rather than resistance to this little Death.

In rehearsal this felt better, but not always quite as real. It was an exercise in surrender, and this is not always an easy thing. I was ever reminded by this ritual theatre that I needed to surrender, no matter how difficult my situation. And what I was going through -though most painful at the time- was really nothing compared to finding out like Oedipus that you have killed your father and married your mother, especially in Ancient Greece's moral climate.

However Fate was relentless in Her severity with me at this time. Each time I surrendered to my circumstances, the Gods would throw another curve ball at me, and just as I was beginning to come to terms with my situation it would get worse again. There were of course many mutual friends within the dissolving partnership, and my relations with some of them also became strained. It seemed the epitome of a progressive breakdown in our clan that had been slowly occurring over the last few years.

Each time some new obstacle or emotional problem arose it became more difficult to surrender, and my faith in the dark Goddess was wavering that my prayers for aid and mercy seemed to come to naught. But I persisted, engaging deeply with the character of Oedipus as a reflective lesson for my own Fate's winding briar-beset path.

The apex of my private ritual activity at the time was on the Autumn EquinoX (March in Australia), also coinciding with my birthday and only about a week before the production's premiere. I had realised the need to take magical action outside –yet still in relation to- the 'play' –to implore Hekate for help. The ritual was performed in the large park across the road from where I was living, in a circle of 8 trees which had become a magical space for me during my tenure there. Some rehearsals for Oedipus had also taken place in that same natural circle in the park.

Basically it was a rite of 'crossing over'; the EquinoXes are seasonal X-roads of the year, when from that equipoise of light and dark the days become shorter and the nights longer. In this case it was actually a 'double crossing' though, in that I was soon to also cross over to the other side of the world, where in the northern hemisphere instead the nights would become longer and the days shorter form that same crux-point. And Hekate –as most of the readers of this book are no doubt well aware- is the Goddess of the Crossroads and of crossing over…

Considering what a difficult time I was having with everything and everyone I knew in Australia, I was of course relieved to be going- albeit the fact that I was going again had much to do with some of the problems arising- and very much felt the need to step into another reality.

The ritual was short and simple, but powerful. With my twisted Gazelle-horn-handled magical dagger from Egypt, I drew a crossroads in the dirt between the four quarter-spaced trees of the circle. I cast one side to represent the southern hemisphere and the other the northern. I took the crescent blade and cut- with some difficulty as it was not very sharp- an X on my chest over a section of the 13-point web tattooed there, summoning all my pain and grief up into that action so that it flowed out in a flood of release with the blood and tears that dripped onto the earth at the centre of the crossroads. *'Cross my heart, and hope to die, Die to hope anew...'*

I implored Hekate and also Hermes –that other Greek deity of crossroads and crossing over, also God of travel and dear to me- to aid and guide my passage, that I may cross over from pain and dissolution into some new and joyous circumstances, releasing the old to allow the new...
And then I stepped over one of the symbolic X-roads lines I had etched in the ground, and felt a sense of relief.

Late the next day I returned to the park to do some yoga, and noticed a bottle-top someone had dropped in the circle. It was right near the central X of the crossroads, and was branded with Hermes' winged caduceus which is used as a glyph by the Mercury (Roman name of Hermes) Cider company! It lay between the two small starling wings –worn on my ears as Hermetic 'earwigs'- that I had left there as an offering in my ritual...

Of course my ordeals were far form over. My rite had given me hope for change but I was still deep in grief and had quite a while remaining in Australia, where most of my personal relations seemed somehow tainted and even a promising new connection turned out to be a veiled psychopath. I focused my energies on the Oedipus production.
It was only a few nights before the play opened that I reached another crisis point. I felt like I was dealing with my situation far better than I had similar ones in the past, and yet this could not save the relationship. It seemed that the more I surrendered and accepted the blows I was being dealt, the more successive blows were dealt to

me, relentlessly. So it got to a point where I questioned the very myth that was so intrinsic to the final scene in the play:

I had long resonated with the story of Shiva lying down before Kali in Her bloodlusting battlefrenzy, and this halting Her rampage. It made sense to me that the same energy that can cause such destruction could be channelled in a more positive manner if not fought as an adversary but instead surrendered to. However now it seemed that the more I surrendered, the more this furious and devastating force continued to tear me apart, even that my surrender seemed to encourage its destructive nature.

So I began to wonder if I should change the ending of the play to reflect this new outlook. It was of course very late timing to make such a major change, but since no other performers were really involved in this final scene and I was also director it was possible, in fact I thought it might be better not to even tell the rest of the cast and crew, leaving them as surprised as the audience. The production was only running for two nights, so I decided to do the first night as scripted while trying to resolve how to change the ending on the second night.

I was happy about the idea, as I had felt quite bound to the script with this play. Usually our Metamorphic Ritual Theatre productions had only loose semi-scripts (often collectively devised) or even just basic plots or concepts which performers/invokers semi-improvised around, and there was almost always some spontaneous or unrehearsed ritual element. Oedipus Tyrannos was an exception in that being written all in verse with very specific intentions it was our first fully-scripted play, and such had initially felt less ritualistic because of this. However the overspill in my own life had become so marked that it soon seemed (at least personally) even more magically charged than looser pieces.

The issue then arose, of course, of just Who wrote the script anyway? —it being about Fate and much of it semi-channelled; in fact I'd had a sense of it being my own Fate to rewrite the Oedipus myth for several years before I'd actually dared face the challenge of reworking such a literary classic. So now I had begun to feel bound to the script and its reflective challenges in my personal life, and to alter the ending could be an effective reassertion of my free will.

In my Butoh dance class the next day, during the climactic group improvisation I found myself in a spontaneous swirling dance with a man of heavier build than myself. Somehow in the flowing momentum of our movement I picked him up around the abdomen and held him under one arm while I began to spin, dervish-dancing around and around faster and faster. Around my wrist I had a thin leather cord clad in the spine of a snake, which I had consecrated to Kali at one of Her main temples in Kalcutta, India the year before. At the apex of our unlikely natural choreography this snapped and serpent vertebrae went flying in every direction across the room, even as the centrifugal force also cleaved our collaboration and we fell apart.

The first night of performing Oedipus Tyrannos before an audience felt a lot more intense than any rehearsal. It was a new moon and was indeed a ritual, and most of the emotion I expressed was very real, regardless of how practiced the rhyming lines were.

Particularly potent was the final dance with Kali-Moirae. I had released so much in the process of the play and this came now to a sense of completion and transformation. My surrender before Her was much deeper, and afterwards I felt a great relief, almost serenity.

So I began to wonder —if the ending as scripted felt so good, surrendering to the Goddess like this despite all Her apparent severity, why should I change it on the second night after all? And yet what I had felt a few nights prior had been valid also, and perhaps also needed expression.

I remained unsure about just how (or even if) I should alter the ending on the second night until just a few hours before this final performance began.

The woman I had recently broken up with turned up to see the play, bringing along her new partner as if to rub salt in the X on my chest. She had opted for the stability this connection offered, disenchanted with my polygamous ideals which were now temporarily faltering in the challenge of the situation. What was the good of being able to overcome possessiveness if others could/would not?

In the final scene, Hekate-Moirae spoke Her lines from *The Book of the Spider* from the webbed screen:

Unless you have found resonance of frequency
With my web's angles askew
Invade not its rays

Unless thou art thus kin
Stick to my spiral
Released only by my venom

But if you choose instead to dance with me
Still you may become my mate
And be devoured yet
But in ecstasy, of ThanatEros' boon
In the Loom of Maya, into the Womb of Gaia

Her three-faced visage morphed, the six arms becoming those of Kali-Moirae. Blue-black thighs dappled with flickering flames, the skull-bedecked Goddess began to dance, and as in the script Oedipus began now not to cringe and struggle but to dance with Her.

But when one of my (as Oedipus) legs was lifted high in the stance of Shiva Nataraj (*Lord of the Dance*), I presented my twisted gazelle-horn-handled knife and with its crescent blade I suddenly sliced at an invisible strand and my leg fell free. I teetered then another arc of the blade freed my wrist from etheric cords of fate. I slashed again and shook my limbs in newfound release, freed from the tale of Oedipus and his torturous destiny, then dropped the knife and turning away from the dark Goddess I began to stride down the long aisle between the pews.

The audience turned their heads to follow my exit, as did the shocked lighting technician and the black-robed Chorus who were waiting on the edge of the stage for their final lines.

But as I reached the door I hesitated, then turned upon my heel and walked back up to the aisle. Taking a vibrant Hibiscus flower (sacred to Kali) from a side-altar, I placed it devotedly upon the platform at the projected Goddess's lotus feet as I knelt before Her. Then I climbed up and lay upon this platform. As Her passionate dance ended, my chest shuddered beneath Her pounding feet. But my head was tipped back with an expression of ecstasy.

This was true surrender. Not surrender because I had to, because I was bound to, but because I chose to.

Several moons later in the UK I met a devoted priestess of Hekate and herbalist witch, and the alchemistry between us was wyrdly immediate. Moonths later still in the USA, I ritually tattooed Hekate Triformis on the back of her neck. I found new kindred clan in Seattle and Portland, and new magical and creative alliances were forged. I saw congenial polyamory lived out, and my faith in humanity was renewed.

Caught as I was in the immediacy of my grief during the reworking of Oedipus, I could not have seen then the pattern of the greater web, or our dark Lady's wider plans.

OEDIPUS:

So devour me, Fate, I surrender to your whims!
Even to your apparent caprice
For why struggle with the inevitable
When it can instead be embraced
...And now it is bliss –this release!

Time, Fate and Spider Magic

11.) *If you lament too long*
Upon what is Lost
You will miss the opportunity
That void invites to fill itself

12.) *When the intended does not occur*
Fill the gap it leaves
With a new and unexpected ecstasy
Adapt to be adept
For the Will of Truth is greater than the self
And all Spells work - it's just a Matter of Time

V OF CUPS
from THE BOOK OF KAOS TAROT

Traditionally this minor arcana card is often called
'Regret' or 'Disappointment'.

Verses 11.) and 12.) remind us that when we expect something and it doesn't happen, we can be so caught up in our lamentations that we miss other potentials, or even fail to see what is actually already there.

This is shown visually in the **5 of Pentacles** card of the Tarot (left), where the figure is so focused on the spilt cups that the protagonist fails to notice the other cups that are still upright, which represent other potentials or possibilities.

However there is a void which occurs when expectations are thwarted.

It is a potent magical exercise to deliberately and immediately fill such a void with unexpected activity -that waysome other, less predictable result will be acheived employing the powerful energy of the desire and its deterrance.

Thus one can *'Adapt to be adept'*.

Traditionally this minor arcana card is often called 'Regret' or 'Disappointment'.

I lost this card from my personal deck years ago when it blew away in a wind-storm during a tantric tarot tattoo rite in a treehouse (see **LIBER TTT Part I**- www.crossroads.wild.net.au/ttt.htm) -and I didn't replace it since I 'had no regrets to be able to regret its loss'.

Years later I discovered the validity of Regret, its purpose in helpingus to avoid making the same mistakes again. A new copy was made and the card re-integrated into my deck which I began to re-design as a result of the experience which reminded me of this.

While doing some of my first web-mandala circle-work, I became aware of the power of Dis-Appointment, of a missed appointment or expectation in time, and of how this void can be filled with an alternate ecstasy rather than lamented.

A good example is the following verse, because it concerns the subject directly as well as being a demonstration of it via the circumstances of its receipt: The verse would not have been written at all if the intended goal had been more immediately achieved, so the invoked energies of the Scribe Thoth were more effectively employed in this manner. This transmission was inspired from a working (performed over a year after receipt of the final verses of *The Book of the Spider*) employing hand and eye, quill and page, as sexual metaphors. The ritual failed to culminate in the manner originally planned on its new moon enactment, but this was all part of the journey. This resultant verse concerns adaptability to circumstance, the tantra of surrender, and the subtle relationship between Will and/as Love:

The Scribe of Min surprised
The book which Opened pages to his pennae
Was Not the one of Knowledge carnal
This he already knew so well
He thought he knew it all by heart
But 'twas by heart he was deterred
From plans of Will and Lust and Art
Instead to learn to listen
To secrets which lips above
Nor secret(ion)s lips below aglisten
May not impart

The Will of the pennae
Instead surrenders to the pages of the heart
As they unfold
Telling a tale that can never be told
In ink but only by blood
The pennae can only point the Way
Surrendering to the flood
The fire of will and fleshly quill
May incite the sheets to turn
But the pennae it shall drown
Before that book will burn
And though one part be missing
When gathered are the pieces of our lord
Scattered across the mounds and vales of the land
That part can be risen only
By Isa's Artifice of hand
When all the rest are brought together
To form the Whole Man
If the Feathered Way be trusted
The Intent must be Adjusted in accord
And a Nu Will forged
So this now is my Will: the eye and ink inward-turning
The sacrifice of yearning-

This WILL NOT be executed
Upon the little death
This WILL to NOT
Cross boundaries expressed
To be incited Is Not to be invited to exspell
Instead be Still
And dispel its spell
-ing in the Words distilled
When pennae engorged with ink to spill
Desires too strong to write its Will
The lessons that it learns from book of heart
Are blank with pure intent
'Til pen will turn within and glut
'pon ink on flesh's folds unspent
And try to tell that tale untold
With vain sad strokes of mystery
This page can bare-ly hold
Yet Ink is thus spilled still
The Quill unfilled and thus fulfilled
in unexpected avenue
Both Art and Will to Heart remaining True

So it seems there is a greater purpose to our actions than we may consciously realise with our immediate desires at a given time.

Similarly, there was a degree of initial frustration involved in the ritual that resulted in receipt of verses *7.)* to *13.)* of *The Book of the Spider*, and it was by allaying this feeling and thus allowing the working to continue (for 3 nights instead of the planned 1) that it eventually culminated with even greater intensity.

This too then is a powerful point, for: '...*all Spells work -it's just a Matter of Time*'.

So don't go spoiling potentials due to dis-appointment badly expressed or frustration exploded, so that later when it is time for them to manifest they have a rotten throne onwhich to earth, and can no longer be effective

This is potently demonstrated by the final two verses below, which were written weeks after the verse above, when the original intention culminated unexpectedly after all:

Til when All intent is forgotten
The furrow tilled with ink begotten
Nu forms in Will's Nigredo
The spattered death
Of resurrected libido
Thoth I INvoKe
Tahuti I INvoKe
Anubis I INvoKe
From the missing part Nebet Hetepet awoke
Atum spawns Black Young
To the farthest stars they are flung
On the strands that the hands
Of the Hathors hath strung

To me it is an essential tenet of the idea of 'Chaos Magic' that one should be able to roll with chaos, to fill the gaps of disappointment with new ecstasies, to 'twist and dance with Fate's strike' and thus deal with the apparently random nature of the Universe.

I say apparently random because I have been led to believe there is an inherent order beneath the chaos, a greater pattern that is so vast and complex and apparently unpredictable that from our usual perceptions we can perceive but a simple strand of this vast weave. That is why I consider myself a **ChAOrder** Magician..

Occasionally in ritual, meditation or other states of gnosis we may step outside time for a moment to see its great ebb and flow, glimpse the bigger picture or even the void from which it springs. The rest of the time, if we can just trust that there is a greater pattern beyond our perceptions, and have faith in the spirit of the universe, for **'Vishvamata'** -a name of Kali in the *Yogini Tantra* which means

'Mother of the Universe'- to ultimately nurture us despite apparent severity, and somehow guide us to our ultimate destiny and purpose, rather than struggling with our course. It is with out perceptions - our attitude towards our circumstances and thus relationship with our fate- that we co-weave our destiny.

'..a *Matter of Time*' suggests (with the emphasis of capitalization) also the timing of Matter, i.e. howlong it takes for results to eventually filter down from abstract intents expressed to the material plane.

And it is important to note here that although from my experience that final line is true, Spells do not allways 'work' in the way expected.

13.) MahaKala and Ghuede are two masks of one essence

For Time cannot exist without Death
And Death cannot exist without Time
He holds us in the grip of Sex
Knowing our urge to procreate and to beCome
Is our impulse also towards our own dissolution
Shiva, surrender, even as you dance!

MahaKala is the Hindu God of Time, and **Ghuede** is the Voudon Lord of Sex and Death, who in that pantheon is a black joker, a grinning skull with top-hat and cigar. While MahaKala is not usually depicted as skeletal or with a bare skull Himself, He is usually shown bearing a kapal or skull-cap bowl, is often draped with skull garlands like Kali, and sometimes holds an entire skeleton, presumably a mortal victim of all-devouring Time. He is also sometimes shown with three legs -one to walk the earth, one to traverse the underworld and one to span space itself.

MahaKala ~ Ghuede

In this picture -begun in Dharamsala, India, drawn most of a year after the above verse yet illustrating it perfectly- I have combined the Hindu form of MahaKala with His (semi-derivative) Tibetan form, and also somewhat with this Voudon Lord of Sex and Death,

Ghuede, in that I have depicted His entire form as a skeleton, yet dancing with all the vigour of short stark life, his phallus releasing the elixir which is MahaKala, the Great Kala or emission from the yoni of Kali, and with-which to Her dark embrace he reTurns only to be begotten anew...

<small>(In relation to this cyclical concept, see *"Begotten"* at the end of **'Loom of Lila'** on the DVD accompanying the hardback edition, and also my painting *'Kalas from Kali'* -the esoterotic centerfold of **SilKMilK Magizain s p o o l # 3**)</small>

For the 'kalas' are emissions from the yoni of the Goddess, different energies as represented by the different secretions of the Shakti/priestess in the various stages of her lunar cycle, thus also the rays of time. Herein is the key to this verse, for would not MahaKala as 'Great Kala' (Maha is simply Sanskrit for great) then be the ultimate secretion, the semen or impregnating life-force itself?

Traditionally there are 15 kalas of the bright fortnight (represented by Lalita and Her Nityas) and 15 of the dark fortnight (represented by Kali and Her Nityas), yet there is purportedly a sixteenth 'secret' kala. Since the entire lunar cycle is covered with the 30 nityas this then would have to be 'beyond time' or eternal- thus it is the seminal life-force which propagates the cycles of birth and death, the seed or potential of timemit ... This exists always, for MahaKala is ultimately the God of Eternity as well as Time.

And yet this sixteenth kala is supposed to be an emanation from Kali also. My feeling is that this is MahaKala Himself as Her child, the Time which is spawned (/emitted) from the Void and to it returns.

It may seem strange on a literal level that Mahakala is both child and lover of MahaKali, yet these are Gods, the very essences of the universe merely deified in (semi-)human form for our apprehension.

On a cosmic level, Kala is phenomenon (form) and Kali noumenon (void), so He returns to Her womb via the seed He implants there, which is Himself in potential, to beCome form once again. Thus the whole cycle of birth and death and recreation is represented in these figures of eternal procreation and dissolution.

These fractal layers of microcosm and macrocosm are suggested in Verse 13.} above, where the little death of orgasm is equated with a bigger death, for a conscious male knows that every time he emits semen he is sacrificing a portion of his life-force. Yet he may surrender to this (as Shiva -ofwhich Mahakala is the ultimate form- surrenders to Kali, She who dances on His heart), knowing he is thus producing a new being -whether physically or an astral thoughtform- and propagating the whole cycle of timemit.

These sexual associations of MahaKala and His obvious relationship with mortality affiliate Him with the Voudon Lord of Sex and Death, Ghuede (although the latter is generally depicted in a more lighthearted manner, it is not without a simultaneous profound reverence); and also to ThanatEros, the composite deity mentioned in an earlier verse.

However the avoidance or at least postponement of 'big' (physical) death is intrinsically linked to the 'little death' of orgasm, for conscious management of sexual energy is a key to health and even immortality.

Ancient Taoist and Tantric techniques of semen retention, if performed correctly and with sufficient regular pranayamas accompanying to keep the prana and apana circulating rather than stagnating, life can be extended, as well as perceptions opening to reverse time-flow and awareness of our immortal souls beyond any single incarnation. So the great kala when turned inward to inseminate one's own nervous system, beComes the God of

E t e r n i t y as well as timemit ...

To fully orgasm without ejaculation is not an act of suppression, it is rather another form of surrender, yet one often succeeded by continued enthusiasm rather than oblivion. And so the final line of *The Book of the Spider*: '*Shiva, surrender, even as you dance!*' suggests this combination of retaining the vigour or life while experiencing the surrender of death. For as in the hymn attributed to the *Martandabhairava Tantra*, Mahakala is the same as Mrityunjaya, Shiva as Conqueror of Death.

Beyond the particulars of tantric techniques however, this could also be seen as a general philosophy of life (one which said techniques may help to activate)- to embrace both creation and destruction with equal measure, allowing the flow of dancing with one's fate, by surrendering to this flow. A part of this is also knowing when to emit externally, for science has shown that ejaculation allows our cells to regenerate -without death there is no change.

My whimsical **'Chaos Clock'** video (on the DVD with the limited hardback edition of this book, also available separately from www.crossroads.wild.net.au/inspiral2.htm) ends with a more primal Mahakala mantra. The making of this film was ironically a voyage into the depths of regulated time for the purposes of expressing its transcendance. On a deadline to finish it before my first trip to India, I spent at least a hundred compressed hours in making the 8-minute clip. The nature of film as a medium is intrinsically related to time and its manipulation, since it may be compressed, expanded and replayed indefinitely. But to make it involves many real-time hours in which the computer tells you precisely how many minutes each effect will take to render. By the end of it all I was truly ready to leave such precision technology behind for a journey into the timeless and unknown (being my first trip in many years with no agenda but to explore).

In my 2005 India Journal **'In Mata's Pyre'** (iNSPiRALink. '06) I describe my eventual reunion with MahaKala, through a series of synchronicities which led me unwittingly to a great and ancient Temple of His at Kalinger in the jungles of Madhya Pradesh. There I stood astounded before His image carven in the stone of a cliffside many millenia ago. I had been disillusioned with much of modern India, with its glitz-glamour tinsel-temples and its unexpected sexually-suppressed orthodoxy (so far from the Vama Marg Tantric imagery I was familiar with); but here at last was primal Shiva, garlanded with skulls, naked, raw, and with a mighty erection reaching for the sky. No modestly-veiled Goddess or garishly-painted concrete Shiva was this, nor an abstracted stone lingam wreathed with flowers and ironically worshipped by prudes - this was the stark reality of life and death, of Time Himself, chiselled into the rock of the Ages. I fell to the ground in sheer adoration, feeling blessed that I had been brought here by His own circuitous yet unpredictable course...

Following is the verse which Justin Patrick Moore -*Hieromemnon of the Silver Dusk*- sent to the ChAOrder's email-list just after the Arachnean tantric rite which resulted in my receipt of verses *(7-13)* of *The Book of the Spider*.

It was amazing to emerge from a three-day isolated invocatory trance with my partner to find this congruent poetry written synchronously with our rite, though its recipient knew not consciously of our activities, thus evidencing the '*Qulielfi Copper Mindfire*' of psychic connectivity through the astral and virtual webs of the Silver Dusk... :

The Spider

A poem by Justin Patrick Moore

*Spider, spider burning bright
in the luminous lunar light.
Fateful creature of earth & sky
spinning silk of space & time.
In what womb, moist and wet
were thy eight eyes placed & set?
How did you carry the fire
of words and web that so inspire?
And what poison that tips thy fang
can pause the life of what it stang?
Who to you so gave the power
to be the master of that hour?*

TimE, Fate and Spider Magic

What the silk? What the thread?
In what forge was your spirit bred?
What the pincers? What spreading glance
dares upon your weave to dance?
When heaven opens up its hall
and the pits of hell are revealed to all,
will you tremble upon your skein?
Or mark with ink your destined reign?
Spider, spider burning bright
in the luminous astral light.
Fateful creature of earth & sky
spinning silk of space & time.

And back to the final (?) Verse of *The Book of the Spider*:

14.) **Liminal Rites are my Twi-Lights**
Love and Lust are my learnings
Truth and Trust are my twin torches
My path is twisted, ever-turning
My twi-fires are ever burning
Guide of Longing, Light of yearning
Queen of Night

I feel a slight reticence to add a fourteenth verse to the Book of the Spider in this new edition, as thirteen is such an apt number of stanzas for such a work/play. However, this verse is undeniably related and to call it 13B would be but a parody of the 12B floors some buildings used to have because of the superstition of 13 as unlucky.

This verse was received as a part of a series of working to explore the Tunnels of Set (reflexes on the Nightside of the Tree of Life of the dayside tarot paths). My second progressive exploration of all the Tunnels, about a decade after the first, my purpose this time was

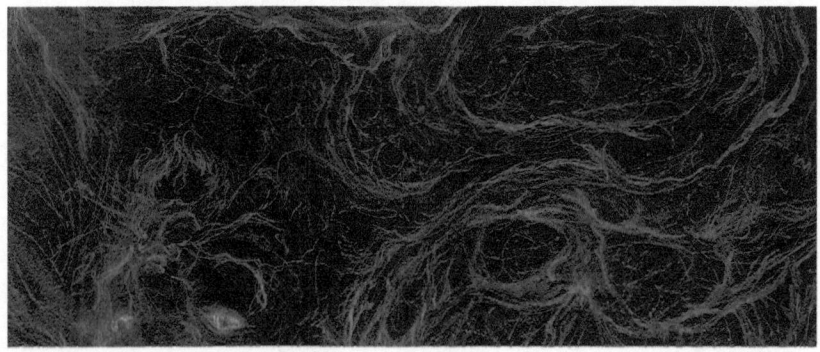

to find more imagery and concepts for a large picture on black paper I was working on for **Solve** *(Fulgur Limited 2012)*, the Black Book of my Tela Quadrivium Alchymic book-web.

(The full illustrated accounts of these Nightside Workings can be found in the esoteric journals **Pillars I** (part 1) and **Qliphoth Opus I** (part 2))

Perhaps unsurprisingly, in the Tunnel of Qulielfi I received as well as imagery these further lines which seem to be an extension of the Book of the Spider.

In my astral journey the tunnel itself seemed to be formed of crescents, almost like a four-dimensional representation of the Qulielfi sigil from Crowley's *Liber CCXXXI*. There were thick textured webs binding together these arcs, and Hekate-Arachne appeared within this tunnel. Her two torches though burning brightly only seemed to light the environment dimly. The verses She whispered to me are quite self-explanatory. The idea of twin torches as '*Twi-lights*' seems particularly significant, expressing the liminal and crepuscular nature of the transmissions and Her role as illuminating guide as well as denizen of such spaces i n b e t w e e n

Another strand in relation to this '*Book of the Spider* r' Tome as Lair and wyrd text-ile:

While completing the third s p o o l of **SilKMilK MagiZain** -a print vessel of the HermAphroditic ChAOrder of the Silver Dusk with a decidedly Arachnean (and also Pan-ic) flavour- I became intensely aware of the physical funnel-web spider in the corner of the window of my new bedroom- a big shiny black one, very beautiful. Towards the end of my intensive editing process on the MagiZain I noticed that it had extended its intricate webbed domain downover the surface of a small picture by my friend Zaen which I

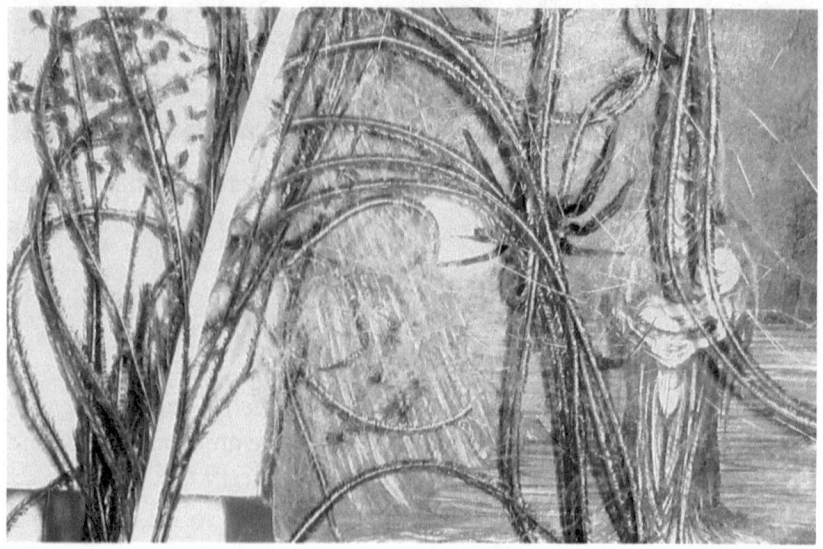

had placed under the windowsill -a picture of a black arachnean priestess, rising twixt two dark cliffs from a sea of blood, with a wyrd white alien baby cradled in her arms. I wondered why She had woven over it, then one day noticed a large white egg-sac She had placed right next to the white baby in the picture. *Wyrd!*

A few weeks later, just after Solstice, I was printing out the first prototype of the just-finished **SilKMilK** s p o o l #3, and mentioned the spider to a contributor to the magizain who was present. When I went to show her the eggsac, we found it had opened, and dozens of tiny little spiders werecrawling all over the webs. (As expressed in the first one, each s p o o l of SilKMilK MagiZain is limited to 1000 copies, being for the 'Thousand Young' of Shub Niggurath, Great Black SpiderGoat of the Woods).

With '*I am the FunnelWeb Spider, And My Lair is My Tome...*' echoing in my reeling head, I set about adding a post-solstice post-script to the new s p o o l.

When I went to the Binders (even more mysterious *Fifth* Fate?) to have the new s p o o lbound (which was bound to happen), I noticed that the paperbark tree on their front lawn was riddled with funnelwebs, their spiralling tunnels disappearing into the peeling sheets and textural layers of the wyrd tree's papery white bark.

I recently moved out of the room and house I was occupying then, and unfortunately had to leave the funnelweb mother behind. I did translocate at least one of her surviving children to my new home, as it had grown in size and woven webs through various talismans on my Kali altar.

During the second (this is the third) revision of this tome you are reading, I heard from the person now occupying that room that She in the corner of the window was about to have another litter of spiderlings.

There was a startling premonition of the synchronous SilKMilK birth, though at its time I knew not that it was such- rather I was just intrigued by the vision's inherent symbology, which draws together several threads previously spun in this tapestry:

On a new moon I used to often visit the Moonbase Astral Temple of the Horus-Maat Lodge, where many members globally astrally converge at this time. On the December '05 new moon I visited in a lucid post-coital state, and here are some relevant extracts from my subsequent ritual report:

'The regularly-morphing guardian Sphinx that greeted me at the entrance was this time distinctly Greek (female) in appearance- in particular the one in the myth of Oedipus, for She asked me (as test for entrance) the classic riddle, but with a variation:

'What has three legs?'

Since the rest of the traditional Greek Sphinx riddle (*'...in the evening, two legs in the afternoon and four in the morning?'*) was missing, I replied, *'All of the time?'*

While this was intended as a query rather than answer, She said, *'That is correct'* and stepped aside, and I realised that the answer is Mahakala, who as God of eternity is indeed *'all of the time'*!

As Hindu God of Time and thus both mortality and immortality, Kala is often depicted with three legs (one in the World, one in the Underworld, and one in Space) as in my **MahaKala-Ghuede** picture.

The main chamber of the astral temple was abuzz with energy. As I proceeded to the egg-shaped chamber, the magickal Word I had been faintly picking up became clearer - not Gulliver as I had first thought but perhaps Gwilliver, but it still didn't seem completely clear.

In the egg-room were many foetuses, all cocooned. I sensed they were the many thousand things yet all one thing - the magickal childe N'aton (Nema's channelled name for the awakening collective consciousness of humanity) as both collective and individuated consciousness, exemplified by the different names lodge-members were calling it/them this Hod new moon.

Now I sensed a great presence around the egg-room, which was akin to an egg-sac. There was a great black spider tending its many/one young, wrapping them carefully. I recognized it from its microcosmic physical-plane look-alike in the corner of my bedroom window as a funnelweb spider, and that the Temple and in fact the whole lunar crater leading to it was its funnel web.

It was only the next day, half asleep in the back of a van on the way to the ocean that I realized what that astral trip was all about:

'Gwilliver' is very similar to *'Quilielfi'*, the name of the tunnel on the Nightside of the Tree of Life which is the reflex of the Moon path - well the temple is on *'the dark side of the moon'*; and it is from an arachnean denizen of this nightside tunnel that I received verses from *'The Book of the Spider'*.

In this transmission the spider of Qulielfi had informed me that it was a funnel-web, that it comes through the 'spaces inbetween' and is attracted by sex and by blood 'especially that from the triple chamber' (both had been involved just before the astral journey).

Also the later verse I received early in '05 concerns Mahakala, thus relating back to the Sphinx's riddle at my entrance into the funnelweb's lair/tome.

The really significant connection is that the tunnel of Quilielfi concerns psychic activity, so the association with N'aton and the Magickal Childe/Children makes sense in relation to this...'

Of course when a week or two after writing this report I discovered the egg sac in my room, the full extent of this psychic connectivity clarified!

Spiders seem to have an impeccable sense of natural timing, and of connectivity. It seems that what they sense upon their delicate webs extends far further than just insects landing in them. Even the subtlest vibrations seem to be felt on some etheric level, and thus it seems their archetypal symbolism of being the weavers between different levels of reality goes beyond metaphor.

I have had spiders turn up in the most specific places at the most precise times with portentous omens, and I know many others who have also tuned into this phenomenon. When I was creating my Kali-Arachne Statue (**APPENDIX E**) the amount of spiders that I found crawling on Her individual limbs as I crafted them bordered on the absurd. (There is even an eensy weensy one crawling across my computer screen as I write this!)

The North American Indians seemed to recognise this intuitive propensity for synchronicity in spiders, revering *'Grandmother Spider'* as the greatweaver and Her species as representative of the wondrous (and delicate) interconnectivity of all life, of the earthly ecosystem, and beyond, into the great web of stars above.

It seems strange then, perhaps, that many people find spiders 'scary' or horrific. Certainly they are creepy, but to me only in a literal sense! Perhaps it is people who find synchronicity itself uncomfortable that fear them, those who would prefer it if things were not so connected and thus one would not have to face indirect consequences; Fate is, after all, truly Wyrd. But I feel there is more to arachnophobia than this:

*S*piders are carnivorous and although this is common among many species of animals that people seem to have less fear of (even when they are large enough to actually eat humans), it is especially threatening that they catch insects in their webs, then devour them later at their leisure. No one likes to be trapped and helpless (other than in temporary sadomasochistic consensual play -part of why spider imagery is more popular in gothic and fetish scenes), and to feel that one may be trapped by Fate is an especially uncomfortable concept. But as we have already investigated in the preceding verses, one can be weaver as much as woven in.

Nevertheless, female spiders also eat their mates, something that many men may find quite intimidating (unless of course it is taken only as a sexual metaphor). Females are obviously the dominant gender of the species, and although this often seems to be the case with humans as well, it is often only evident from the inside of (or at least close knowledge of) relationships, and men usually like to maintain at least the illusion of dominance -so spiders as an archetype of the primal all-devouring feminine are a menacing image to them.

It is little wonder that many men feel threatened by the archetype of the devouring arachnean Feminine eating their mates, although in the human species females often drain the male's energy in a less overt manner. Women generally seem to have a far greater -or at least more enduring- sexual appetite, as their orgasm is not creation of the life-force-expending seeds of potential new life that a man's is. For a male the 'petit mort' really is a little death, a true sacrifice for new life, whereas the female creates her eggs more cyclically rather than in the act of sexual union.

Men wishing to overcome this primal and somewhat justifiable fear of being consumed, should learn to focus and direct their energy via techniques of taoist and tantric semen-retention and prana-circulation, to meet this archetype of *'femme fatale'* as an equal. Extended love-making for the purposes of ecstatic union and the gnosis thereof rather than for purposes of procreation can only be maintained (beyond youth's natural exuberance) equally with this kind of knowledge and understanding.

It is probably actually a similar fear many women have of the 'devouring feminine'. Those who do prefer to be submissive or to at least appear so reject this primal aspect of their gender. It is slowly changing, but women are often still expected in our society to be civilised, refined, polite and petite. The raw and primal archetype of bestial and consuming female passion that spiders represent is still not socially acceptable in many quarters of modern western civilisation, even though the more refined aspects are still quite evident in these creatures also, as exemplified by their delicate tapestries.

So it is with the Goddess Kali:- Her common image with tongue dripping blood, dishevelled hair, adorned with skulls and severed hands, is hardly attractive to most people, other than perhaps in a subconscious semi-instinctual fashion. This is the Kali Yuga (Age) however, and the archetype of the primal feminine is returning, as evidenced by the increasing 'femme fatale' imagery in popular culture. However most people still react with fear to the image of Kali, and this is part of the reason for this iconography itself. She appears terrifying, bloodthirsty, and so we must overcome our fears to see beyond this outer visage, to find the nurturing Mother within.

The skulls and hands She wears are representative of the egos which have been slain by Her merciful sword (or lunar crescent scythe), which returns one, if surrender is made, to the blissful perfection of the void. In AdyaKali's state of truth once She has cut away all that keeps one from the essential -psychic interference, emotional baggage, distracting thoughts, ambitious agendas- there is no Time. This is why She is the devourer of Mahakala.

So the affiliation of Kali with Arachnids goes beyond the mere multi-limbed imagery, or even the devouring yet creative (weaving) aspects- She is the Destroyer of Fear, or more precisely She confronts one with one's fears, giving one the choice to face and overcome them, or to flee. Well, attempt to flee, for often avoidance will only progressively increase one's awareness of the tightening threads of fate and karma around one, until eventually one must turn to face Her.

Significantly, I have known several people who have overcome arachnophobia while working with Kali, even if it has been a lifelong (often conditioned) fear. The beginning of release of one of these - an American in-it-I-ate of the HermAphroditic ChAOrder of the Silver Dusk -is an interesting tale of synchronous weaving and potent wyrd omens:

Lodan Seth was astrally initiated to the ChAOrder in a ritual linked with the Launch of the limited first ('Hekate') edition of this book. A **Metamorphic Ritual Theatre** performance was created around a reading of verses from *The Book of the Spider*, with Three Fates danced separately then forming a composite eight-limbed arachnean kama-kali (ritual posture), and it seemed like an appropriately significant time for his initiation, after a period of correspondence (ironically I was unaware of his fear of spiders).

During a discussion for the performance a few weeks before its enactment at the book launch, it came up that some real blood should be used for the verse which mentions it as 'prime attractor' of Arachne. After all, this was ritual theatre not just theatre.

As in the Book, blood *'especially that from the Triple Chamber'* would be the most apt, and one of the women was willing to offer if she bled at the appropriate time.

While this was expected it could not be relied on, and the question of any other blood being drawn was left unresolved when we adjourned the meeting. On the way home just afterwards I picked up a parcel from my postbox, which turned out to be the various items requested from Lodan to link to his initiation.

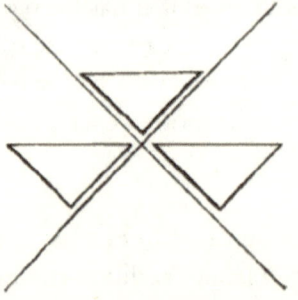

I opened it to discover that on the three corners of one of the magical papers he had sent, were three downwards-pointing triangles - something which immediately reminded me of the 3 Fates symbol as we had been working with it in the ritual dance *(pictures at left)*- and each one was daubed with a spot of his blood!

Thus the offering was already made before it was even (consciously) called for...

Needless to say the astral link was quite powerful with the ritual, and Lodan later revealed that he also recovered from arachnophobia with some ongoing magickal work with Kali that he began that night.

The clincher was when we later realised that his birth name is the same as that of the person who took the part in our synchronous *Book of the Spider* ritual theatre of first being a victim of fate, then rewinding timemit gnidniwer to instead dance with and embrace his fate...

Another instance of someone overcoming arachnophobia occurred during a workshop I held on Spider Magic: Attendant was a middle-aged 'born-again Witch' who had maintained her day-job as a receptionist in a Christian institution. She expressed fear of physical spiders but had come to the workshop after enjoying an earlier one I'd held on Tarot for Conjuration.

During the workshop I had participants draw little spiderweb maps on their notepads, in preparation for mandalic webwork (as described beyond **THE THIRD GATE**). A very small spider alighted out of nowhere onto her page, and she was surprised to find that -having direct evidence of the creatures' atunement- she was not afraid of it, but rather laughed with delight as it crawled across the little ink spiderweb she had drawn there...

There is an interesting tradition in English folk magic of eating Spiders to confer Invisibility upon the consumer. Although not a practice I would personally indulge in (for love of arachnids more than any matters of taste), its relevance to my Book of the Spider and its message is twofold:

Firstly it seems to relate to the idea of taking Fate into one's own hands, devouring it rather than allowing it to devour you. After all, spiders consume their mates after (sometimes even during) intercourse, so I suppose it is fair enough to turn the tables on them. I'm sure the rite can be performed in an ecstatic manner!

This could be partly a recension of folk medicines in the middle ages involving wearing or eating spiders to ease fevers, but I believe it to go deeper.

It is a classic shamanic experience in many ancient cultures to be consumed by one's 'power animal' thus becoming at one with it and in subsequent journeys it taking on the role of spirit guide.

I know several people who have had such visions with spiders consuming or cocooning them, and often a physical spider bite soon after or before will consolidate the experience.

The reversal -eating the spider- is as valid, although to perform such an act on the physical is mostly symbolic of intent, despite its literalism.

Secondly the alleged result of invisibility relates to the dark Fourth Fate- invisible yet implicate.

By consuming your Fate, you are becoming it, taking it into yourself. You become the *'Fourth Fate'* who co-weaves your own allotted destiny...

Weaver and Cutter in the central webs of
MetaMorphic Ritual Theatre's first **Labyrinth** installation, Eostre 94.

What is this 'other' that we seek to contact with such techniques as described in my receipt of *The Book of the Spider*? Is it a being or beings from another dimensional reality, or is it actually the equally alien reaches of inner consciousness, the buried treasures of the deep subconscious mind surfacing briefly into our awareness?

When one realises True Will, it becomes apparent that there is ultimately little if any difference between these, except in terms of the angle from which such is perceived. Fate -as irrevocable destiny separate from and pre-determining an individual's path- and Will - as an individual's assertion of their own path- are reconciled and cease to become opposing or contrary factors.

There is no longer any difference between personal and universal Will, when one is aligned with Truth.

So how does one realise True Will? Crowley -continuing a Hebraic tradition via the term used in such operations by Abramelin the Mage- expresses it as being a result of the *'Knowledge and Conversation of the Holy Guardian Angel'*. The Holy Guardian Angel is supposed by some within the Typhonian Tradition to be the Future Self, guiding one towards one's full potential (i.e. Itself). This idea is succinctly presented by *Michael Staley* in his essay *'Supping at the Angel and Feathers'* (-**STARFIRE Magazine I;5,1994**).

If this is the case -and I also am of this viewpoint- then the Guardian Angel is one's Fate itself; and to make contact with it is to embrace one's destiny and realise that it is only one's higher/deeper self which 'pre-determines' our path.

This future self concept takes us back to the issue of time-travel, and it is thus revealed (through a complex and reflective series of interwoven angles and interstices) just how what may have seemed for a while like a vast tangent actually demonstrates the methods of time-travel to which such a web matrix may be put to use.

It may have seemed that this 'contact with Other' I have described was tangential to the issue of astral or etheric time-travel, but ultimately it is an example of its operation in reverse: the 'other', Guide or Guardian Angel/Daemon/Spirit -here seen as arachnean weaver of Fate- is only glimpsed by the present self because it has travelled back on a Ray of Will within the Web of timemit to communicate.

Whether 'it' performed this consciously or not, is perhaps less relevant to us now as to how we open ourselves to its contact and conversation.

The idea of sending one's current or present self along the web in much the same manner as this Angel or Future Self travels back will also be discussed, and practical techniques to apply these concepts then being presented past **THE THIRD GATE**.

To further illustrate and clarify my case of the Holy Guardian Angel being virtually synonymous with Fate, I will present some of my own experiences with such contact. This early contact with my Guardian Angel in Arachnid form was one not initially of ecstasy (though this did come when I realized its True nature) but of abject horror:

One of the major avenues of The HermAphroditic ChAOrder of the Silver Dusk for expression on the Outer is our **Metamorphic Ritual Theatre Company** (www.crossroads.wild.net.au/morph.htm).

Via public rites which are a combination of pre-rehearsed theatricals and spontaneous interactive ritual, we subtly initiate those of our 'audience' ready and willing (and to varying degrees according to how ready and willing the various candidates are) to the mysteries while simultaneously entertaining and thus seducing them into a state of receptivity for this potential gnosis.

To date probably the most intricate and effective performance rites we have created were the Labyrinths constructed and conducted at Festivals in Victoria, Australia on Eostre 1995, 97 and 99.

These were not merely 'performances' but totally immersive sculptural installations, complex mazes woven with ropes, string, fabrics, and ether in-which potential initiates could lose or find their paths, and along the Way interact with various deities and mythic archetypes via our hierophants and psychopomps who were possessed by (or in some less successful cases merely acting) those Gods and Spirits they had invoked.

TimE, Fate and Spider Magic

There was a ritual framework to these events upon which the more spontaneous elements and interactions were strung. Guiding or controlling the major interstices of passage between the various chambers of the Labyrinth were The Three Fates- Spinner, Weaver and Cutter -as incarnated in the performers who invoked them for the rites.

Upon entrance to the Labyrinth -by crawling through a long stretchy red fabric tunnel adjoined to the wooden labial entrance- the Spinner would offer the initiate their thread or lifeline, and request they Spin the *Wheel of Fate*. This determined which elemental path (fire, water, air or earth —spirit was only the way out) they would set out on, by where the revolving flaming torch on the Great Wheel stopped in relation to the pentagram at its base.

(cf. my **Wheel of Fortune** illustration).

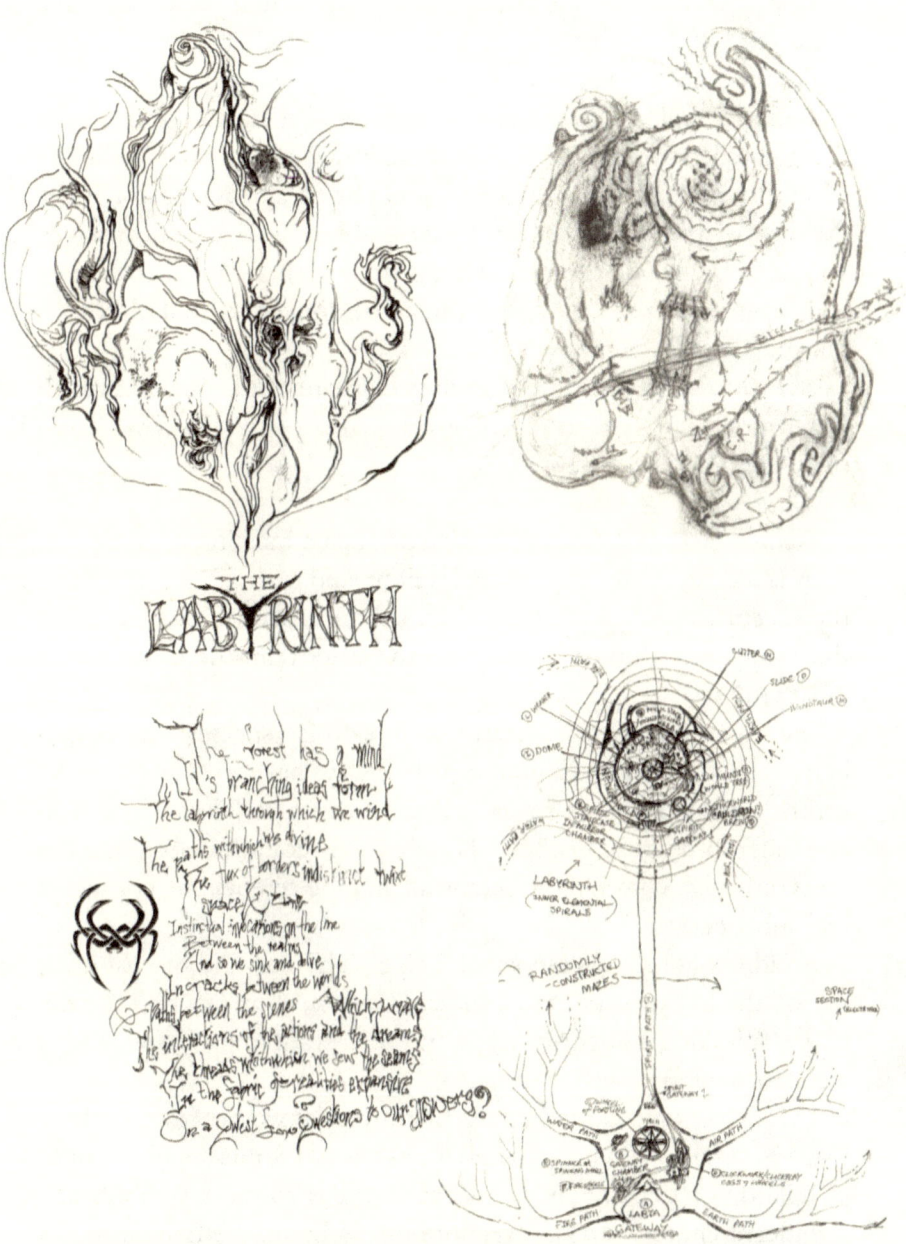

3 *Metamorphic Ritual Theatre* Labyrinth *Maps:*

Outer etheric form (trance drawing before the inner map was designed) -*top left;*
Inner Map of installation layout for first Labyrinth Eostre 95 -*top right;*
Inner installation layout for 2nd Labyrinth Eostre 97 -*bottom right.*

As well as Clotho, our Spinner also represented **Ariadne** in the context of the Ancient Greek Labyrinth myths. Each night a new initiate would be chosen as the hero Theseus and be given a shimmering golden thread to help them find their way through the convoluted outer mazes which surrounded the central spiralling labyrinth. This is like a shaft of sunlight to aid one through the darkness of the Labyrinth -for it is inevitably one's own subconscious and deep mind one explores when lost in such a liminal shadowed and mysterious zone, so a thin thread of conscious ('solar') reason may be a vital reference-point indeed.

After drawing the first planning diagrams of our Labyrinth installations, we were struck by how much it looked like a brain and brain-stem (*see previous page*).

Golden-Orb spiders are reflective of such a meeting of lunar and solar essences, the interaction of intuition and reason. Like all spiders they seem to sense vibrations on a subtle subconscious level, but their webs are spun of golden thread rather than the usual silvery lunar strands.

The symbolism goes further, for this species are often hermaphroditic and their golden webs always have an X shape in the centre, a veritable cross-roads as if the weaver is Hekate Herself in Her saffron-coloured robes. This X-roads could be seen like the pons or bridge between the cerebrum and the cerebellum, conscious and subconscious realms.

Ariadne's golden thread which helped Theseus find his way back out of the Labyrinth in the Classical version, seems to become the entire spiralling Labyrinth itself in the case of the Golden Orb's wondrous glinting web.

In 2011 scientists made their first artificial womb from Golden Orb spider-silk. While the material was chosen for its super-strength in relation to density and its durability, it is to me a symbolically significant choice too. For far more than a brain, the Labyrinth has always represented the womb.

The name Labyrinth itself comes from the same Latin root as Labia, and the passage through and into its depths is a return to the source and a journey of shamanic death and rebirth.

Indeed, even many years after our Labyrinth installations, some of the ritualists still had people approach them in the street and say how their journey had changed their lives, giving them a glimpse into deeper magical realities so that they returned with a renewed sense of self.

The original Labyrinth of the Minotaur was on the island of Crete, and small figurines of the bare-breasted Goddess of the ancient (pre-Greek) Minoan civilisation there have been discovered at Knossos -the purported palace of King Minos- and are now housed in the nearby Heraklion museum. She bears a snake in each hand. The convolutions and spiral coiling of the serpent seem reminiscent of the Labyrinth's patterns. Ariadne was once an important Goddess of the Minoans, rather than the Classical version of her being the mortal daughter of King Minos (whose desire for gold was perhaps solar 'reason' taken to such extremes that it becomes unreasonable?). As a probable Goddess of fertility, perhaps the initiation She offered a thread through was into Her own womb of life, little death and rebirth, and thus She bore the serpents of kundalini and its winding passage up the spine and brain-stem from base to crown.

Ariadne married Dionysos, who is linked in Indo-European prehistory as an ancient horned God of ecstasy to the original Shiva (Pashupati, Lord of the Beasts), consort of Shakti the Hindu Goddess of the serpent-power.

Feel the snake slither in its nest, Dionysos!
Feel it rise From betwixt your thighs to your chest, Dionysos!
Feel the buzz of bees in your skull,
Of reason be bereft, for Dionysos!
   -verse from **'Solve et Coagula'** (Metamorphic Ritual Theatre, 2011/2012)

Further into their journey -in which if desired they could change elemental paths at the Crossroads- they would meet the Weaver (Lachesis of the Three Fates) in Her chamber. She would weave the initiates' individual strands into the Web of Fate where their different lifelines converged and crossed in variegated patterns of conjunction.

Eventually the Cutter would cut the initiate's thread when they were killed by the **Minotaur**, their bestial shadow-self which would confront them in the centre of the inner spiral. The manner of their death would be reflective of their attitude to this meeting. If they wanted a fight the Minotaur gave them one, but usually he would 'slay' them simply with a touch, or an embrace. For the Minotaur was probably a classical recension of the bull-God Dionysos, who was terrifying or ecstatic according to ones' apprehension of His primal mysteries.

Once cut away from the great Web -an intense experience for many who had by that stage of the journey a deep association with their thread as their lifeline- they would ascend a seven-stepped spiral stairwell while facing various reflections and refractions of themselves in a multi-faceted cylindrical chamber paved with mirror shards and fragments on all sides. Thereby they would re-turn to the First Gate and be 'reborn' through the Labyrinth's vaginal passageway Out into the rest of the festival and 'normal' reality, left with an impression of the undercurrent workings of their life journey via the parallel and metaphorical microcosmic world we had immersed them in.

 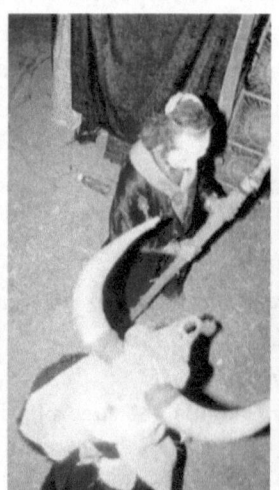 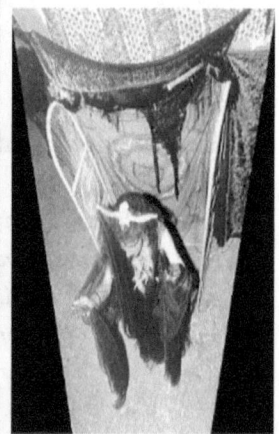

Above: Photos by *Milo Angel* from MRT's 2nd Labyrinth (Eostre 97):

In-it-I-Ates on the central geodesic dome (left); Gatekeeper and Minotaur (centre)
The Cutter at the Entrance to the Mirror Chamber (right).

(More in-depth accounts, photographs and maps from these Labyrinths can be found at www.crossroads.wild.net.au/lab.htm or in **'Alternative Australia'** edited by Alan Dearling, *Enabler Press, 2000*).

As you have probably glimpsed, these Labyrinth installations and rites of Metamorphic Ritual Theatre introduced to many of its potential initiates the possibility of directly apprehending their own Fates, so it is little wonder that similar effects to perhaps even greater depth were reflected back on their creators:

Creating these Labyrinths was a major task for all involved, especially myself as a primary organiser, director, designer, sculptor, performer and priest/ess thereof. Each consecutive such endeavour, despite its success and the gnosis and learning achieved, was concluded (especially while packing up!) with a decision to not take on such a vast amount of concentrated activity again.

Then again, a few years later, I would find that although more participants had joined to share the workload, the work had also intensified into greater complexities with more funding and materials allowing the realisation of further layers to the structures (both physical and magical) which had already been established, and I was back in the same overburdened position.

The third time around, even in the early stages of pre-festival preparation, I was struck suddenly by a feeling of immense horror. Realising I had once again taken on the organisational role in such a vast project, after twice resolving not to do so, I had wondered just what was compelling me -apparently against my own will as I then perceived it- to involve myself in such complexities yet again.

I was struck with a sense of awe and even dread as I perceived the vast eight-limbed Shadow of Arachne Moirae looming over my dwindling egoic self. The Goddess of Fate, I knew, was the real instigator behind the Labyrinth -as incarnating in the mortal women whom I was on the outer apparently helping motivate to embody Her Triple aspects. I felt suddenly as if I was but a pawn of Fate, a puppet on Her strings, an insect in her web.

Oddly this feeling came upon me in the rather mundane and public environment of a crowded café, while discussing the plans of the imminent third labyrinth with a lover. So vast and apparently sinister was Fate's shadow oppressing like a great shroud about me that I began to whimper then even cry with fear. I rushed forth from the café into the street and sought refuge in an alleyway, where I crumpled into a heap of abject despair upon the ground.

My partner came and comforted me, though as when the feeling had first hit me inside, I was still unable to communicate effectively what was ailing me, so wrought was I with purity of the emotions involved.

Eventually bracing myself I managed to express my fears, and even this began to allay them. My partner's empathic and profound responses (and she too, as my mirror was an agent of the Triple One at that time) helped further, and as I gradually calmed (breathing deep, no longer cowering)

I realised that yes, only I had taken on this project, and though I had done so as if compelled by outer forces, they were ultimately only my own inner guides directing me towards the realised expression of my -and Our as the Spider Clan executing these designs- innate potential. She, I realised, was but a womanifestation of my own anima -the female within me. On levels beyond the physical, I am as much the Triple Goddess as any genetic female, and a puppet only of my own innate, intricate plans whose full weave is oft unbeknownst to my own conscious mind.

Once I realized and accepted this, I was swept up on a wave of great love for the Spider Mother which outreached and overwhelmed the fear I had felt earlier. I was ecstatic in her nurturing and deadly embrace, intoxicated on her medicinal venoms, swaying in the alleyway enraptured with impassioned relief and love. I was Her, my Fate and I were One.

May I go so far as to call this another 'technique' then of contacting the Guardian Angel or Anima/Animus?: That of following one's artistic impulses and creative compulsions even in contradistinction sometimes with reason and against the apparent 'better judgement' of the conscious and logical mind.

There is a parallel here again with the creator-destroyer Goddess Kali: Kali-Ma Who is usually first perceived by the initiate to the tantras as a terrifying creature, a bloodthirsty and predatory devourer. But as we now know this is only Her outer image which tests the mettle of the potential devotee, for if the initiate persists and faces their fear, they will move through it to find the benevolent and nurturing great Mother Kali, still terrible to behold but oh so beautiful in her wild and ecstatic dance, from which winds forth the 'Play of Form' (*Lila*', deified as Lalita, the Bright Goddess of the new and waxing cycles of the moon).

There may be some confusion engendered by my use here of the term '*Anima*' -this is a term (introduced by Carl Jung) for the female within the male, and like it's counterpart for women -the 'Animus' or male within the female -it is the implicit reflection, the hidden part of the self which complements the explicit physical self and thus completes one's being. The quest for communion with this hidden anima or animus is one of the ultimate goals of the Hermetic Art of Alchemy: it is the '*Sacred Marriage*' or **Alchymic Wedding** with Self, the symbolic union of Sun and Moon.

Why then am I using the term Anima in relation to and almost interchangeably with the concept of the 'Holy Guardian Angel'? Are they the same thing then, different perspectives from different Hermetic systems of the same basic reflection?

Perhaps, to some extent yes, but it's not quite that simple. I do believe the Guardian Angel to be the Future Self- and yet there is for many some overlap here with the quest for the anima or the animus. If the goal of the Alchemist or Magician is union with this other within, then assuming this is to be achieved, the Future Self will have a more realised anima/animus than the present self. So the Guardian Angel may often appear as one of opposite or even multiple or flexible gender this seems to be a fairly common occurrence in experiences of conversation with the HGA.

For me it is particularly pertinent because I have worked deliberately with not only finding my anima on spiritual and magical levels but also womanifesting her on the physical plane to some degree.

The overlap between the intrinsically related operations of the *'Alchymic Marriage'* and the *'Knowledge and Conversation of the Holy Guardian Angel'* is also a result of the nature of reflection and duality -this 'other' self is obviously not the usual or obvious extant self, so it is often seen in terms of opposite yet complementary self -and opposite gender is an obvious apparition of this, thus the Angel often appears in this reflective image -allowing also a dynamic tension which can be sexually resolved on astral or etheric levels as a part of the 'conversation'.

Both of these magickal Operations —The Alchymic Marriage and the Knowledge and Conversation of the Holy Guardian Angel- are usually associated with the Sphere of *Tiphereth* on the Tree of Life, further suggesting their parallels.

We can relate this microcosmic and personal anima/animus idea back to the complex relationship between Kali as Goddess of the Void and Kala as God of Time, perceiving the divine and macrocosmic reflection in their union.

Their usual place of congress is the Smashan or Cremation Grounds, that carnal Crossroads between incarnations, where they dance and fuck amidst the corpses, jackals and vultures.

MahaKala is ultimately an aspect of Shiva, so the great dance and union of Shiva and Shakti resonates through yet another strand of Hindu cosmogony.

Why have sex amidst the burning bodies? Although this is sometimes ritually enacted by extreme sects such as the Aghori in India, generally it is intended as metaphor rather just being macabre for its own sake: Kali births Time as well as fucking and devouring Him- so with their union in the Smashan it is All present simultaneously -the entire cycle of Time: -Death, sex (little death), birth, life, sex, death... the co-existence of all these extremities within a singular 'place' brings all into perspective -there is so much evidence of Time that there is no Time, so much rapid change and movement it appears as stillness- there is no Time only Eternity, the ever present Present in continuous creation and dissolution.

As Kalika Kali is '...*of the form of the void. ... Her yoni is the Wheel of Time (kalachakra)*' *(-Shaktisamgama Tantra)*. That the Kalas emit from this Wheel which is her Yoni, the Greatest of which is (the) Maha-Kala itself, shows that Time is the product or offspring of Kali.

So here the arachnean anima image I presented with my own story is reversed: -the male is within the female, even as the female is within the male. And to extend the metaphor, we are created by fate, even as we create our fate.

One of the inner teachings of the Sabbatic traditions in the west is that the fourth or hidden path of the Crossroads is actually the male God within the Great Triple Goddess who is invoked at this place of convergence; and He is a black God of Death —Thanatos (Greek), Herne (Celtic) —a dark aspect of Cernunnos, Irlik Kahn (Siberian) -or in the Eastern equivalent, the similarly Black God Mahakala (Hindu and Tibetan) -Time is only created by the cycles of incarnation.

As a God of storms, rage and ecstasy, Odin/Woden upon His eight-legged steed Slepnir amidst the horde of Valkyries is often correlated with Cernunnos as Lord of the Hosts who also ride furiously across the roiling night sky upon the Wild Hunt. Considering this, it is interesting to now look back at my suppositions about Odin's relationship with the Three Norns earlier in this manuscript —as co-weaver of his Fate after his ordeal on the Tree, he also becomes akin to a Fourth Fate or hidden dark aspect of the trinity. And there are many similarities between Odin and Shiva, who was also originally horned ('Shiva-An') and primal, Lord of the Storm as Rudra the Howler, and associated with Sacrifice and surrender.

It was when my Metamorphic Ritual Theatre Company unwittingly scheduled a performance of **'Le Pendu'** (The Pendulum, an old French name of Tarot Arcana XII, *The Hanged Man*) on *VijayaDassura*, the 'Tenth day of Victory' at the end of Durga Navaratri, that I realized the correlation of the reflective Hindu Goddesses also: For after nine nights ('navaratri') of performing puja to Durga in the three days of Her white (Sarasvati) aspect, three-day red (Laxshmi) aspect and three-day black (Kali) aspect, I hung once more by a single ankle, intoning,

'For nine nights have I hung from the World Tree...' while below (/above?) spun wove and cut three Norns in white, red and black.

Perhaps by now I may have engendered some confusion in the reader as to the identity of this 'fourth fate' or hidden aspect of the Crossroads trinity? For whereas earlier I described it's various masks in feminine terms, I now reveal a possible masculine identity of the Dark God as inner anima of the Triple Goddess of Fate and Time.

So which is it? Well- either, neither, both. This dark entity has no fixed mask, it is an elusive absent present Elder who awaits our choice -Whatever identity we wish to apply, in resonance with our own True Will: The Fourth Fate is our own individuated part in the crafting of our destiny...

As *Jan Fries* reminds us, *'In the Edda (Icelandic scripture) we are told there are many more Norns, some of them Aesir, some elves and some dwarves. Perhaps we should conceive destiny as a complex weaving that is done by many Norns in many places, each of whom processes space and time in her or his own way. Ultimately, this leads to a model in which every mage functions like a spider, building a mandala of realities and projecting it on the substance of the world. Indeed we are the Norns of our own lifetimes.'*

(-*'Helrunar'*, Mandrake of Oxford, '93).

Fate is never definitive, but a weblike span of possibilities and potentials which we become more conscious of as we find our True Will within its vast scope.

Like the Spider as Her ultimate zootype, Kali is ultimately of a devouring nature, so She is the Destroyer of Time (Kala) as well as its Creator.

The *Niruttara Tantra* says (2, 27):

"*The cremation ground is of two kinds, O Devi, the pyre and the renowned yoni.*"

SHIVA-KALI YONI-LINGAM

MahaKala is destroyed in the fire of His loveplay with Maha Kali. So this is the message of *The Book of the Spider* reflected in the Hindu pantheon: Kali birthing and devouring Time, Her mate.

She frees us from the restrictions of Time, She releases us from the web of Her own creation.

Besides physical death as the measure of cycles of incarnation, this can also be looked at as a metaphor for states of gnosis. Deep trance states, induced by extensive meditation or deliberate ritual practises, can induce no-mind. We may go beyond Time, outside the Wheel of Fate. Yet the rim of the Wheel is also its very centre, its axis axle, and so it is by making love with our Fate - entering the Yoni of Kali and penetrating to its core -that we transcend Time. The axle penetrates us also, as dualities merge in the meeting of numenon and phenomenon.

Once we have truly done this, even once for once is then known as all-ways, we know the mutable nature of time, and our perspective is freed. We may move upon the rays of the web with ease, no longer attached to the sticky spiral of 'regular time'.

Looking at the HGA (Holy Guardian Angel as the Future Self, the Question arises as to which Future Self? For assuming we have some choices or control of our destiny, do we not thus have an infinite array of different potential possible futures?

Indeed, and this returns us to the concept of the Web; -reduced to eight or even sixteen rays (kalas) merely as a simplified model, it is really multi-dimensional (a spiralling funnel) rather than flat, with innumerable strands of possibility reaching off into the ether…

So perhaps the Guardian Angel is our greatest potential, our best possible avenue in the intricate and often confusing maze of existence, what we are meant to do in the universe; and so finding alignment with that is the attainment of True Will via communion with our Other which is Self, in the Great Work of Becoming…

The HGA changes form and face with ease -at different times S/He has appeared to me with different masks, different genders and even different names -for the future is an indefinite and constantly shifting thing -not a single moment but a flow of flux and gradually-realized fruition.

I have focused here upon Hir appearance to me as a Spider because it is the relevant mask to the nature of this book, as Mythic Archetype of Fate deified and embraced as the potential and inherent divinity of the Self.

Former as well as Future Selves can be contacted along the rays of the Web. I have travelled back to meet former incarnations, finding this especially effective on fly agaric mushrooms as they give one an enhanced awareness of cyclicity. Soon afterwards I picked up deliberate sigilic keys one of my former Selves left in his artwork; confirming my experiences in the light of normal consciousness. Similarly I have left such keys in my own work so as to continue the work in my next incarnation. Establishing this kind of continuity of existence beyond the constraints of individual incarnations is a major way of transcending time, or rather the limitations of a single lifetime, by perceiving eternity and the continuing thread of one's spirit through multiple and variegated existences.

The day after Winter Solstice 1998 I combined two substances which individually had given me the most intense experiences of my life -fly agaric mushrooms and DMT. While of a similar intensity, my experiences with each separately had been vastly different. The combination, taken ritually within a sacred medicine wheel, was mind-blowingly effective as a method of travel. Here are some of my diary entries from the time, written only a few days later:

'Using the snake-encircled spiderweb as a map of time, I leapt on a ray and travelled back to meet my former self in a c rack between the worlds.

Fly agarics tend to increase awareness of self and of the cycles of fate. One becomes almost overwhelmingly aware of the infinite spirals of existence; the circles of time can be felt coming around.

On previous intense journeys with these mushrooms, this clairsentience of imminent events has been combined with an incapacity to affect the course of The Wheel of Fate. This time, however -due to a slightly decreased dosage, a developing familiarity with some of the spaces traversed, and greater focus from daily meditation, chanting and a recent 6-month period of entheogen abstinence- I was able to assert some control over my experience, rather than feeling I was on a ride I couldn't get off! I have been learning how to roll with Fate, how to recreate our destiny with the subtle power of Adjustment...

(note: this is an oblique reference to the archetype of Maat/Moira, the hidden fourth Fate of tarot Arcana 8 'Justice' which Crowley renamed 'Adjustment'.)

'...Around this time I was in the process of redrawing my **Wheel of Fortune** tarot card. I tattooed the Wheel of Fortune on my ankle as part of my ongoing journey of Tattoo Tarot Tantra (www.crossroads.wild.net.au/ttt.htm or IMPious #3) and as an anchor for my rite, so that I could return to the circles of time after going to the 23rd Arcana with DMT, a substance which when smoked sends one hurtling into the Other, into somewhere/somewhen else inexplicable to our normal perceptions. If you look at the spider-web as a map for time-travel: the spiral is 'normal time'; but sometimes we can get on one of the rays and jump to another part of the spiral...:

'My two most intense fly agaric trips have both been on the night after winter solstice. Thus I continued this cycle, but from the Crossroads of the wheel I took DMT and rode the frog to the 23rd Arcana, another dimension altogether, outside the circles of time and the wheel of the Tarot.

'Even before I took the DMT, I was able to move on the web like never before, by becoming a CHorus *b e t w e e n* the multi-Verses of possibility and moving emit ni sdrowkcab. Submerged deep in the Well of Remembrance (fly agarics bring the subconscious mind to consciousness, sometimes allowing access to previous incarnations) I went back to meet my former self, who has left me keys in his art and writings (discovered as progressive clues gradually over six months or so) to remember my previous incarnation and continue the work. This was an incredibly beautiful and empowering experience, the full nature of which cannot be revealed. Suffice it to say that he was looking forward to meeting me as much as mih teem ot sdrowkcab gnikool saw I.

I was re-minded of the **Last Laugh Foundation**, which exists outside the circles of time. Moving away from my ritual circle into the Egg-house my friends Ken and Zya built, I re-newed my re-member-ship in this immortality foundation by reclaiming my inheritance as a continuous soul. I re-dis-covered the sigil (tattooed about five years ago and recently re-emerging as a sentient symbol and a powerful mantra) of the foundation above my ankhle, which is now tattooed with the wheel, one of the upper spokes (rays of the web) just barely touching the symbol. Two days after the journey a piece of my former self's artwork, last seen about 2 years ago, finally arrived in the mail. I had requested it be sent after having a vision months ago of drawing a symbol under the rim of the table in the picture. The sigil is indeed there, and what-is-more it is Ward H, the triple symbol of the Last Laugh Foundation, confirming in 'normal reality' my fly agaric experience.

'During the solstice ritual I did a lot of work with Tarot, "dealing with both hands", both forward in timemit ni sdrowkcab dna, using the double current of Crowley's 'Book of Thoth' (Aeon of Horus) and my own personal deck '**Book of KAOS**' which is be-coming a tarot of Arachnean Maat Magick. Thus I was able to re-trace and re-weave my own destiny. I have only begun to re-cord this. I am developing a method of divination/affirmation/confirmation via Kaos Tarot, wherein the future is re-aligned by 'writing' as well as 'reading' the cards. After all, what is the use of prophecy if not to re-direct that foresight as necessary, form-u-lateing a more satisfactory out-come. Due to the nature of Fate, however, our redirections were of course all-ways meant to be!

'Thus I re-dis-covered the power of the Word, with which one can, in a true state of uncensored divinity, shape reality as one Wills. Then when I took the DMT, while activating another sigil, I went to Arcana 23 and fully real-ized how much -in its beautifully and subtly twisted way of ravelling and unravelling -the tapestry of time and space all-ways turns (inside)out to be ex-act-ly and perfectly as everything was all-ways meant to be...

'...Since solstice in-form-ation has continued to flood my synapses. I seem to have opened some kind of floodgate to the akasha which I have maintained access to even after fully grounding back into 'normal' reality...'

To elaborate on some of the ideas touched upon in this rather exuberant diary entry:

Backwords speech has been an effective technique for me for moving sdrowkcab in the timestream. It alters our usual forwards-oriented linear perspective. Oddly on the fly agarics I found I could talk backwords quite fluently (or seemed to be able to, although there was no one else immediately present to confirm this from a normal perspective). Since then I have over the last few years developed this faculty purposely, and can now speak sdrowkcab (phonetically rather than as written) fluently in my usual state of consciousness also – perhaps I jumped forward on the web back then to grasp this now-learned ability pre-eminently, or was it just that the mushrooms gave more immediate access to an innate though usually subconscious process of reversal?

I have found that my subconscious and conscious minds have had less separation and more obvious interaction since I began learning backwords speech (phonetically rather than as written, i.e. reversing the actual sounds rather than spell-ings), although aside from such general and admittedly subtle effects it has not done so much to effect my awareness as I would have hoped, considering the amount of time taken to learn to yltneulf sdrowkcab kaeps

However if practised occasionally it does serve to alter one's perspective somewhat of time and apparent linearity.

What really fascinated me about the idea is when I discovered the work of *David John Oates* with what he calls 'reverse speech'.

After realising some of the 'backwards messages' on albums seemed unlikely to be placed there deliberately, he began to examine reversals of recordings of political speeches and even common room conversations. Discovering apparent messages in these also, he came up with a theory that we subconsciously express underlying truths related to our forwards speech sdrowkcab. Notably in political speeches, these messages -which seem to occur around every 15-20 seconds of conversation- seem to contain essential motives or facts when the forward content is indirect or ambling.

Oates' theories have not been accepted by the scientific community at large and many have criticised his inconclusive ideas. Of course anything relating to the subconscious is difficult to prove; however what intrigues me is his concept that reverse speech is the 'language of truth'. For Oates does not seem to be an esotericist and yet this idea segues perfectly with the aeonic theory of the Maat current moving backwards in timemit, for Maat is the Goddess or Neter of Truth!

So regardless of the degree of validity to his work (and he does seem to be somewhat of a marketing strategist), DJ Oates seems to have tapped into some strata of subconscious expression. The idea of Oates' critics that his studies merely demonstrate pareidolia, the tendency of the human brain to perceive meaningful patterns in random noise, does not in my opinion actually entirely dismiss his theories, rather adds another interesting angle:

Is Truth in the Ear of the Listener, or from the mouth of the speaker? Ultimately it must be a combination of both anyway, when the quantum concept of the perceiver-created universe is considered...

Of course various cultures have explored the multi-directional possibilities of language a long time before DJ Oates ever investigated the phenomenon.

The ancient (older than Sanskrit) *MalayalaM* language, originating in Kerala (southern India) and also spoken in Malaysia, contains words which are spoken forwards and words which are spoken sdrowkcab, and the words which are the same both ways are considered words of absolute truth -for example AmmA, their word for mother, and also the name of the language itself! Such words are called in English palindromes.

There are more directions to write or to read than two however, as demonstrated by several vertical Asian scripts (e.g. Japanese), and so we have Magic Squares, which read the same left-to-right, right-to-left, top-to-bottom and bottom-to-top; usually presented for magical purposes from medieval or earlier times. The oldest known one is the 'Sator' magic square which appeared in the ruins of Pompei:

S A T O R
A R E P O
T E N E T
O P E R A
R O T A S

One proposed translation/interpretation of this square is
'To sow and to reap, the work of the wheel', a message which seems to be echoed in its cyclical form.

We used it in the second track of our **Labyrinth CD** (a translation into immersive soundscapes of the ritual journeys through our installations), and in the process of re-cording it discovered an interesting facet of the square's magical properties: The original track of chanting the words from the square was reversed, and we found it sounded the same backwards as forwards. It was therefore palindromic not just visually but also phonetically and sonically; and was perhaps designed also to be chanted?

Walter DeLong proposes **TEXET** as an alternative central Word for the SATOR Square, after an in-depth examination of the Gematria involved. His theories were affirmed by multi-linguistic Gematria scholar *David Allen Hulse*.

Implications of Latin *Texte* (to weave) from which we derive our Text. Perhaps TeXeT implies the weaving of Fate forth andna kcab ini timemit

Certainly visually the square appears more perfected with that central X aXis which suggests the X-roads extending diagonally to tighten the wordweb's spell.

The square can also be rotated with ROTAS at the top for example, but of course it still reads the same with all the directions reversed.

The inclusion of **ROTAS** in this Magic Square brings us -self-referentially- to more of a Magic Wheel: ROTA (the Wheel) is a rearrangement of the letters of TARO(t), also cyclical as the Uni-Cycle of the Major Arcana 0 the Fool rides. The palindromic mirrororrim of ROTA is ATOR, which I have recently discovered relates etymologically to both Spiders and their venoms, and to poisons more generally, including their medicinal qualities. Just as I arrived at this section of the Text in my revisions for this edition, my friend Elix sent me this:

attercop (n.)
"spider," Old English attorcoppe, literally "poison-head," from ator "poison, venom," from Proto-Germanic *aitra- "poisonous ulcer" (cf. Old Norse eitr, Old High German eitar "poison;" German eiter "pus," Old High German eiz "abscess, boil;" Old English atorcræft "art of poisoning") + copp "top, summit, round head," probably also "spider" (cf. cobweb and Dutch spinne-cop "spider").

Amptes & attircoppes & suche oþer þat ben euere bisy ben maide to schewe man ensaumple of stodye & labour.
[Elucidarium of Honorius of Autun (Wycliffite version) c.1400]

For form evolution from Latin to French, cf. raison from rationem. The Latin word also is the source of Old Spanish pozon, Italian pozione, Spanish pocion. The more usual Indo-European word for this is represented in English by virus. The Old English word was ator (see attercop) or lybb. Slang sense of "alcoholic drink" first attested 1805, American English.

For sense evolution, cf. Old French enerber, enherber "to kill with poisonous plants." In many Germanic languages "poison" is named by a word equivalent to English gift (cf. Old High German gift, German Gift, Danish and Swedish gift; Dutch gift, vergift). This shift might have been partly euphemistic, partly by influence of Greek dosis "a portion prescribed," literally "a giving," used by Galen and other Greek physicians to mean an amount of medicine (see dose (n.)).

-The Online Etymology Dictionary, www.etymonline.com

Ator is also of course similar to Sator in the Rotas square, for the Sowing contains the Spider's venom. Another possible permutation of the four letters of ROTA, TARO and ATOR, is TORA -The Holy Book. The Wheel, the Trumps, the Spider and the Book. Hmmm, there seems to be something essentially arachnean and bound up with Fate in these four letters, and its formula seems intrinsic to *The Book of the Spider*...

Numbers seem to hold interesting reflective properties also, especially in their correspondence with the Hebrew letters in Qabalistic Gematria.

An example pertinent to this work is 31 and its reflex 13. 31 is central to the Thelemic gnosis, being the key toCrowley's *Book of the Law/ Liber Al vel Legis*, unlocking its various Qabalistic puzzles as a third of 93, the number of both Thelema (Will) and Agape (Love). This Key was discovered by Frater Achad in his *Liber 31,* and the name Achad itself -the Hebrew Word for Unity- equals 13 (A =Aleph =1, Ch =Cheth =8, 2nd 'a' not written in the Hebrew letter version - AChD, D =Daleth =4; 1+8+4 =13).

Achad's **13-star of Ma-nifestation** *(above)* has 3 layers of interlocked 13-pointed stars. 13x3=39, which is the reflection of 93, the result of 3x31. So we have a kind of small magic square of numbers rather than letters. 13 and 13 as a composite palindrome, 131, is the number of Pan (the horned essence of the PanDaemonAeon) and of the Mithraic Time-God **AION** :

The Gnostic and Mithraic God **Aion** is a lion-headed God entwined by a serpent, the Greek name coming from Alexandria in Egypt. Aion - also associated with Greek **Chronos** and appearing in similar forms as **Zurvan** in Persia - represents Time, but particularly Infinite Time, or Eternity.

So here the DNA-patterned serpent which encircles Hir body is also encircling the Cosmic Egg - or is it two snakes? Or one and a phallus? The serpent-twined egg is an Ancient Orphic symbol, and in some Greek mystery schools the similar God **Pales** hatched from such a vessel, as did related **Abraxas**.

Gender is sometimes ambiguous in such images. As in a notable Roman statue of the Time God S/He symbolizes also the antithesis between fire and water and has four arms representing the four winds, with four legs for four directions.

One of these arms is both cracking out of the egg of eternity - into linear time? and yet wielding the crack itself as a lightning-bolt (a Jupiterian aspect Aion sometimes bears) - the flash from infinity to form, Kether to Malkuth - which as phallic Vajra complements the yonic Bell in other hand.

Already a syncretic and multicultural deity due to diverse origins and variations of form and name, Aion has here been conbined with **NaraSimha**, a lion-headed God of India, presiding over the s p a c e s in between - as in the classic Vedic tale where He conquers a demon as 'neither God nor Man nor Beast' (rather, a hybrid of them all), 'neither night nor day' (dusk and dawn with their twilight magic), 'neither outside nor inside' (even as here S/He is neither within or without the egg, but in perpetual rebirth); and, as I discovered from asking for an explanation of a Sekhmet-like stone figure in Kajuraho - also 'neither man nor woman'. For sometimes this gynander appears in feminine form as **NaraSimhi**.

-From Orryelle's gold book **COAGULA**

An image resonating through many ages and culture, another aspect of this archetype is Ancient Egyptian **Nefertum**, the divine child of Sekhmet and Ptah: He is often shown with the head of a Lion, or with a blue Lotus crown, and is a God of beauty, perfumes and incenses. Sometimes - in the complex web of mythology differentiating along the length of the Nile and over many dynasties - Nefertum was considered an aspect of **Atum**, the original hermaphroditic creator-being. So here again we re-turn to the source, ever-born from itself in cycles of TimemiT.

When Atum later came to represent the setting sun, Nefertum as a child upon an opening lotus represented the rising sun at dawn.

Presiding over twilight, S/He/they are God/dess/es of the s p a c e s in b e t w e e n...

Thirteen is a number of great significance to this tome in that it is the number of the annual lunations and corresponding menstrual cycles. A lunar zodiac -as traced from the Druidic Tree Zodiac by James Vogh in his *'Arachne Rising' (Granada, 1977)* -had Arachne the spider as its thirteenth sign.

This lunar zodiac shows the more subconscious and inner aspects of the psyche and as such complements the more overt solar zodiac we know so well today in our outer reason-based society.

Apparently the Greek myth of the Minotaur is a code for this 13th sign, devised to hide its existence when the patriarchy suppressed the feminine lunar current. It is the tale of half a pair of Twins (the hero Theseus) -Gemini- and half a bull (The Minotaur- he was also half-human) -Taurus- meeting in the Labyrinth (Arachne's Web – most Labyrinths have a spiral formation). For according to Vogh, the dates of the lunar Arachne star-sign correspond with the first half of Taurus and second half of Gemini in the solar zodiac.

We recreated this rituality in our Labyrinth installations, having Theseus come in each night to slay the Minotaur and close the proceedings. This initiate would then become the Minotaur in the following night's rite (there were 3 nights of ritual in each of the 3 Labyrinths), in the ancient pagan tradition of the new Horned God/King slaying and replacing the old. In ancient Thrace (mostly now Bulgaria) the king was a living avatar of Dionysos, and he was ritually slain at the moment of orgasm during coitus with a priestess, so that the spirit of the God would be carried through to His successor in Her womb.

Besides its seasonal origins, this cycle was also applied in our final Labyrinth to the greater Wheel of the Aeons.

For Gemini is especially relevant aeonically in that it concerns the Twins- and the Aeons of the Son and the Daughter -Horus and Maat- are twinned, i.e. Con-current, though seemingly reversedesrever in the time-stream, past and future constantly interlacing as the eternal present.

In the final rite on the 3rd and final night of our 3rd and final Labyrinth, these Twins merged to create the Hermaphroditic

Baphomet as the New Horned God/dess of this twinned Pan-Daemon-Aeon.

Completing the revision (for this third edition) of this book upon the island of Crete, after visiting the ancient Minoan site of *Knossos* today, some more light is shed upon the ancient origins of this Labyrinth, and our theatrical version seems now as much a return to source (the nature of the labyrinth itself) as a 'rewrite'. It seems that Ariadne was originally the Goddess of the Minoan culture which preceded the Classical Greek mythos by several millennia, and it is quite likely that She was the officially-unidentified bare-breasted Goddess wielding a snake in each hand whose statuary was unearthed at the site - the first known 'snake-handler' before classical (and stellar) Ophiucos. In later (patriarchal classical Greek) mythos She was denigrated to the mere mortal role of King Minos' daughter, and the minotaur seems to be a recension of that ancient Bull-God from Thrace (an equally ancient or perhaps even older culture on the other side of what is now the Greek mainland) whom She married -Dionysos. This God of drama, ecstasy and intoxication had a bisexual and effeminate yet distinctively masculine nature, and was represented also by the black goat -shades of hermaphroditic Baphomet?

I have read that Vogh's 'Arachne Rising' work was a 'hoax', but on re-evaluation of its precepts in this light I have to question this. Certainly he made some things up, but there is an undeniable and valid esoteric continuity in the work, as well as considerable information that is correct according to earlier sources (e.g. Greek and Celtic poet and scholar *Robert Graves*). So while the specifics of his spidereal zodiac may be contemporary rather than ancient, its foundational idea of the thirteen-moon calendar is real. The whole Arachnean 13th sign as he presents it is about psychic and intuitive powers, so to dismiss the work as irrational or unscientific is to miss the point.

It is only after the publication of the second edition of this book (including the above paragraph) that I read that Vogh created the book as a very deliberate hoax, with the intention of demonstrating that people will believe anything. I find this incredibly humorous, for it seems he was a scientific-rationalist out to debunk unscientific or poetic speculative texts. The irony is that in my opinion he did the opposite, by demonstrating his own ability -obviously usually suppressed by his rationalist attitude- to tap into mythic sub-strata and intuitive connections- the spidery threads of the subconscious and mythic-symbolic deep mind. And this is exactly what his book- beyond the specifics of false scholarship- is essentially about. To write a whole book about it he must have had some kind of deep interest in the subjects, something he was seemingly unable to admit even to himself.

The womb-like Labyrinth -with its serpentine twists and turns- was anciently a symbol of Hekate (another Thracian deity), Metis (one of the conjectured origins of the name Baphomet as Baph-Metis) and Medusa, aspects of primordial femininity suppressed by the origins of the Patriarchal dominance (on the outer) in later Classical Greek culture. These earlier ancient female archetypes, who in their serpentine splendour represented the unbridled primal power of women, were replaced by Athena, the new more 'civilised' Goddess of Culture and the Arts whom the Athenians devised as springing from the head of the All-Father Zeus after he consumed (suppressed) Metis. Obviously a male mental projection of womankind as even evident from their own myth, Athena replaced her primal successor/s: Medusa (her image apparently imported originally from Libya or/and from Sicily, isle of the Titans) and Metis. Both have names relating to ancient female 'Wisdom', and were probably only later divided into separate deities/aspects.

Serpentine Medusa became a monster in the re-writes (the beginnings of His-story as we knew it), who was destroyed by the male hero Perseus with his sword (magickal weapon of air and the mind -divisive and analytical reason).

Parallel is the myth of the chaos serpent Tiamat chopped up by Marduk (her segments becoming T(he)-I-Am-At of linear timemit). For it is the snake or serpent more than any other creature who most repeatedly represents time and cyclicity in the creation myths of ancient cultures.

Tiamat was divided into portions by the Sword (the mind with its perception of form through the function of duality) of the solar hero Marduk. This division is the separation of fluid or natural time into the very specific and set time of the modern western world. It was in fact the Babylonians with this mythology who began the current artifice of our 12 (hour) and 60 (minute) based time system.

The modern western world (and its unfortunate imitators in the east, north and south) is obsessed with the structure of specific time. Every minute and second is calculated precisely and used to define our activity daily and thus constrict the parameters of our existence to pre-set schedules and regiments, to impose order and control.

Considering Her limitations as a male projected ideal of femininity, it is good to see Athena confronted again by a more primal feminine force in the myth of **Arachne**. As told by the Roman poet Ovid (in his marvelous 'Metamorphoses'), Arachne was a mortal woman who dared challenge the Gods when it was suggested her skills at weaving were equal to those of Athena, the very Goddess of such arts. Arachne not only proved her match at the Goddess' craft but also dared depict the deceptions of the Gods and their hierarchy in her tapestry. For such Promethean defiance she was turned into a spider, and banished to the rafters to weave there forever after.

An adaptation of this myth formed the foundation of the first ever Metamorphic Ritual Theatre (under that name) production, *'Arachne Ascendant'*. The illustrated framework of this play (from IMPious Magazine #1) is included as **APPENDIX B** in this book because of its relevance to the whole Arachnean gnosis; but also because it makes an important point about the re-turn of primal feminine powers. From the perspective of Athena (and her Father Zeus) the transformation of the mortal Arachne into an arachnid (a name derived from the character's name) was a dire punishment, to regress to animal form. And yet many of the earlier Goddess archetypes were unashamedly bestial, expressions of divinity within -rather than separated from- the carnal.

Regardless of the historical validity of his hypotheses (or not -there are theories that even its supposed origins in Fraser Clarke's 'Druid Tree Zodiac' are semi-fabricated), by positing Arachne as the 13th star-sign of the lunar zodiac Vogh has re-elevated Her to the stature of Cosmic Goddess which She deserves.

For as the American Indians so recognised with their 'Grandmother Spider', the span of the natural world stretches from the microcosmic spiders weaving in the branches of trees their webs between heaven and the Earth with its delicate eco-systemic strands, to the great web of stars above us. All is a wondrous web of interconnectivity, and She is the Goddess of Fate who binds it. That those born under the influence of the Arachne star-sign are speculated to be more psychically aware suggests other, etheric strands beyond the more tangible webs of the world of form. And yet it is this realm of matter which transmits and houses the subtler weave.

So Arachne becomes both Animal and Goddess, divinely carnal. As such She is a healer of the split between flesh and spirit propagated by the Christian myth of 'The Fall' from heaven and divine grace (which was only really a fall in consciousness brought about by such propaganda itself).

The monsterised and 'slain' serpent-Goddess Medusa re-turns as the spider, another primal feminine zootype. Her web connects heavens back to earth, healing the division of the chaos-serpent Tiamat into these separate spheres and its microcosmic reflection in the modern disease of the body-mind-spirit split.

The more stellar aspects of Arachne's fractal web reach their apex of scale within our corner of the universe in the great spiral arc of our Milky Way Galaxy, and that dark rift at its centre. Now as we re-align with this 'Womb of the Great Mother' in the culminative Kali-Yuga (the final Age or Yuga in the Hindu system) -we're coming back home to Ma.

Only a few weeks after our first performance of 'Arachne Ascendant' (**APPENDIX B**) astronomers (rather than astrologers such as Vogh) announced the discovery of a '13th star-sign' constellation, and called it after an image formed by the pattern of its stars '*The Snakehandler*'.

A strange reflection of the Arachnean constellation which is (according to Vogh's placement of the Spider) almost directly opposite it in the sky from a geocentric viewpoint, this also reasserts the serpent and the spider as complementary archetypes of primal femininity resurfacing. For the spiral coiling of the snake forms the web of Time as woven by Fate through our cellular MEMories with the twisting serpentine strands of DNA, 23 strands of chromosomes on Maya's loom...

8

Time Ate itself at 8 o'clock
Two hands stopped
8 hands splayed
The clockface displayed
Sudden Shock
Constancy had a seizure
The cuckoo lost its balance at an alarmiiiiiinnnngggg rate
But there was nothing, is nothing to measure this by
For all measure was Ate
8-handed, Chao-tick
Where becomes when, There becomes then
Where begoes then, And there docomes when
When Time was 8
Time stood still

...time sat down, time chilled
Stasis flew by!
Stagstagstagnancy staggstaggstaggered on
Upon it's beaten track
...While entropy held back

Time 8 itself at Ate o'clock
All Time was Ate
I must be coming now I'm late...

(from '**Clockwork Clockplay**'by Orryelle)

Hekate Triformis

THE THIRD GATE

Jewelled Spider

Earth glows, stars shine
Light plays in the necklace of Indra
Spelling out the stories of appearance
of that which is manifest
of bright becoming dark
and then bright, again
Behold the matrix glittering
Watch it contracting and expanding,
continuously spiraling
in all glories - Diamonds All -
each in all
and all in each
Catch the cables to the ace
Jewelled Spider at her mandala-loom
Feel the pull towards the centre, everywhere
and all-ways
(Circumference, found no-place)
S-u-s-p-e-n-s-i-o-n of time and space
And gone, without a trace
That sorrow!

- Verse by Mermaid
(RIP 2013)

(http://home.earthlink.net/~mermaid93)

As suggested in the diary entry I presented in the previous section: With backwords language and other techniques (to be now progressively elucidated), former and future selves may be contacted along the Web.

As well as past physical incarnations (if you believe in such), you may also follow genealogical bloodlines or even contact spiritual ancestors -your inspiring or kindred magical or artistic predecessors- who may often be difficult to separate from the line-Age of your individuated soul in motion through timemit. This is a common mistake, accounting for why there are so many

claimed reincarnations of Cleopatra or Crowley and so few of Mike Clark the greengrocer from Texas. Ultimately perhaps it doesn't matter, as we have established some kind of inspirational connection through the web of DNA with those souls who have made a prominent mark upon the akasha- the exact nature of these connections is not necessarily so important as what we learn from them - but beware of the hubris (ego pride) which may result from such 'revelations'! What really matters now is what we are doing now, and if such information helps motivate and inspire our work or play in our present incarnation, then it is useful -otherwise it has little real meaning and can become gratuitous.

Beginning with past incarnation or even spiritual ancestor work is not recommended as a starting point for practical use of the Sixteen-kala'd Web however.

The most immediate use of the spiderweb map is travel along the rays -rather than just the spiral- within one's Current incarnation, visiting various nodes of Choice -interstices of the Web, where the rays intersect the spiral- to realign our Fates. There are two major ways of approaching this work:

The first is by creating nexus points outside time, which reside, as all recordable phenomena ultimately must, within the exterior framework of normal time. We may thus create vortex or tunnel points in our normal time realities, by creating rituals at specific points in our continuum, linked through the greater cycles of the cosmos —most obviously that of the sun and the moon through our heavens.

Thus if we perform a rite at a certain time of each moonth, if the rite and the trance created is powerful enough, we may be able to more easily access this state at the same time of each following moonth. Thus we use Time to transcend time, getting off the Wheel by going to its centre.

As discussed earlier in this book, the best time of the moonth to perform such rites is usually the dark of the moon, the transition from one lunar cycle to the next.

Larger cycles may be used for similar, and often greater, effect. The obvious points in the solar annual cycle are the Great Sabbats of the Year, and here we have again the Eight rays -for there are Eight days of major cosmic significance in the annual cycles we perceive from Earth.

This ancient seasonal magic, that of the eight-fold year, is celebrated in Witchcraft and the Sabbatic traditions: the two *solstices,* when the days and nights are at greatest variance in length, and the two *equinoxes* when they are of equal duration, are points of very tangible observance. Equinoxes are good for rites of Balance and Equipoise, under the auspices of the Goddess Maat with Nox and Lux evenly-weighted within her scales upon the year's fulcrum, while summer solstice is best for outer work and celebrations, and winter solstice as the longest dark is best for inner work and extensive shamanic journeys.

Then there are the Sabbats between: *Imbolc, Samhain, Lughnasad/Lammas* and *Beltaine.* I will not go into the seasonal and traditional significance of each of the Sabbats here, for any good (and even many bad) books on Witchcraft delineate the basics of these.

Other times of more personal significance can also be used, even arbitrary dates chosen and thussanctified by the very choice. The important thing is to create some kind of continuity between these points, so that they become significant workable nodes within the web of your existence.

Then when applying the second method of spiderweb time-travel

-that of ritual application with a spatial metaphor as described shortly- they are established as interstices.

Birthdays are a good natural example -to varying degrees most people celebrate or at least notice these when they come around each year -and they are treated as somehow special -sanctified.

We step outside our usual patterns, to celebrate or acknowledge something because of the resonance throughout the entire web of a significant event -in this example the very birth of the individual whose timeline is concerned. In the same way any date of situational or even self-imposed significance can be sanctified and used as a recurring 'marker' along the calendrical web.

I have created a vortex outside of time on the day after winter solstice, a date originally accidental as a result of a miscalculation, but sanctified as a result. I took fly agarics for the first time on this day, a rather large dose of six (another miscalculation, based upon erroneous information I was given), and had an extreme (overwhelmingly so) inter-plane journey. Amidst other strata there were pieces of physical reality that seemed out of place with the context of the trip, but were actually, I later discovered, out of time:

The following year I ended up taking fly agarics at the same time (again I aimed for solstice, and by circumstance had the trip the following day, then remembering that it had actually been the day after solstice the year before also) in the same locale and went back into the vortex. Pieces of the previous year's journey appeared out of nowhere (nowhen?) and I realized that the incongruous phenomena I had experienced in the first trip were actually splices of this second trip which had somehow swapped place through time with those from the previous year!

Since then I became more deliberate with my annual date with this Vortex, trying new entheogenic substances and combinations thereof —such as the later DMT and fly agaric one described previously- on the day after solstice.

While such sacraments do alter our perception of time in rather immediate ways and are thus sometimes useful for such work, they are of course not necessary for effective ritual utilisation of the

Spider's Web. In fact I have found that since employing these substances a few times I have enough inherent awareness now of the true malleability of time (as a thing which is crafted by our perceptions) that for any kind of specific work, it is usually more effective not to take any sacraments, so as to be more capable of conscious reality manipulation with perceptions focused and less chance of delusions.

Although psychoactive sacraments can temporarily provide an extended perspective, they are usually less reliable and consistent than other techniques of gnosis which may require a bit more work, and it is only if you can find lasting keys from their temporal gnosis that they may be useful beyond the immediate.

If you do choose to experiment with shamanic plant entheogens, research them well (effects are often personal or untranslatable, but dosage and other necessary information is vital), receiving guidance if possible directly from someone who has worked with the substance/s in question and have them or at least someone un-intoxicated as your (non-intrusive except if required) guardian during the excursion; exercise caution with dosage and care with setting, and do not expect to do anything much in particular the first few times you try an intense new entheogen, except explore.

Let the spirit of the plant/s take you where they Will, indeed you may have no choice but to surrender and this is the bliss they offer for the beginning of your relations with them. Only later may you expect to become familiar enough with the perspectives they confer -and the realms to which they provide keys- to traverse them with conscious intent and directed Will; And even then only effectively if other meditational and magical practises are maintained.

And I again stress that use of the following techniques -especially while first trying them out- is probably more manageable without any such sacraments. I have only ever worked with strong psychedelics a maximum amount of 4 or 5 times a year, and found them most effective after prolonged periods of not using them and exploring and developing methods of gnosis without substances in-between.

Before outlining some basic techniques of web-work, I would like to relate a brief personal example of how useful they may be, and thus also demonstrate the practical immediacy of the system by expressed experience:

While writing the bulk of (the first edition of) this book I was contemplating a major decision in my life. I had been planning for a good 5 moonths to go to Europe that year (2002) and had been gradually working towards this goal, in terms of finishing various projects in Australia and also networking ahead (navigating yet another kind of wwweb) for my proposed travels.

However as I was beset with various obstacles and delays I began to wonder if it was actually wise to go that year at all, as I also needed to be over there mid the following year for a specific project; matters of affordability and practicality arose. I was trying to think ahead and mentating on my dilemma until it began to become aggravating to my psyche. Tarot readings only provided more data to fuel the dilemma rather than resolve it, and I was constantly intellectualising on the (un/)feasibility of my journey.

Unlike the previous time I had travelled overseas, I was very settled and comfortable in Melbourne and my home there, happy with my abode and my circle of relations, and as winter set in I was delving deeper into my own magical universe, so world-travel seemed ever more remote and would require a process of severe up-rooting.

I was writing the first draft of this book sporadically during this period, sometimes almost as a distraction from my over-hanging decision. Then suddenly one day it occurred to me that my theory and practise should not be so separated! It had been quite a while since I had worked with the web-travel techniques I was leading up to describing, and it was suddenly obvious to me that I should apply them to my immediate situation.

As soon as I went into ritual space, the answer was immediate. By taking the process into my magic circle and examining it from an intuitive and spiritual rather than just a mental angle, I was able to make a definite decision, and purchased my air-ticket to Europe the day after!

An additional benefit was more consolidated material for this book, as a result of further realisations from this process.

Jumping around in this narrative in much the same way as the ray-hopping it elucidates (like some kind of hyper-texte-ual voltiguer), while editing and expanding the original book five months or so after writing the above, I affirm that my Journeys in Europe for four months of 2002 were wondrous and profound, and indeed exactly what I needed to do at that time. When upon return to Australia I first re-entered the backyard earthen circle where I had performed the spider rite which aided my decision to go, I felt a light tickling sensation in my navel. I looked down to discover a tiny lime-green spider had immediately nested itself there, as if in consolidation.

By mapping Time onto a spatial plane, we allow ourselves to metaphorically navigate it within the microcosm of our magic circle.

The purpose of this is in a way the purpose of all ritual: It is active. We can think eternally about something and never get any closer to a decision or result. When not ready or able to yet fully enact something on a larger scale, we can 'model' it microcosmically to determine not just how we think about something but how it actually feels.

The spiral as discussed can represent the progression of time, the rays are astral short-cuts to different points of the spiral -in much the same way as the spider moves along these rays with ease while the insects caught in its web stick (quite literally!) to the spiral.

The points where the outward rays intersect the spiral represent the choice nodes of your path. They are the cross-stitches in the tapestry, decision points or X-stream events from which various alternate paths diverge.

There are many different ways to set up the eight-fold mainframe of your web, and which you use in each individual case is to be determined by the nature of the working and what you wish to explore and effect.

I have included a diagram as an example of how such a web can be constructed, but the lengths of time can be varied according to what you wish to (and feel capable of) explore.

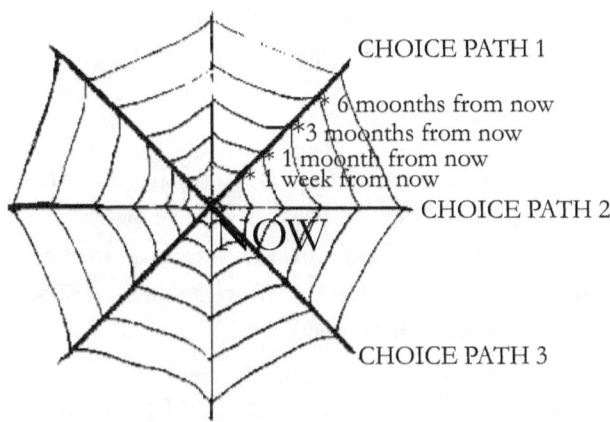

Select a scale for your model according to the span of your purpose, considering also the span of your inner vision (though also stretch this progressively if it seems limited), in terms of more immediate time-frames being generally more accessible and vivid.

If you wish to explore a previous incarnation or astrally travel back through hirstory, then the rays could be representing whole life-spans or even aeons. If you are wishing to determine something about your immediate future, then scale the model with the spaces between the nodes as days, weeks, moonths, years or decades according to how far you wish to travel.

I recommend that you start with a fairly close and immediate scale, as often the further your mind's-eye reaches the more vague and elusive the visions and other sensations will be.

It is probably not good to become too set or specific about the structure, as this will occupy the logical mind and distract from visionary trance states. Pre-determining the scale before entering ritual space is also recommended for the same reason —you may in some cases even want to draw it out on a piece of paper first —a map of a map. Then you are ready for ritual practise (although I recommend reading through and digesting all of this properly before beginning the Work):

Begin by casting your circle, in whichever manner you see fit, using whichever system or elemental/directional Godforms you resonate with.

(I find *Nema*'s six-fold Maatian banishing (in her *'Maat Magick'*, *Samuel Weiser*) particularly effective for this kind of work as it is Aeonic in nature, expressing the formula of Pentagramm-aton through the evoked elemental Godforms and therefore orientating your circle in both time and space simultaneously.)

Once the circle is cast sit in its centre and perform at least 13 rounds of *Sodashi Sadhana*, a kind of *Kumbukka* (breath-hold) Pranayama, or 'alternate nostril breathing', to begin to induce an altered perspective of time.

This is a breathing technique of primary significance to the tantric traditions which is of special relevance here. The Tantras say this allows one to extend life and to move beyond time. It is indeed effective for such, circulating energy through the entire system, which is purified in the process, and offering an immediately apparent altered state (if performed effectively) which often does confer the sensation of cessation or extension of time.

It is a simple exercise:
Breathe deeply in through the left nostril, blocking the other with thumb or forefinger, hold the breath (with both nostrils blocked) for as long as is (barely) comfortable then release and exhale through the right nostril. The breath should be held here too after the exhalation, before the entire process is reversed to take it back in through the right and (after another pause) out through the left nostril, then back again, and so forth.

For deeper trances this pause of breath should be progressively extended with repeated practise, it is the 'instant beyond incident' or moment beyond (normal) time. (In 'Maat Magick' Nema suggests an effective mantric sequence using variations of the Word of Maat *IPSOS'* in combination with this pranayama).

In India one of my yoga teachers specified that the proportionate length of inhalation, exhalation and pauses is important for physiological balance, and should be at a ratio of 1 (inhalation) to 3 (hold) to 2 (exhalation) to 1 (hold). For example, one could slowly count to 10 on the inhalation, 30 on the hold, 20 on the exhalation and 10 again on the second hold, before reversing the sequence to take the breath back through to the original nostril. The same can be done -once the practise has been done often enough to make such extensions comfortably- with a sequence of 15, 45, 30, 15.

For advanced practitioners, the perineum muscle can be contracted and released like a pulse to both count these proportions and increase the gnosis by sending more prana up to the head.
This Kumbukka ('breath-hold') Pranayama is an effective daily practise as well as being useful in ritual, the former also building greater potency for the latter.

Another effective breathing and energy exercise to use at the beginning of a spider-magic ritual is simply deep breathing energy and attention into each of your chakras progressively up the spine - at least seven deep breaths focused on each chakra, using the abdomen not just the lungs by pushing your stomach gently out on the inhalation and pulling it in on the exhalation, keeping the entire body, neck and face relaxed.
You may want to cease this at a certain chakra to remain in the mode of its attributes, according to what energy is suited to the particular working you are doing. For example, with the rite I performed in relation to my decision as to whether to go overseas or not, I instinctively stopped the exercise after the heart chakra breaths. This put me in an appropriate space for making my decision from an intuitive and emotive rather than merely intellectual vantage.

Trace the Spider Web map within your magick circle as a great mandala. If outdoors you may etch it into the Earth with your feet while dancing the spiral slowly outwards to its periphery, or sprinkle cornmeal or other grains along your path in the manner of the creation of a Veve (basically a sigil or symbol on the ground or floor —the term comes from the vodoun tradition in which veves are a kind of diagrammatic house for a particular spirit).

If you feel adept at such things you can just visualize the web, but actually creating it physically —at least the first few times- will probably make your work easier and allow for more specific navigation. Regardless of whether you create the image with grains, earth or just your third eye, you should also create and define it with your movement —spiralling out from the centre to the rim of your magick circle. Larger spirals are often more effective as the spiralling motion and the gnosis it entails will then go on for longer, and also simply because there is more room to play with for the rest of the rite should you need it. If working within a smaller or confined space,

make the spiral tighter but still with many loops so that you are still spiral-dancing for a considerable time.

While creating the initial spiral you may want to chant:
T i m e m i T, T i a m a i T, T i a m a t, Tiamaat, TeyaMayeT, Tiamat, TIAmAt,
T'IAmAt, Th'I-Am-At, The-I-Am-At... ... ...'

Tiamat is the Great Serpent of Chaos at the bottom of the ocean of Time, and this chant represents Her division from fluidity (natural time) into segments ('The-I-Am-At' of specific orientation in time) through the delineation of history as described in the previous sections of this book.

It only recently (third edition) came to my attention that there is an Ancient Egyptian Goddess called **Tayet**, who presides over the weaving of the linen bandages in which mummies were enwrapped. Weaving -and especially mummification which seems akin to the preservation of their prey in silken cocoons- is a distinctly arachnean attribute, so it seems apt that Her name (phonetically when the mantra is chanted) pairs with that of Mayet (the World Order, earliest name of Maat) in one warp/weft of the palindromic TiaMait/TeyaMayet. Again, the spider and the serpent together form spirals and rays...

When you reach the rim or periphery of your circle, spiral slowly back into its centre again - defining more clearly the pattern you created in or on the earth on your spiral out. But do not dance forwards in to the centre, but rather sdrawkcab, retracing your steps in reversion of your original spiral.

This is a technique common in *Vodoun* –to dance backwards widdershins (anticlockwise) calls the spirits to you, as etheric mirrors of physical reality.

While doing this chant:
'The-I-Am-At, Th'I-Am-At, T'I-Am-At, T'IAmAt, TIAmAt, Tiamat, Tiamaat, Ti aMa a t,
TeyaMayeT, T i a m a T , T i m e m i T' etc. ...

This is the reversal of the previous mantric current, the restoring of Tiamat to Wholeness and fluidity, to primal Chaos and natural time. It should be begun in a swift staccato fashion to define the segmentation of 'The-I-am-at', and gradually slowed into fluid continuous chanting as you reach the centre. You may want to also echo this transition with your movement.

When you reach the Centre of the circle allow the Tiamat chant to fade into silence. Be still and feel yourself as the still axis/axle of the moving Wheel of Fate around you. You are the calm Eye at the Centre of the Cyclone, the *Ain Kia*. Closing outer eyes, now also place your palm flat upon the centre of your forehead (third eye). This is the meeting of *Ain Kia* and *Kaph Zos*, for the Eye (the Hebrew letter Ayin, and the Kia within the Sabbatic tradition) is at the centre of the Wheel (which as Major Arcana X is the Hebrew letter Kaph, represented by the Palm of the Hand or sabbatic Zos).

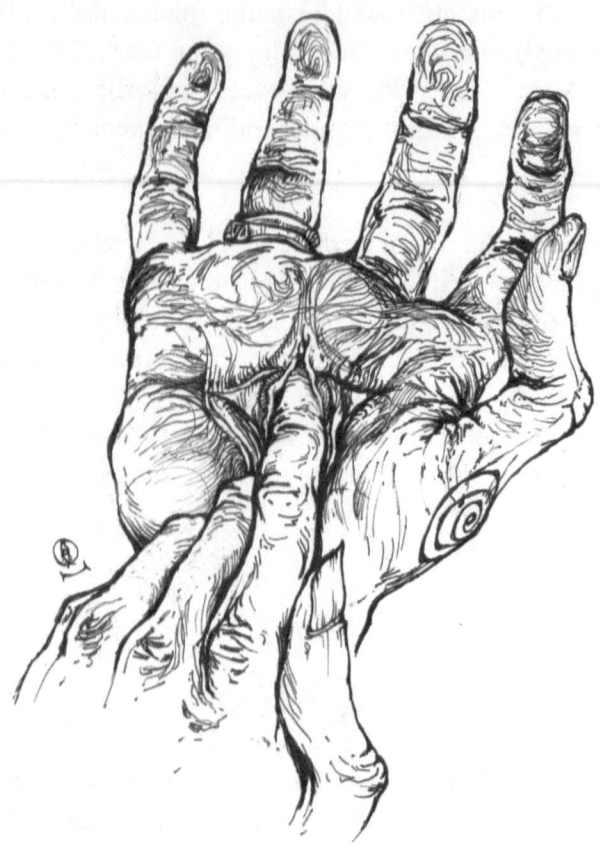

You are beyond Time. It is from this Hadit-point which you are about to operate, enabling easier astral movement. Draw your palm away from your forehead while opening yourself to inner sight, activating your third eye (Ajna chakra).

Begin to perform the **Bes-Kali mudra-mantra (APPENDIX A)** at this point, to attune yourself to the primordial current of the *Dreamtime* or Nameless Aeon (called by Peter Carroll the Shamanic Age), and to feel the power of Kali as the Creatrix of the Web you are about to exude into the circle.

Know that while in the Centre of the Wheel You are MaHa (Mother of Breath) Kali, weaver of Time and Creator of your own Fate.

When you inhale the '*Ah...*' of the mudra-mantra, hold it for a while, pulling your tongue right back into the orifice of your throat in a deep self-matrimonial kiss. Pause, hold, feel the cra ck between inspiration and expiration.

When you need to breathe out do so forcefully, expelling the breath with the '*...Ha!*' and with it a directed ray of energy, an astral kala to form a Ray upon the web, an Arrow of your Will.

Turn to each of the eight directions, and project a ray in each, using the tongue and breath for propulsion. The retractions of the tongue on the inhalations of '*Ah...*' between draw in energy, forming the inwards-pointing arrows implicit along the spiral. If using grains sprinkle these out upon the exhalations, 'drawing' the external rays.

The points where the outward rays intersect the spiral represent the choice nodes of your path/s.

In terms of future self workings especially, the choice nodes are never set realities. They are various potentials. They can be compared and contrasted to enable decision-making, by using them to represent alternate strands of outcome in your life. Knowing that the future is ultimately indeterminate is a part of empowering yourself as the crafter of your own Destiny.

Once the entire web (spiral and rays) is cast, take some deep breaths right down into your belly and, knowing that the centre in which you stand is the eternal NOW, step out from it into the Web of Fate.

Walk directly and deliberately out along one of the rays to your chosen choice node (interstice twixt ray and spiral) prospective. Close your eyes and imagine or visualise (for want of a better term, though any or all of the senses can be employed rather than just sight) yourself at this future point in your life -whether you have set it as a moonth, a day or even an hour from now- and experience it as profoundly as possible. This may seem as much a process of deliberate conjuration as divination

if the visions do not appear easily and spontaneously, but it does not matter —you are indeed creating your future reality as much as perceiving it! -And as you become more aware of the forwards dna sdrawkcab flow of timemit and the nature of True Will, there will ultimately cease to be any real differentiation for you betwixt Divination and Conjuration.

After experiencing (which may include vague feelings or emotions as much as or even instead of specific sensory phenomena such as visions sounds or smells) the first choice node, return to the Centre.

Breathe deep and step out onto another ray, and walk -being aware of the divergence of your path from the previous, though both issue from the same NOW point at the centre- to a parallel node (spiral and ray interstice) and experience an alternative future to the previous one. You may orient these rays before stepping onto them as specific different paths of events and circumstances.

I will continue to use my earlier Rite of Decision as a demonstrative example:

I cast one ray as the path of going to Europe in my immediate future, and experienced some vague visuals and feelings of what this potential reality would be like, then cast another ray as the alternative of remaining in Melbourne (Australia), and stepped out to the parallel node of about a moonth from Now with this option in mind. The sensation was one of frustration and even stagnation, which surprised me as prior to the rite I was feeling not only comfortable but very creative being there. By the time of the actual flight (which I booked the day after the rite), I was already beginning to feel the first twinges of such frustration. So you can see the usefulness of such projections...

Another technique I have found effective for web-working is reverse speech, the verse fo esrev-er eht

This is good for an entirely different kind of working, that of regression or moving into the past rather than the future. It can also be combined with backwards dance and movement in the manner I described with the casting of the inwards spiral.

This has implications for what Peter Carrol terms, '*Retroactive*

Enchantment?. The past seems not quite as malleable as the future to most of us, but as it too is created by our perceptions and there is no real 'true' history, a certain degree of adjustment is possible. It is dangerous territory as problems may arise due to discrepancies between our own 'memories' and those of others, so the consensus perception of others should be considered to avoid aggravation of this. Remember this is astral work, and don't confuse the planes.

So in practical terms retro-active enchantments are only really effective for altering personal (and often private) choices and thereby revoking habit patterns or embedded guilt strata. Changing the course of history (or even personal hirstory) as we know it is more difficult, although some writers and other propaganda artists have managed it.

In Greek legend there is a story which demonstrates such reversal –and thus extension– of time:

In Homer's epic tale of *Odysseus*, the hero's wife *Penelope* weaves a tapestry upon her loom as he travels the seas over seven years. She promises her numerous suitors that only when her weaving is complete will she give Odysseus up as lost or dead and take a new husband. But each time as by day she almost finishes the tapestry, she unravels it back by night, creating an eternal flux of suspension. For She represents the Three Fates of her culture's mythoscape, and she is suspending Odysseus's destiny til such time as his course may re-turn him to her loom/womb...

To use any re-cording device, be it audio, video or even the ancient pen, is to re-cord the cords already woven, so as to wind back like Theseus in the Labyrinth the Golden Thread of passage. In this way we reinterpret and thus recreate with our perception 'history's' 'set' events.

(A warning here that there is a danger of becoming obsessed with re-cording and fail to move on, caught in a Choronzonic stasis of repetition and analysis.)

(A warning here that there is a danger of becoming obsessed with re-cording and fail to move on, caught in a Choronzonic stasis of repetition and analysis.)

We may make contact with our former selves —becoming something akin to a guardian angel for them- or even younger stages of present selves in some cases, but this is very dependent on the receptivity of these former selves or stages of a younger self. As the visitations are astral, the earlier self often will not be able to perceive your attempted contact. It is best to choose times of non-ordinary perception —ritual states, meditation or moments of extreme emotion, whether terror or ecstasy- major decision or crisis nodes in the younger/former self's life to attempt such communications.

Dream spaces are potential access points but the chances are that the former self will not remember the experience when awakening (though this doesn't mean it won't have some subtle effect via the subconscious).

If we take reverse time-travel to its extremes we may ultimately access those states which A.O.Spare refers to as '*Atavistic Resurgence*', where primal and bestial aspects of our ancient natures may be accessed from the core of our cellular memories —beyond the personal into animal selves and even plant or (in one very strange journey; no oddly I wasn't on anything that time) fungal selves…

A particularly potent method for astral travel emit ni sdrawkcab is the **'8 Gates'** Pathworking initially shown to me by *Rain Fisher Wolf*. He received the journey 'straight from faery' and after he had passed it on to me ironically (since it is for accessing deep memories) could no longer remember it himself, leaving him with the feeling he received it primarily for me.

Well I have certainly made much use of it, having adapted my first major journey with it (during a solar eclipse just after he told it to me) into a ritual theatre piece I have now performed eight times, and subsequently passing it on in group workshops and rituals. I now present it more widely, as the DVD accompanying the hardback edition of this book contains a hypnotic audio induction of the pathworking for ritual use, and also extracts from theatrical performances of my own journey with the working.

I adapted the journey into a theatre piece because it was already a great story directly as experienced, with no need of elaboration or re-plotting. The way the different lives I explored linked up on the web was wyrd and wonderful, and later use of the working with others yielding similar results leads me to the conclusion that one is often likely to find links between different lives as the particular fragments re-experienced are remembered precisely because of their evident associations.

Thus we trace the intricate weave of inteconnectivity betwixt our different incarnations through the tapestry of timemit.

My first performance of '8 Gates' as a theatre piece was as an improvisational secondary solo short play after the rehearsed group production for the launch of the first edition of this book.

Although the story and its messages were clear to me, I had no real idea how I was going to adapt my journey for theatre, but wasn't sure how to rehearse a solo theatre piece (my first of any length) so decided to just wing it on the night. It flowed very well, and many preferred it to the much more predetermined and rehearsed play it followed. What really made it easy to choreograph immediately on the stage was that there was an eight-rayed spiralling web on the floor from this preceding piece, and when at the end of the less visual path-working (I asked the audience to close their eyes as I spoke them into the trance) I arrived at the 8 Gates themselves, I realised to my delight that there they were mapped out before me on the floor as the spaces between the rays! For each journey into a different self (animal, plant, human, etc.) I simply stepped into the appropriate space and played it out before returning to centre and current self.

And thus a new way to use the spiderweb mandala was devised, and the 8 Gates Pathworking evolved from a merely astral experience to a more active physical exploration of different selves. It has been used in this way since with groups as well as individuals.

Thank you, Ra'en!

Generally future workings are more effective and accessible to the mage's consciousness as realms of alterable potential than the past, and the more immediate the more accessible.

How one uses the spider web model is ultimately up to the

individual sorcerer. What I have outlined above is only a basic guide or template for your own mutation and development. You will find your own personal 'settings' and techniques as you play with it, according to the nature of your work; and these may continue to change and evolve...

Complexities I have begun to develop with it personally I will not describe, as they will probably only confuse the reader and detract from their own personal paths of developments from the basic template I have presented.

The emphasis is on *Practise*. Some of this may not seem to make much sense as words, but if you go and put yourself into trance by the various methods suggested -or even by another/s entirely- and ritually create the Web, you will find your own gnosis and may progressively develop your own methodology within its contours and interstices...

But take heed also that while practise of such magic is useful, obsessive work is not. As with tools such as tarot, it is important not to get too caught up in the maps and systems and possibilities and potentials inherent, and thereby actually inhibit rather than enhance their real-isation. I don't do such workings often, only when a major choice node in my life warrants it.

Having said that, more regular experimentation with these rites is more pertinent in the early stages of the work, as we may develop methods thereby.

Astral potentialities are interesting reflections, but regular-speed physical time travel is important too! -and the former is only really useful if it's results are then effectively applied within the latter, on the plane of manifest reality.

One idea I will suggest, without outlaying a specific means of working with it, is that the elemental quarters cast in a circle could be used in combination with the minor arcana of the tarot, with their elemental suits correlated along the web-map.

Personally I have found tarot useful in combination with web-work, positioning the actual cards along its strands; and encourage individuals to devise their own methods by experimenting with such combinations (though only after more fundamental webwork has been established). For tarot too is a tool which can be used for *conjuration* as much as *divination*, as I will now divulge before returning to this more physical mandalic web-work:

Oracles can be used for **Conjuration** as well as **Divination**, one leading quite naturally to the next. After all, what is the point of investigating potential fortunes or future possibilities if we do not then have the power to adjust what we have foreseen if unsatisfied with it? Otherwise the sole purpose of divination —other than the mere satiation of curiosity- would be only to prepare ourselves for what is to eventuate.

But is not this very preparation, this expectancy and readiness itself going to then effect those eventualities when they come? For -as we have already explored through **THE FIRST GATE**- the nature of any incident is very dependent upon our perceptions of it. In this way we apprehend and thus co-create—through our perceptive angle on events- our own destiny with the Fates, Gods, spirits or Neters (or for the less religious, with the blind Chaos of circumstance itself). For Fate does not preclude free will.

If our fortune is thus affected by our apprehension of it through divinatory oracles, why not then consciously craft our fates with our wills, using these same divinatory tools for conjurational purposes?

We may divine to bring up from our subconscious the most likely potential outcomes of our current path, then use this divination as a springboard for altering the course of these paths of destiny if dissatisfied with their direction. For any 'future' result in an oracle is never set in stone -until eventuating it remains a potential, one that may shift slightly even just from looking at it. So we can often adjust this most likely outcome even more consciously and specifically, by adjusting our current circumstances or way of being to re-navigate our future course.

What follows is a very practical system of techniques for using the Tarot –this ancient Book of symbols and archetypes being one of the most popular and potent oracular tools (and one with which I have much familiarity and faith)- as a tool to make such adjustments, to 'write' rather than just 'read' your fortune. I have used these techniques quite extensively myself, and have also presented them at several **Tarot Conjuration** workshops where (and subsequently) other participants have also found them most effective, even if initially being unsure about the idea of 'meddling with fate' in such a manner.

To such resistance I can only assure that if it is one's belief that fate is so fixed that one should not interfere with its course, then the result of such wilful activity can at the worst only be that things can't get any worse than already pre-ordained, so you may as well at least attempt to make them better!

I have never experience any negative results from these techniques, nor been informed of any by those with whom they have been shared thus far. I would however, recommend that they be used with care and caution, the idea being to prompt a deep exploration of what one really does (and does not) want from what the cards bring to the surface, rather than a flippant reshuffling of fortune without due consideration.

Remember, if you make adjustments and they do work, but you then realise that wasn't what you really wanted or needed after all, you are only yourself responsible and cannot blame your 'misfortune' on Fate, God/s or even on that classic scapegoat the Devil, which is probably what scares some about such work.

This system of Tarot Conjuration is ironically based loosely upon -and inspired by- the common card game **'Snap'**. Ironically because there is evidence that our modern deck of playing cards used for such games actually evolved from the Tarot, the suits of diamonds, clubs, hearts and spades (with their four court cards and ten numbered cards) relating directly and respectively to the elemental suites of pentacles, staves, cups and swords. So we are returning a playing card 'game' back to the source of the tools it employs.

Although who knows for sure? —perhaps such techniques have been used with tarot cards long ago, and the games themselves are also but vestiges thereof?

The idea of applying 'Snap' to Tarot readings began as a joke: A rather out there friend of mine, known by the name of Phineas, was unhappy with some of the cards in the outcome position of a tarot reading I did for him. He immediately began to select other cards at random from my deck and slapped them on top of the offending outcome, with a triumphant cry of, '*Snap!*'
'That's better...' he then said and we both cracked up laughing, descending from there into even greater absurdities.
However, even as the Magician card follows the Fool card in the Tarot trumps, there is often underlying meaning in the Fool's playful jests and spontaneous whims, and so upon later (more sober) contemplation of the idea I realised how it could be utilised effectively with the application of a mage's intent. From there, progressive experimentation from this basic seed idea has led to the development of a powerful system of self re-programming and conjuration methods using the Tarot.

It was quite some time before I even clicked just why the basic rules (with some minor adjustments) of 'Snap' are effective in altering a Tarot reading. As in the card game, one should only replace the unsatisfactory card with another card of either the same elemental suit (whether it be cups, staves, pentacles or swords) or else if of another suit, then of the same numeration. For example, the 5 of staves could be replaced with the 5 of swords, or with the 8 of staves, but not by say the 8 of swords. The reason this works for reading adjustments, I realised, is that there are *affinities* between these cards,
relationships which make the adjustment feasible. To replace the 5 of staves with the 8 of swords is unlikely to be easily achievable in reality (despite the ease with which it may be done physically in the mere map of the reading), because they are so vastly different from each other in nature. There is no affinity to easily bridge the vast gap from one to another.

But to replace the 5 of staves with the 5 of swords is much more feasible and possible, because they are aligned through their enumeration. All of the 5s, regardless of suit, share the martial qualities of Geburah, Sephira 5 on the Tree of Life. Similarly all of the 2s share something of the essence of Chokmah, and even regardless of Qabalistic considerations, have a dualistic and twinned/pairing aspect relating to the number two in general.

The other means of adjustment, via same suit rather than same number, is also about affinities, but of a more elemental nature: The 5 of staves could be replaced with the 8 of staves or even the King of Staves because they are both of the suit of staves/wands and therefore of the element of fire and its qualities of passion and creative energies. The 8 of swords has little affinity with the 5 of staves as neither its number, nature or elemental qualities are aligned.

So it becomes clear how and why the basic rules of 'Snap' work applied to a tarot reading.

However, regardless of elemental or numerical affinities, little result is likely to be achieved by simply changing only the cards themselves. Tarot- as with other divinatory tools- is a reflection, a mirror in which the initiate may scry to unveil aspects of self and circumstances which s/he might not otherwise be consciously aware of. If we then wish to alter the pattern revealed, we need to do so within our lives and our selves, using the reading/writing of the tarot as only the map which it is, a guide with which to view and transform the territory of our circumstances. We can conjure with Tarot in terms of using it to consider and clarify what needs or wills to be done, but we then need to apply these revelations to our 3-dimensional existence.

Having made this vital point, let me assure you that Tarot can be a powerful tool to point the way and set the course for such real-world applications of conjurational adjustment, a navigational instrument if you like for passage and fortune through timemit, though not the journey itself.

Extensive use of such techniques –and their results- may indeed blur the very distinction between the concepts Divination and

Conjuration themselves, tapping us into the time of everflow and giving us glimpses of the true intersectional nature of absolute presence.

When we perform a tarot reading, the cards we are most likely to be discontent with are those in 'Outcome' (/near future/results) or 'Future' positions of a spread. Most feel that the past is unchangeable (true to some extent but our perceptions of it may definitely be altered- and where else does the past exist other than in Memory?) and most of the cards around present circumstances are already in effect.

The important thing with this work is to trace back the dissatisfactory Outcome or Future result to discover its origins and source in more current cards of the spread; i.e. The most effective way to change the future is by changing the present.

It is a good start to 'Snap' an outcome or future position card you dislike, to replace it with something more resonant with your goals and ideals, but this is only the beginning of the work.

We must then search out the root of this unsatisfactory future potential in the present to effect any real change. So in positions of the reading such as that of the underlying 'Foundation', and the initial card laid and those crossing and/or covering it i.e. affecting and influencing it, 'self at the moment' and such positions should the origin of the problems be sought. I usually use a 13-card variant of the common *'Celtic Cross'* tarot spread, but similar positions as those I have just described exist in most spreads. Regardless, one is basically looking in the cards which signify the present situation and current aspects of self, to see what may be evident there as a source of upcoming future troubles —or rather of their potential. The 'Guidance' position (if you use one) also often suggests further insights into origins, although it is rarely a card you would want itself to change. Likewise with the oft nebulous yet ever-revealing 'Hopes and/or Fears' position: clues may be found as to what to change in the more immediate circumstances.

Aspects of Self (often represented by court cards) evident in current positions are always the best place to start, as the surest way to change your circumstances or environment is to change yourself and thus your perceptions of and relationship with them. If nothing jumps out in your present situation cards as needing changing, try tracing origins via affinities: If the offending Future card is the 3 of Swords, say, then look at other 3 cards or swords cards in your present as likely candidates for the seeds of the problem.

So when you have found an origin for your potential future problem, Snap this card also, again of course with one of affiliated number or suit. Unlike the card-game, it is not necessary however to do so with any kind of speed or hastiness, since you're not competing with anyone else (unless you feel the Gods or Moirae are impatient to beat you to Their own desired outcome!)

Although swiftly slapping down the next card in the deck you come to of same number or suit can be a way of reaching a more intuitive response from your deep mind if you are the type to struggle with over-analysis, it is generally better to slowly and carefully consider the changes you are about to make before you actually lay down the card, so that when you do so it is an act of surety and affirmation of the changes you are committing to make in your actual life.

You may want to go through several different options before deciding, pulling several different cards of the same suit or number from the deck before you actually determine which of these is either the more suitable option, or the more feasibly achievable one. For consideration must be given to the achievability of the changes you wish to make- there is little point in altering cards which represent changes you are not realistically able to enact in your life.

Do however give yourself some credit, for the degree of transformation possible is only partially to do with circumstances, and usually primarily in proportion to the degree of your will, determination and especially perseverance. You can plot the course of action with the cards, and from there determine a methodology (there may be clues in the guidance position card) to effect it.

The fact that you can't usually change much merely by changing the cards and not yourself too was demonstrated to me quite graphically (and comically) during early experiments with these ideas. After the initial 'snap' revelation I had in my foolish head that I could change my fate simply by changing outcome and future cards I wasn't happy with.

The reading in question was performed outside where I had been sleeping on the verandah of a gypsy palace, and the question in the reading concerned some complications in my love life at the time. Quickly changing three cards, I felt satisfied I had averted glimpsed impending disaster, and wandered off. Later there was a strong wind gusting through the grounds. I returned to the site of the reading, where I had left the spread laid out as affirmation. I found that the three replaced cards had all blown off, revealing the cards underneath again. The rest of the reading had remained intact despite the wind but for a single covered card which most related to the difficult situation. I eventually found it in my bed.

And yes, all the things I tried to avoid by covering them with other cards came about. The positive result was that I then looked more seriously into the idea of 'writing' tarot, and refined the methods as outlined here.

The only 'moral' to this tale is that one should not mistake the map for the territory. If I had truly considered the changes I wished to make to my self-predicted fortune, and worked out how I was going to enact them, then things would have probably worked out differently. Subsequent refinements have been more successful.

Tarot reading is good for bringing to your full conscious attention where you are at, what you are doing and where you are headed. Subsequent Tarot 'writing' is effective for working out what to change aspects of this to (if so desired), and what changes need to be made now to change the outcome. The rest is up to you.

So how does one actually effect the real-world changes this method suggests, one may ask. That is something I can't answer precisely, for it depends very much on what change it is you wish to make.

Only you may really know, but the cards (both as they were and as you make them) can of course offer ideas and navigational routes. The important thing is to persist: although affirmation is powerful, just the decision to change is not always enough. It's a good start though!

A good way to remain conscious of a commitment to continue exacting the decided change is to place the cards you replaced the unsatisfactory ones with on your altar, or another place where you will see them often, so you are reminded to maintain decisions made beyond the initial reading. You may also wish to meditate on their imagery and symbolism.

I have not as yet written of how one works with the **Major Arcana** or Trump cards using these methods, and some readers are probably wondering by now since the trumps do not exist in modern playing-card decks, other than the Fool as the Joker. Since the usual rules of the card-game Snap can thus not be applied to changes of Major Arcana cards, one must judge affinities more intuitively and/or logically rather than by specifics of numeric or elemental attributes of cards.

It seems important that a trump (major arcana) should only usually be replaced with another trump card, since these are such major and significant aspects in a reading and the life it reflects. However if you really feel the need to 'tone down' a major arcana to a minor arcana card which has some kind of resonant affinity with it, I don't really see why not.

I don't think that just any trump card should be used to replace any other one. Many of them are vastly different from each other, and it seems too contrived for instance to replace the Hermit with the Tower; although it does of course depend on what you feel of your capacities and is contextual to the circumstances. Ultimately there are of course no rules other than your own, just be sure to keep your play with the cards aligned with what you can then actually change in yourself and enact in the world, or it will become merely an act of delusory wishfulness without real results.

Decisions to *not* change anything after much consideration can also be important and powerful.

If you think you don't want something and via a process of working with Tarot in these ways - including investigating other options via the methods described- you realise you actually don'twant to change the way things are going after all, this in itself still creates a subtle yet often vitally powerful effect on your life: For whereas before you may have been unhappy with your lot, wishing for something else; now after really assessing alternatives and thus perhaps realising just why you are doing what you are doing, you will be more at peace with this fate and rather than struggle with it, embrace it. Thus even though your actions or circumstances may not change directly, your experience of them still will, through a shift in perception and acceptance of underlying purpose.

This of course reiterates the earlier and central core of this book, in that even when Fate does seem unalterable in terms of circumstance beyond our control, still we may change our experience of it with our perception and acceptance of it, aligning it with our True Will.

All of these techniques I have presented for the use of the Tarot for Conjuration are practical in as much as they may be applied to physical reality, insights gained and decisions made then affecting the manifest world. However, it is still cards on the table, and while a little active it is primarily mental and philosophical, and many will find it more effective to actually move around within a magic circle, with physical and even theatrical ritual to embody rather than just contemplate the various potentialities of one's Fate. And so I return to the use of physical web-mandalas, which may be employed to actually walk through rays of change you may have discovered via the tarot work, and thus further activate their course, redirecting your destiny as you see fit. Or else of course the mandalic webwork may be used as a method unto itself (as described earlier), more direct and tangible than cards for conjurational re-routing of fate-lines...

Since the first edition of this book I have experimented in pairs and groups with using some of the techniques I initially outlined for solo work. Casting a web is extremely effective with eight people performing the **Bes-Kali AHA mudra-mantra (APPENDIX A)** simultaneously, one ray each while standing in quarters and cross-quarters of the circle' then walking the spiral out together, and this can even be desrever to close at rite's end (as can be seen in the beginning and end of **'Loom of Lila'** on the DVD); just two people can also perform it effectively, facing each other on the inhaled, 'Ah...' then turning suddenly back to back to exhale the 'Ha!' together and project a ray of intent; then both ritualists may rotate their position and repeat this to cast rays in another direction, forming a crossroads and, if desired, the spaces in between.

I initially felt that exploring past incarnations using a web mandala/veve would be impractical in a group situation, as peoples' individual journeys could interfere with each other, especially if expressed aloud or with movement. Nevertheless, we tried it and I was amazed by how well it flowed. Wyrdly, participants' separate experiences were mostly actually enhanced rather than distracted by those of others working simultaneously around them.

Particularly, this has been done with the **'8 Gates'** pathworking as elaborated earlier.

I held two Spider Magic workshops at the new year Confest Festival '04, within a web installation woven twixt four trees. The Crossroads was aligned with these and the diagonal rays, time spiral and spaces in between also projected, as we mapped time onto the spatial plane within our magick circle with a spider-web mandala veve of flour.

The first workshop was an introductory session where I explained the concepts of spiral time and fate as true will, and demonstrated how the web mandala may be used for individual exploration of paths of potential.

The second was more a practical ritual, and again the right people came:- about half present were people who all knew each other well and had even worked ritually together, but those few strangers who turned up from the workshop noticeboards also had strong wills and a focused application to the working.

My last-minute decision to gate-keep rather than go into full trance myself also proved to be an apt intuition, as some people walking past were disturbed by a participant's expression of their experiences with emotional purging and I was able to let them know everything was alright without the workshop being interrupted.

I was delighted how well things flowed, considering that most of the techniques and methods I presented had been developed in solo rites and not before tested in a group context. Rather than interrupting each others' journeys, they all actually interwove in a non-direct but wonderfully synchronous manner:

One person's goblin-like expressions in the fungal gateway filtered through into another's experience in the Plant gateway next door. Her sounds meshed with his memory of being a forest ecosystem as animals seemed to scamper across his many limbs in a kind of frenetic energy passage from the altered perspective of his slowed-down temporary floral consciousness.

Another's experience -of beginning to be born- did at first seem to be disturbed by another's confrontation in the same Human Lives Gateway, and she began to retract, remaining on the verge of incarnation; but afterwards I told her (from my peripheral observations as Gatekeeper) that she had actually rolled onto the ray/line b e t w e e n the Human Gateway and the Spirit Gateway - where realms between incarnations could be experienced- and thus got stuck on the cusp of incarnation...!

It was fantastic how immersive this workshop seemed to be for everyone involved, especially for a semi-public ritual.

I was then eager to explore this group application of 8 Gates further in a more private Silver Dusk new moon circle. Wyrdly Ra'en who had originally shown me the pathworking came along to the ritual, so it was good to have the original concept loop back on him in a developed application years later...

So after warmup chakra tone chanting, Ra'en cast the 8 Gates, calling in the spirits of the Mineral World, the Plant World, the Fungal World, the Animal World, the Human World, the InBetween, the Black Void and the White Light; while I sprinkled flour to mark out the central Crossroads of our web-veve -chanting for Papa Legba to Open the Gates, and another participant called in Hekate as Crossroads guardian while Darren drew the diagonal eight rays betwixt the Gates with salt.

Then everyone sat around the periphery of the now highly-charged space while I led the pathworking, timemit ghourht sdrawkcab gniklaw dna gniklat

When the first (tsal ro) of the Forgotten Nine had rowed us to the farther shore of the Styx's still black waters, we stood still en-tranced and entrance-d into the circle's centre via the spiral dance and staccato-to-fluid progressive chant of *'...The-I-Am-At ... T'-I-Am-At ...Tiamaat...'* slowing with our movement into the centre...

From 'there' (no-time) we each stepped into a different gate of being, except for me -I returned to the potbelly stove at circles-edge as gatekeeper/guardian.

I had been unsure how the working would go with this many people (there had been just four at the Confest workshop), but as with last time the individual journeys of each -though some quite vocally and animatedly expressed- seemed to strangely complement and even interweave rather than interfere with each other.

Jake and Darren were both wolves together in the same (animal) gateway at the same time, aware of each other but just sitting alert rather than running together. Rain at one point went into the same gateway briefly and was also a wolf.

T explored a human life that she could not really pinpoint -the visions were not clear, but the emotions were strong and quite disturbing.

Ground and T each explored the white gate briefly -despite Rain's original warnings to me years ago that this was not necessarily a good idea as it represented dissolution into the all. Perhaps they were assured by my own dissertations (despite not having tried that gate myself yet!) that the working is 'only on the astral'. They found their experiences there difficult to relay but apparently both disconcerting and reassuring?!

Ground also explored the Black Gate which he found 'peaceful'.

Rain went on a huge journey with the whole working, experiencing several fragments in different gateways which interconnected oddly in much the same manner as my original experience with the pathworking on a solar eclipse which I had later adapted theatrickally.

He began in the Plant Gateway as a Great Oak (his 'power-tree'), during which he emitted a strange low slow moaning sighing sound; then experienced himself as a human who ate powdered fly agaric and sought to slay a dragon. I can't remember in which order, but he also was this fly agaric in the fungal gateway (akin to my own experiences with this gate's sElf and human sElf's consumption thereof. I Amanita. I Am-an-eater...), and was the Dragon he sought to slay, bewildered and outraged by the attack. The man was broken by meeting the Dragon's gaze, realising the dragon was himself.

After 'flying' around the entire circle as this dragon -which he later said he sensed as pervading all gates as some kind of core being- his great swoops carrying him out in an expanding spiral to its periphery, he re-turned to the plant gateway and his beautiful slow oak moan song. Ra'en felt his journey to be a mythic and symbolic one rather than actual past-life experiences.

This seemed the general flavour of the work that night, perhaps because of the group aspect?

Nevertheless, the veils seemed broken down sufficiently with our casting that the difference between individual-personal, mythic-archetypal and collective-akashic selves seemed nebulous anyway. The significance was in the power of the experience rather than its particular nature.

As circle guardian I did not observe people's reactions or expressions closely, being there only in case I was needed rather than wanting to interfere or spectate. My focus was therefore spread loosely across the whole web in self-contained alertness rather than scrutiny of individuals. So I noticed the patterns between different ritualists more than the facets of each person's journey. At one point I became extremely aware of the beautiful harmonies that began to emerge. Separate and very individual vocal expressions from different quarters of the web began to merge and flow into a strangely synchronised whole.

I am not sure how consciously aware of each other they were, but the various chants, cries and sounds of participants tuned together into a beautiful song for a while...

Towards the end of the working Jake left the circle and joined be by the fireside. After a while I felt it was okay for me to then enter and briefly explore one of the gates myself. I ventured into the fungal gateway, finding myself rather abruptly (after being outside the circle's collective spell) immersed in a very different reality-perception.

It was nothing like my previous experiences in this gateway as a fly agaric mushroom. I am not sure what kind of fungus I was, but perhaps a whole collective colony of something as I felt very 'spread out' and I think very very small -I seemed to be experiencing reality on a molecular level -I can only describe it as perhaps the gradual permutation of moisture through a microsystem?

Everything was gloopy and slow, I could only express it with very soft squelchy popping sounds. Deciding almost immediately to return to the centre before I went any deeper and lost my thread of normal 'observer' consciousness, I found it took quite a while to slowly 'permeate' back to that perception-space...

One thing I noticed of significance is how Ra'en's experience synched with the overall pattern of the working, in relation especially to our casting: -the spiral (winding through the eight rays which formed the Gates betwixt) was created with our dance inward and chant of the 'T'-I-Am-At...' to '...TiaMat' chant. This symbolically restores the great Black Dragon of the Deep TiaMaiT (TimemiT / TeyaMayeT) to wholeness... Now in Rein's vision the Dragon rather than being broken into pieces mirrors the beast within its prospective slayer, and he instead is 'broken' (though in spirit rather than body). So the dragon remains whole, and spirals back out...

When I conveyed this to Reign he revealed that he had not consciously realised this pattern.

We closed the Gates and the circle and banished, sweeping out the flour and salt of the veve-web.

Other ritual elements may be effectively used in combination with the spider web model. You can call in appropriate Gods or spirits to effect changes upon the different nodes according to their energies.

Vodoun (and its African and South American variants such as *Santeria, Candomble, Ifa* etc.) has a particular affinity with this kind of work, as such veves (symbols drawn upon the ground or floor to call in the loas or spirits) are used in these traditions. The central symbol of the Vodoun traditions is the **Crossroads**.

The Lord of the Crossroads **Legba -Eshu** or **Ellegua** in the Santeria tradition- is entreated first in most rites, as it is He (or sometimes She –Crossroads God/desses of many cultures are usually of ambiguous or flexible gender and age) who Opens the Gates for any further magic to be wrought. Most other veves are drawn upon or intersected with the central Crossroads.

The Spiderweb is no exception –in fact the Crossroads are of course its central pinion or framework, forming the (elemental) quarters which are then split diagonally to manifest the Eight Arrows out (and the Eight Spaces In Between).

If you have an affinity with the Vodoun pantheon (and many who have a feel for spider magics are likely to find one if that current is explored) you may wish to entreat Legba, Eshu or Ellegua with prayer and offerings when you cast the Crossroads of your web.

Some other such Gatekeepers from other pantheons are **Hermes** (Greek) –who is also indeed a Lord of Time-travel, **Hekate** as Lady of the Crossroads and lunar-arachnean archetype, **Anubis** (Egyptian), and **Ganesha** (Hindu) who should be entreated first before any Hindu or Tantric rite.

There are specific *Loa* (Vodoun Spirits) related to Spider Magic. Primary amongst these are the African *Anansi* -the ancient trickster 'Grandfather Spider'; and *Baron Zaraquin*, an Arachnean Lord who usually comes in the form of a Scorpion (another arachnid), but sometimes a spider, human, or any combination of the three. Sacrifices/offerings may be made to either at the Crossroads to aid with this work.

There is also a major 'family' of Loa often considered arachnean- the *Ghuede*. Ghuede as presented earlier in this book (including visually) is the Vodoun lord of Sex and Death, but He has several variant forms which are sometimes seen as separate aspects of one being, and sometimes as a group of related spirits. Their arachnean qualities and the affinity of Ghuede with Mahakala consolidate the concept of time as a web.

The most spider-like of the family is **Ghuede Nibbho Araignee** (left), a gynander /transexual deity. (*Araignee* is French -as often used in Haitian and New Orleans Vodoun- for arachnid)

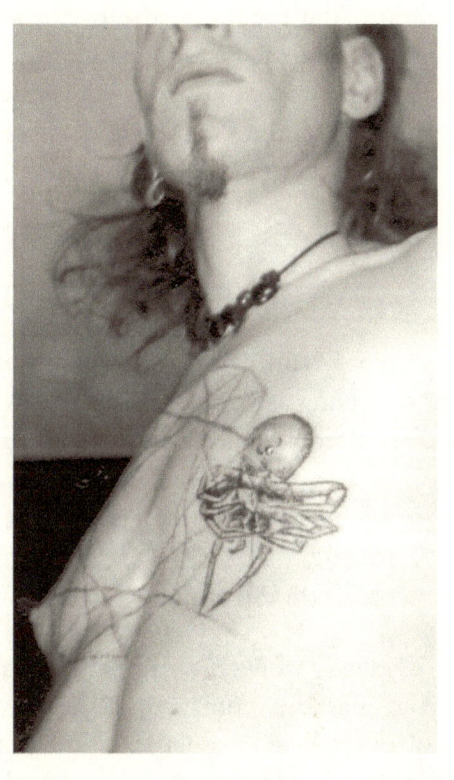

I called this loa when I had my chest tattooed with *Achad's 13-point Star-diamond of Manifestation*, including a hermaphroditic Golden Orb spider (members of this species are often hermaphroditic) weaving its angles *(right)*- and found Hir a potent energy to deal with (for the full story see **SilKMilK s p o o l # 2, iNSPiRALink.**)

The tattooist- an Anglian witch- had worked with this loa before with some interesting manifestations such as large white tropical spiders mysteriously appearing (in England!) and warned me of the dangers involved in working with such loa, when the clickclack of his needle-tipped chopsticks, used for traditional oriental hand-tattooing, reminded him of the wyrd clicking sound they had made. I took little heed of such cautions at the time, having already done some work with Ghuede, but have since come to understand them, as more long-lasting results of such work have gradually unfolded.

So I pass on the caution: the *Vodoun Loa* can be very severe and unrelenting and are not to be trifled with, especially the more intense ones such as the Ghuede.

They should not be entreated without appropriate sacrifices, and if none are offered may just take their own.

Only deal with them for important work -they make no bones (or many bones?) of having a joke at a practitioner's expense, which may contain useful lessons but is not necessarily pleasant.

Sexuality can be used directly rather than just implicitly for these rites if it is your Will. Rather than just with tongue and throat (although this should also be included amongst them) via *Khechari mudra* (the tongue in the back of the throat as in the **Bes-Kali mudra-mantra**) and vocal intonation, the Kalas may also be cast forth and kcab ward from the genitals to initially project and define the Rays of the Web. Here are some ritual ideas of how to utilise this energy with spider-web rituals:

If you are genetically Female:

Invoke **Kali Ma**, your chanting of Her mantras gradually intensifying as you begin to sexually stimulate yourself. One of the most effective is the 23-syllable Kali Vidya:

'Hrim Hrim, Hum Hum, Krim Krim Krim Dakshine Kalikaye,
Om Krim Krim Krim, Hum Hum, Hrim Hrim Svaha'.

Drawing in energy from the spiral of the Web around you with your ecstatic contractions, begin to form the eight invisible introverting rays or kalas. These are inspired upon the inhalations which alternate with the extended exhalations of the eight extraverting ecstatic expiring kalas.

The kalas should not be projected outwards until through continuous deep breathing and masturbation a deep trance has been attained. Project each one when you are close to orgasm, In then Out along the Web but allowing the energy to then subside and bide your time until the next Ray is cast, high-tensile strands strung with the anticipatory tension of tantra (in the loom). Know that You are Tefnut/Mayet (a part of TeyaMayeT/Tiamaat restored), primal Goddess of Moisture.

E-voke Maha Kala, God of Time before you. As the Web tightens and the pulsations grow, Invoke Maha Kala. As He enters you devour him, in-drawing in the process of this inhaling inspiring the final

inverted Kala, in orgasmic contraction. Know that as Kali Ma, Kala is your Animus, even as you project Him back out to be born and borne along the final Ray as the ultimate Maha (Great) Kala in the ecstatic expiratory release of Orgasm.

To fully produce the ultimate Kala from a woman, the energy should be moved successfully up the spine to be fountaining through the Sahasrara (Crown) chakra.

Though this is attainable to anyone who has the self discipline to perform sufficient breath and energy work over a period of time, it is not of course an expected possibility in all ritual circumstances.

Even a weaker connection through a semi-Open Sahasrara will sufficiently leave the ethers with its vaporous wisp of an imprint, which is enough to know the QuintEssence of this Amrita; though of course deeper exploration of the full potentials is beneficial.

If you are genetically Male:

Invoke the Time God **MahaKala** first. His Gayatri Mantra (usually traditionally performed at dawn, dusk, midday or midnight, but still applicable elsewhen) is:

'Hum Hum Mahakala, Praside praside, Hrim Hrim Svaha'

If other pantheons resonate more with you than the Hindu (or you may wish to combine several of these examples), you could invoke the Greek primal Pan Pangenitor, Ancient All-Begetter, Celtic Cernunnos or Egyptian Atum while beginning to masturbate.

With slowing breath and quickening energy, take oneself to the edge of orgasm, and on these outward crests casts forth a wave, a subtle kala from your phallus, brought forth by the hand of your Will. With eight great inhalations between in-draw the inverting rays of the web, with perineum contractions and deep breath spooling their sticky strands up the spine and through your body to dance softly upon the branching delicate web of your nervous system.

E-voke Kali Ma before you, and pluck upon the tensile etheric web with tactile tentativity. With each outwards crest and inwards ebb cast and draw the 16 kalas, culminating in the invocation and inversion of Maha Kali Ma as your Anima, drawing Her in on the final contraction, with energy up to and through the Sahasrara or crown chakra as much as possible. She then leaps back out of You as Tefnut ('Moisture') with any seeds you may emiT. If you do not wish to ejaculate (and it is not something I would recommend doing more than a few times a moonth, though regular non-ejaculatory orgasm properly performed is beneficial) the few drops of fluid which may emerge will still carry the QuintEssence of the Kala prana, which needs no physical vessel ultimately as it can be cast from the Crown.

Know too that this use of sexuality for casting the Kalas of the web is on a symbolic rather than actual level, as with the rest of the rite as a metaphorical map/model microcosm. While some of the actual kalas produced by the human organism may be physiologically produced during the ceremony and sexual gnosis is of course a powerful energy to use magically, it is doubtful that even the most adept tantric yogini could produce all sixteen of them at the same time of the moonth in a single session!

The use of sexuality in such weaving is more symbolic of the true kala emissions which play through the lunar cycles which you are symbolically contracting into the circle and its web-map; sexuality also being useful for raising kundalini and/or aiding the induction of the trance which is necessary for such work.

Of course not all sixteen rays (or even eight) of the web are necessary to most web-workings, only a few paths often being explored to reach a decision or retrieve the necessary information.

Even if not ultimately used in the rite the other beams may be constructed initially just to give the overall design and symmetry of the web —or not…

There are actually nine different types of web that a spider physically creates: Besides the sticky spiral and the high-tensile rays, there is a special type of web for cocooning prey, another variation for creating egg-sacs for the young, a flexible web on which spiders float and ride the winds, and so forth...

To attempt to correlate all of these with the specific Hindu kalas would perhaps be contrived, but the very variety of emission itself is another interesting parallel.

It is rare in *Spider-Web Time-Travel Rites* that more than sixteen rays would be of any practical use, but it is interesting to consider that further divisions create a vivid fractal pattern whose geometries resonate through several different cultural systems:

From the four basic directions and elements we double into the eight-spoked Wheel of Fate or the Chaostar.

From here doubling the rays again we have the sixteen kalas of the KalaChakra Wheel and of the ChaOrder Mandala

Doubling this we get 32, the number of paths and spheres upon the Tree of Life, the ancient Hebrew Qabalah, and also the number of names and forms of Ganesha, Hindu Lord of the Categories

Doubling this again we get 64, which is the number of hexagrams in the ancient Chinese I Ching oracle and the mathematical basis of our very DNA.

Some great cosmic map is implicit here, one which I began to diagrammatically charter once after my first ayahuasca trip, and have not yet consolidated (but perhaps it is better left nebulous and therefore flexible?)...

The Trigrams of the I Ching and their eightfold projections are metaphorically congruent also with the 3-faced Spider-Goddess of Fate and her Web.

This links to the subject of DNA, which has 23 strands. As popularised by author R.A.Wilson and Genesis P.Orridge's Temple of Psychic Youth, 23 is the number of Synchronicity. It is also the number by Gematria of the Hebrew Word 'ChVT' meaning a Thread.

Perhaps it is a means of tapping straight into those nigh-infinite strands of cellular memory?

What is this 'Syn-Chron-icity'? Syn is an Assyrian Moon God, Chronos the Greek God of Time from which the word 'Chronology' comes, so it relates to the patterns of lunar time –i.e. intuitive or felt rather than logical ('solar') time. Indeed, the web of synchronicity – that sensation which occurs with increasing regularity the more we align with our True Will or Fate- is ultimately beyond intellectual apprehension.

Thus it is with Arcana 23, that state beyond our normal perception of Time. For there are 22 tarot trumps, from 0 the Fool to 0 the Fool, and outside (or is it the very centre of the Wheel?) this perpetual cycle of existence, this Uni-verse-all Uni-Cycle which the Fool rides, is the 23rd Arcana, the great Beyond of the Unknown and –at least to our normal perceptions- Unknowable.

It is this Arcana which I have been exploring –using my Key 23 sigil to help me unlock the doors to dimensions beyond the 4th dimension of Time, to the very Quintessence of Magic.

The winds they blow and the tides they ebb
And Arachne ascends Her wondrous web
The warp and the weft, the corpse and the cleft

In the 13th Hour when the harvest is ripe
I lay my Horned Head Before our Black Mother's scythe

In the 13th hour She assumes Her power
On the 13th day of the 13th moon
In the 13th hour She has come to devour
In the 13th day on the 13th hour
At 13 o'clock She assumes Her power
On the 13th moon of 2013
She comes through the spaces
in be twe e n

In the Kali Yuga She receives Her puja
In the 13th year past the 13th Baktun
In the Kali Yuga She dances Her furore
To the fugue of...
PANDEMONIUM!

From Shamanic to Religious through the Aeons
And Now we're leaving the Rationalist Aeon
As we go into the...

PANDAEMONAEON

-Lyrics from Orryelle's **'PANDEMONAEON'** Song
Originally a track of Mutation Parlour's **LABYRINTH CD**, revised in 2013

In reflectivevitcelfer counterbalance on the physical plane of the etheric ARCANA 23, The Silver Dusk executes the Ma-nifestat-Ion of Nuit. For *'The Manifestation of Nuit is at an End'* (*-Crowley,* **Liber Al vel Legis***)*, and the Silver Dusk heralds the End of the cosmic day begun with the first glimmering rays of the Golden Dawn and inaugurated by their emergent prophet of the Magickal Revival, Crowley as the herald of the Shining Son/Sun Heru.

But now as Ma(at)'s (the Daughter H final in the Tetragrammatic formula of the Aeons) Ion or node of an Aeon encroaches, the Work approaches completion. For there is a hidden (Sh!) axis to this aeonic formula, the fifth letter of Spirit around which the more manifest aeons revolve.

The lunar arachnean intuitive artistic magick of the Silver Dusk resolves the light of reason of the scientific approach to magic instigated by the more systemised Golden Dawn. Crowley championed, *'The Methods of Science, the Aim of Religion'* -so now his Arrows of Art shall find their mark - the Winged Eye is the target and its arrested flight shall bring the vision to earth...

Eros is the Archer, Agape is the Key (thrice divided), the End of the Beginning is Nigh. Time's great spiral tightens towards its apex, the axis of infinity and axle of TAROTA.

The Mayan calendrical conclusion signals the awakening of the Great Rainbow Serpent of Gaian Kundalini, fledged Kukulkan/ Quetzalcoatl, Jormungandr arisen, TiamaiT restored.

Yet this 'end' can only be perceived as such from our current linear perspective of timemit. Once time has 'ended' the very concept of ending is irrelevant. What else can this be but re-turn to the ineffable 'beginning' of time and the space/form its loom defines -the Shamanic Dreamtime which has always been, *Beyond*...

The Hindu conception of Time is incredibly complex. The *16 kalas* relate to sidereal zodiacal attributions, and the whole system is precisely calculated from great Yugas or Aeons (though theirs are far vaster than the western concept of aeons) of time down to the minuteae of individual breaths, upon the divisions of the *KalaChakra* (Time-Wheel). While we need not concern ourselves here with the complexities of the full kalachakra system, there is one important factor that must be noted for its practical ramifications: the concept that *'Breath is Time'*.

For although the Eastern view of time is as precise and specific as the Western one, it is this fundamental concept which separates and invigorates it. For the eastern division of time is as much for spiritual as practical purposes —being used to calculate astrological influences within Vedic horoscopes which are intrinsically linked to the Gods.

It may seem strange to western logic that the smallest degrees of the divisions of the Kalachakra system are determined not by planetary influences or the cosmic cycles of the sun and the moon, but by the human breath, since this would not seem to be regular and specific.

Yet ultimately how long we are alive for, how much 'time' we have in each apparently mortal existence, *is* indeed determined by our breath. If we breathe at different rates, time does seem to distort accordingly. When we breathe slowly and deeply, it is because we are relaxed, or if it is done consciously and deliberately, it can induce relaxation when it is needed; offsetting ageing elements such as stress, tension and even bodily ailments such as nausea. So our health and therefore ultimately our lifespan -our allotted time- are indeed determined by breath.

Our breath changes in various physical extremes such as severe climate changes, fear/danger, sexual excitation, etc. These states are those when time seems to distort, to speed up or slow down or seem irrelevant. An orgasm can be like a cessation of time, a no-time (and sometimes no-matter) space beyond our usual perceptions of sequence.

Certainly I prefer the eastern equation of Breath = Time to the western one of Time = Money.

The letters of the ancient Sanskrit alphabet are the garland of fifty skulls Kali wears, with which the tantras (Hindu sacred textes) are woven. They are the breath and measure of mortality, of temporal incarnate inspir-ation before returning to Her void when we expire. Spiders, the Black Goddess' primary zootype, have 'book lungs' within their web-spinning abdomen, page-like membranes with which they breathe...

Breath is the meter of our existence. It can be used to deliberately raise our energy -especially when combined with perineum muscle and/or genital and anal sphincter contractions to draw prana/apana up and down the spine.

The Hindus have a mantra they relate to time: –'*SamHa*'; To them this expresses the sound of theinhalation and the exhalation. I hear it more as 'Ah' and 'Ha' which validates for me a formula I have worked with considerably –'*AhA*' –for this Hekau (Word of Power) used in different ways both conceals (the whispered 'Aha...' of the hidden secret) and reveals ('Aha!!' the lightning-flash of realization), and also contains the laughter which often follows such revelation of secrets; plus AHA contains a layered gematric formula of perfection which I will not go into here *(aha...)*...

Suffice it to say for now that AHA is one of the Three Keys to The Last Laugh Foundation, inner circle of The ChAOrder of the Silver Dusk and an Immortality Foundation which has existed long beyond the fictional constraints of its namesake in Tom Robbins' humorous novel about Pan, *'Jitterbug Perfume' (Bantam, 1984)*.

That this Word AHA also represents the breath is significant. Combined with the Hindu Khechari mudra it is especially effective, as I have condensed into the exercise I call the **'Bes-Kali AHA mudra-mantra'** (**APPENDIX A**).

The region in which this all occurs, of course, is the Mouth, and Mayet/Maat's Word is IPSOS, meaning *'By the Same Mouth'*. It is within the cavern of Moisture (Tefnut) that the Vinum Sabbati Amrita is brewed with self-penetrative Khechari.

The Hebrew most holy name for God is written YHVH, yet according to tradition is Unspeakable. There is a stream of thought in some esoteric schools that this Word is also related to the breath, so perhaps it is unspeakable in that it is merely breathed and the vocal cords are not called into play. God is Breath Itself, also in the Ancient Egyptian cosmology as the life-force of the pranadeva Shu (air), whose Sacred Twin is Tefnut/Mayet (moisture) -one cannot without the other. Certainly this 'unpronouncable' name makes more sense as the Word which was God at the Beginning of Hebrew scriptures, as it seems fairly obvious that breath preceded articulated sound, which grew as a vibration therefrom, only later gaining (an awareness of) 'meaning' as language. Indeed, this is the progression in Hindu cosmology.

It is interesting that the same name YHVH has also become a formula for the aeons -as propagated by the Golden Dawn and Crowley- with each letter representing an element and corresponding great Age in human development, for ultimately the 'unspeakable' name of this formula leads us back to the conclusion that Breath is Time.. And Breath is God/dess —our inherent divinity is realised by our effective use of the Breath. The Hindu Puranas assert that all existence is the breath of MahaVishnu, the Preserver; yet this breath itself is the Destroyer Shiva as MahaKala -Time, which can only emiT anew in the wake of death, cyclically, eternal.

And there is the secret letter (Sh!) within the equivalent Hebrew formula, making the Tetragrammaton into the Pentagrammaton. Even as with Aha, the apparent concealing is also the revealing, for Sh is the sound of the actual Hebrew letter, Shin, the letter of fire and spirit (therefore prana as breath and lifeforce) which completes the elemental formula.

Aeonically, this is the nameless or wordless aeon beyond ordinary time, which is always there regardless of trends in temporal manifestation -the very axis or axle of Time's ever-turning spiral Wheel, the pause between the breaths.

In Jewish esotericism the secret letter turns YHVH (Yehovah) into YHShVH (Yeheshua or Jesus), father becoming son. But as Nema pointed out to me, if you rearrange the letters (and as time is cyclical the 'beginning' of the Word is as apt as the 'end' or anywhere between) you get ShYHVH - which phonetically sounds like Shiva.

So few people know how to simply breathe properly -fully and deeply with spine erect and using the abdomen- despite it being such a basic fundament of health, happiness and life itself.

The simplest yet one of the most effective methods of meditation is just full awareness of our breath, focusing on only that. Regular practise will spill into the rest of our lives as breath-consciousness - and thus true time-consciousness- effects our very state of being. When we feel stressed or overworked, the tendency is to breathe quickly and shallowly. The last thing we think we have time for is to meditate, do yoga or even just breathe consciously- deeply and fully. Yet if we can bring ourselves to do so even- or especially- in these cruxes, we find ourselves more functional.

Time itself shifts and stretches with our breath, and we find ourselves focused again, our perspective altered and panic alleviated. So really when we feel stressed or pressured by deadlines or appointments we don't have time not to meditate, or at least to breathe with awareness.

When one rests, it is vital to do so deeply and thoroughly, especially in the modern world's busy and high-tensile society.

Giselle Sybil and I practised intensive *Embalming* mummification rituals (www.crossroads.wild.net.au/embalm.htm) for a year or so - presented as 4-hour restorative treatments for body and soul, with harmonic chanting, purgative sauna, psychic surgery (astral organ removal and cleansing), sonic balms, temple-style massage, salt exfoliation, dead sea mud and traditional embalming oils. By the time the recipient was wrapped up in linen bandages, they had been so thoroughly purged and relieved of any tensions or anxieties (the lightening of the heart, so as to come into balance with the feather of Maat) that they were able (in almost every case) to fully rest and totally surrender to the womb-like void space of that containment in peace - something that in modern life is rare indeed. An interesting phenomenon I observed with these treatments is that regardless of the patient's energy, persona, body shape, etc. (and there was great diversity), when they eventually emerged from the wrappings they all look and feel essentially the same - like a newborn.

This cocoon-like enwrapment also of course has its arachnean aspect, but the death it allows is one of restoration rather than mere preservation. I believe the Ancient Egyptians- with their mystic emphasis on rejuvenation- performed some of their 'funerary rite' procedures on the living as well as the dead. Whether this was the case or not, they are definitely effective used in this way from our experiences and those of our clients.

Continuing the relationship between spiders and fate, we are reminded that only those rare few who struggle with the enwrapping ever find it difficult. To surrender utterly only serves to remind us within a ritualistic microcosm that, *'What is death but a great mutation to our next selves?' (-AOSpare)*. We are transformed and resurrected, emerging restored and rejuvenated from the cocoon which is in this context really more akin to a caterpillar's pupa of transformationthan a containment for the preservation of prey.

In further development of the embalming process, we had initiates contemplate a Word of Power when performing the *Opening of the Mouth* ceremony at the beginning. This may continue whilst they are enwrapped. Thus when at rite's end this Word is pronounced upon emergence, it allows them to consciously empower their destiny as True Will. Throughout the ritual process they have lightened their heart of mental, physical, emotional and spiritual burdens to pass Maat's Judgement, weighing their hearts against Her feather of Truth, to visit *Amenta* (the Ancient Egyptian afterworld) freely, so that they may return with affirmation of new life and conscious choice.

One may wonder why someone such as myself who is so in love with Kali as the state of being beyond Time would ever put myself in situations of high pressure with goals and ambitions. Yet I am periodically trying to juggle several intense projects (e.g. performances that are also life-size statue and book launches!) and their specific deadlines. Well it is precisely *because* I love the void.

It is nigh impossible to operate in the World of Form without being constricted somewhat by Time anyway; so being a productive artist-magician as much as a mystic, I embrace rather than try to avoid it, and relish the joy and even the birthing-pains of manifestation.

For MahaKala is Time itself, and it is He with His flux and flow who is the lover of Maha Kali.

She is the great Void and He the multiplicity of forms that rush to fill it. Beyond time through time.

When one embraces time and space, making the most of their wyrd and wondrous play of form, then one can also fully release it. After bouts of creative activity the ecstasy of deep rest, of the void and of no-time is incomparable.

And after full immersion in the void, the form that again rises forth from Her womb is once again a thing of newness and beauty. Thus is MahaKala also the God of Eternity.

When Kumbukka Pranayama (described at the openening of this

Gate) is combined with Khechari mudra (pushing the tongue into the back of the throat) and also deliberate contractions of the perineum muscle (between the anus and the genitals) on the inhalations and pauses, even greater effect can be attained. The pauses between the breaths -which are effectively pauses in time, s p a c e s   i n b e t w e e n - can be gradually and progressively increased (deliberate perineum contractions can be counted to keep track of this), for the gnosis attained effectively prolongs our vitality and ultimately our very existence as an incarnate being; and if khechari mudra is used in combination this can be gradually intensified also by pushing the tongue further back each time you practise (regular practice of the BesKali Mudra-Mantra is effective for stretching the tongue's capacity). Eventually a state similar to suspended animation may be attained by Yogis pushing such practises to their extremes (sometimes including the cutting of the frenum lignum muscle under the tongue, although this can be worn away more gradually by consistent practise of the Bes-Kali AHA Mudra-Mantra).

Its more immediate benefits are purification, prana circulation (particularly necessary if also practising non-ejaculatory orgasms) and more fluidic perceptions of time.

Time is Breath. ...AHA... niotalAHni and exHAlation form the warp and the weft of Maya's loom, the great Tapestry of TimemiT through which TiamaiT coils;

The ebb and flow of breath, eternal cycles of Birth and Death, Inspiration and Expiration, Contraction and Expansion, Order and Chaos...

And of the mysterious Spa c e s I n -Be tw e e n -the pauses twixt the breaths- little can be said or seen, they being only perceptible by the wondrous strands of manifest form which frame their chasms...

APPENDIX A:

BES- KALI AHA MANTRA-MUDRA-ASANA

This is a combined mantra (incantation) and mudra-asana (ritual gesture or posture) for invoking or resonating with the energies of Bes, Kali and/or other such primordial deities (e.g. Pan, Shiva-An, Atum); it also stretches and strengthens the tongue for *Khechari*, a Tantric yogic exercise for energy circulation of which the fundaments are included in this exercise. It is useful in ritual (as discussed through **THE THIRD GATE**) or simply as a daily yoga asana.

Bes is the Ancient Egyptian dwarf-God of dance and childbirth who is often used to represent the pre-civilisational Shamanic or Primordial Aeon. **Kali** is the Hindu primal Mother Goddess from which all things sprang. and the Destroyer to Whom they must reTurn.

Both of these ancient deities are usually depicted in ancient artworks with their tongues out, Bes' position being especially rare in Egyptian iconography as He is always shown facing directly forwards, rather than the usual iconic sideways/profile depictions in their art.

MahaKala emerges from the womb of **Maha Kali** in a 𝔐etamorphic 𝔑itual 𝔗heatre performance.

The Asana/Posture:

Stand with left foot facing outwards to the left and right foot facing out right, bend the knees into right angles (or as close as possible -it can be a strenuous posture at first, but with regular practise one can adapt fairly quickly. Echo the right angles of the legs with the arms, also facing outwards to each side in L shapes (as in picture above -the *upper* arms!) . This is the traditional Thelemic & Maatian posture for Bes and is used in *Nema's 6- fold Casting/ Banishing* (which the following can be incorporated into) from her book *'Maat Magick' (Samuel Weiser)* .

Now add

The Mantra and accompanying mouth-Mudra:

After a few preparatory deeep breaths, Pull the tongue as far back in the throat as possible while inhaling deeply. Accompany this with an 'Aaaaahhh' sound, more breathed than spoken.

When this can be taken no further, hold the breath for a while, then expel the breath with a 'Haaa!' sound while sticking out the tongue. Towards the end of this exhalation the tongue is to be pushed out as far as possible, stretching the muscles to their full extent (if it hurts a little you're doing it properly!).

Repeat this process at least three times. Your energy should be in-drawing and contractive on the inhalation, and radiant and expansive on the exhalation. It can be further potentiated by tightening then releasing the perineum muscle and/or the anal sphincter (a yogic lock called Mulabhanda) which helps to move the energy inwards and upwards, then outwards on release.

The *frenulum linguae*, the web-like muscle at the bottom of the tongue will rub against the bottom front teeth.

If this exercise is done regularly (I suggest at least one session of three repetitions each day) this tendon will gradually wear away, allowing greater flexibility of the tongue.

Thus *Khechari*, the traditional ancient Yoga of holding the tongue in the back of the throat, can be performed more effectively, as the tongue can be pushed far enough back to stimulate the pituitary gland (which is also a trigger point to activate the hypothalamus and possibly even the pineal gland via the Pons or bridge between conscious cerebrum and sub-conscious cerebellum).

The tongue can be progressively stretched (or the ligament under it even progressively cut away with regular small snips- I use nail-clippers) so that the 'hymen' of soft tissue at the back of the roof of the mouth is eventually penetrated and the tongue-tipextends up into the back of the nasal passages, stimulating the sensitive soft tissue there.

Bliss results from the increased hormonal secretions (via the pituitary gland) from this practise. This is an upper chakra 'self-mating' exercise which can ultimately produce the *Amrita* or nectar of immortality. Kechari is a powerful mudra and in India it is usually recommended only to be fully explored with the guidance of a guru.

In the simpler earlier stages with the tongue just sitting in the back of the throat or even on the roof of the mouth (still effective), combined with conscious deep breathing, the Taoist Microcosmic Orbit is formed to help circulate Prana/energy throughout the body during pranayamas, meditation or sexual activity.
The AHA mudra-mantra can be also be performed with just the tongue and breath, without the full body posture/asana.

The Mantra **'AHA'** is a Word of the primal/shamanic aeon or Dreamtime, and the double-wanded form of the Pan-ic mantra **'Ha!'** (see *The Book of the Horned One* by *Aion 131*, Concrescent Press 2012) and thus puts one in touch with primal sexual/creative essence.

AHA is a word commonly used for both Concealing (the whispered and secretive 'aha...') and for Revealing (the ecstatic realization, 'AHA!'), in reflection of its indrawing and outgoing qualities in relation to the breath. There are also various powerful aspects In Gematria (letter-number-meaning relationships) to this mantra which are too lengthy and involved to discuss here, but its essential power is that of inhalation and exhalation, contraction and expansion.

I only recently discovered the supreme significance of this mantra in relation to the ancient *Sanskrit* language of India:

Ah and **Ha** are the phonetic (vocal) expressions of the *first and last* letters of the Sanskrit alphabet, their equivalents of English letters A and H -thus AHA represents the entire cycle of TimEmiT, as encapsulated in the microcosm of the breath. It is the Sanskrit portion of the Alchemical **AZOTH** formula, representing the Alpha and Omega (Greek), the Aleph and the Tau (Hebrew), The Beginning and the End.

Additionally, as revealed in a commentary on the *29th Book* of the *Tantraloka*:

Ah is the sound of *Shiva* and Ha that of *Shakti*, so the ultimate union of Energy and Consciousness is expressed. This is the rise of the Kundalini Shakti to the Crown (Shiva) within the individual (represented by **ArdHanAsrishvara** the Hindu hermaphrodite God/dess), an ascent which can indeed be facilitated by advanced *Khechari Yoga* (Yoga = Union).

APPENDIX B
Arachne Ascendant

It seemed as if Arachne had been taught by Athena, the goddess of culture and the arts and inventor of the loom; but she denied this, offended at the suggestion that she had any teacher, no matter how distinguished.

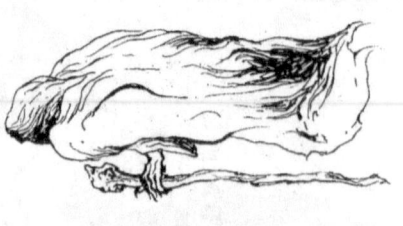

ATHENA (as old woman): "Not all the things that old age brings are to be shunned with advancing years, we gain experience. Pay heed, then, to my advice — seek recognition as the best of all mortal spinners, but admit the supremacy of the goddess, and humbly ask her pardon for your hot-headed words. She will forgive you, if you ask her..."

ARACHNE: "Fuck off you old hag! You are too old, that is your problem, and your mind is obviously feeble. You need not tell me what to do. — Am quite capable of looking after myself!... Besides, if Athena thinks she's so great, why has she avoided my challenge? Why does she not come to me in person?"

ATHENA (revealing her true self): "She has come!"

ARACHNE, though shocked, persisted with her plan and, in her eagerness for a victory she foolishly thought she could win, rushed upon her fate. Zeus's daughter uttered no more warnings; she accepted the challenge and postponed the competition no further. Arachne and Athena stretched the slender threads upon their looms and began in earnest...

In their eagerness, they were not conscious of the labour involved...

ARACHNE: "Let Athena come and compete with me then!"

ATHENA made herself up as an old woman and came to Arachne...

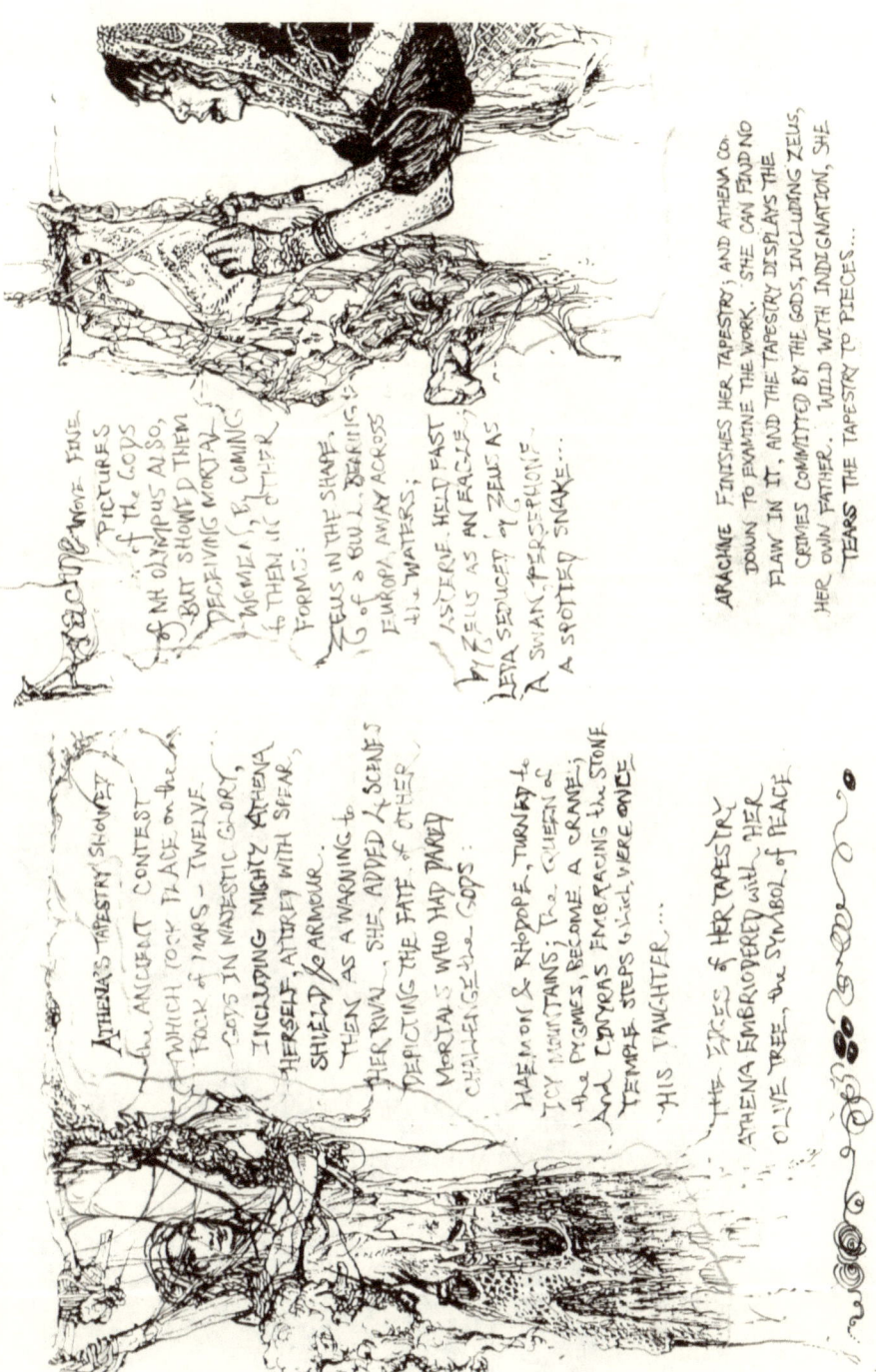

ARACHNE wove five pictures of the Gods of Mt Olympus also, but showed them deceiving mortal women, by coming to them in other forms:

Zeus in the shape of a bull, bearing Europa away across the waters;

Asterie held fast by Zeus as an eagle; Leda seduced by Zeus as a swan; Persephone a spotted snake....

ATHENA'S TAPESTRY showed an ancient contest which took place on the rock of Mars — twelve Gods in majestic glory, including mighty Athena herself, attired with spear, shield & armour.

Then, as a warning to her rival, she added 4 scenes depicting the fate of other mortals who had dared challenge the Gods:

Haemor & Rhodope, turned to icy mountains; the Queen of the Pygmies, become a crane; and Cinyras embracing the stone temple steps which were once his daughter....

The edges of her tapestry Athena embroidered with her olive tree, the symbol of peace

ARACHNE FINISHES HER TAPESTRY; AND ATHENA COMES DOWN TO EXAMINE THE WORK. SHE CAN FIND NO FLAW IN IT. AND THE TAPESTRY DISPLAYS THE CRIMES COMMITTED BY THE GODS, INCLUDING ZEUS, HER OWN FATHER. WILD WITH INDIGNATION, SHE TEARS THE TAPESTRY TO PIECES....

TimE, Fate and Spider Magic

Tattoo Narrative:

Arachne was punished for her aspirations of divinity; instead of being turned into an animal — a spider... but at the same time she is granted immortality as an artist — to weave forever, on some level Athena had to acknowledge her skill.

And such were the wonder of the intricate tapestries that she spun across the trees & the rafters, that humans, peering closely at her catching the dew in her crystalline structures, recognized her great art. And, being the creators of their creators, granted her divinity after all. She was elevated to the stars, becoming to many ancient cultures the cosmic weaver of fate.

The American Indians perceived the spider as the great weaver of the web of stars, whose threads connected heaven and earth. They saw the earth as their mother, and the sky as their father. Was not Arachne, then, the anima of father sky, the female within the male?

In European matriarchal societies the calendar was based on the cycles of the moon (not the sun); so there were thirteen months in a year (not twelve).

Arachne was the thirteenth sign of the zodiac, the weaver at the centre of the web of stars....

ATHENA [shouting]: "Daring to compare your craft to mine! You aspire to be divine? You shall be punished for your crime! You shall metamorphose down! Not up evolution's line! You shall not become a goddess, but an animal —
...A mere ARACHNID!"

[casts spell of transformation with Hecate's herb (cell-bane)]

[aside]: "How dare she imply the gods deceive her? To Arachne]: "But as you are such an adept weaver...
may your looms be the trees and the rafters,
and may you spin your wondrous webs forever after!"

APPENDIX C

LIBER QOPH vel HEKATE

Sub Figura C

Hail Luna, as you rise, X'Yum IxChel, Kia,
Om Chandra Namah
Queen of dreams, Cast your spell,
Of triple veil
Selene Selene Selene

Ar-iadne, Ar-ianhrod, Ar-achne Moirae,
Ar-iadne, Ar-ianhrod, Ar-achne Moirae,
Ar-iadne, Ar-ianhrod, Ar-achne Moirae,
Morrigan(-a), Nornir, Parseae,
Hail Hekate

Of faces three,
Shining from afar,
Spider of Destiny
In your web of Silver Stars

TimE, Fate and Spider Magic

WAXING MOON:

Hail Diana, Huntress,
As you draw your silver bow,
Hail Artemis and Io,
Oh Horned waxing luminous present glow
Nu and numinous maiden crescent shewn

Hail Clotho, Spinner of life's thread
Drawn forth from Nix Night
Turning Fate's first strands
With nimble hands
Twining twixt the dark and bright

Ar-iadne, Ar-ianhrod, Ar-achne Moirae,
Ar-iadne, Ar-ianhrod, Ar-achne Moirae,
Ar-iadne, Ar-ianhrod, Ar-achne Moirae,
Morrigan(-a), Nornir, Parseae,
Hail Hekate

FULL MOON:

Hail MoonMother,
Full and fecund, round and bright,
Isis, We draw you down from the night,
With your cauldron-womb of luminous white

Hail Lachesis, Weaver, Craft your web
Weave the lines between the times
Of Wax and Wane; And tides
Of flow and ebb

Gossamer silver cords
Of dreaming draw together
In your matrix matted of matter and ether
DreamMother, give Birth
As your light shines down to Earth

Ar-iadne, Ar-ianhrod, Ar-achne Moirae,
Ar-iadne, Ar-ianhrod, Ar-achne Moirae,
Ar-iadne, Ar-ianhrod, Ar-achne Moirae,
Morrigan(-a), Nornir, Parseae,
Hail Hekate

WANING MOON:

Hail, Grandmother Spider,
Crone and crow,
Wisewoman, elder, seer,
Help us face, and embrace
Our fears
Hail Hekate of the Crossroads,
Oh old and ominous presence glowing
Your waning numinous crescent going

Hail Atropos, Cutter,
With your waning silver scythe,
You Cut
...the thread of Life.

Ar-iadne, Ar-ianhrod, Ar-achne Moirae,
Ar-iadne, Ar-ianhrod, Ar-achne Moirae,
Ar-iadne, Ar-ianhrod, Ar-achne Moirae,
Morrigan(-a), Nornir, Parseae,
Hail Hekate

DARK MOON:

There is a fourth face, though unseen
There is a fourth path, whom few know
A fourth Fate, who awaits
In shadow

Hail Kali, Blackness,
From whom the kalas of Time emiT
Three Norns converged,
Past, present, future merged,
On the path of Blood beyond the Wheel we surge and scry
To Caer Arianhrod, Castle in the Sky

Hail Nought, Not, Nuit, Maat,
Yours the dark and secret art
While crone's scythe cuts breath and with death
The thread of life appears to dwindle
From No-thing you craft another mask
And re-splice it back, on another track
To Clotho's spindle

Ar-iadne, Ar-ianhrod, Ar-achne Moirae,
Ar-iadne, Ar-ianhrod, Ar-achne Moirae,
Ar-iadne, Ar-ianhrod, Ar-achne Moirae,
Morrigan(-a), Nornir, Parseae,

Hail Hekate

LIBER QOPH VEL HEKATE COMMENTARY:

This verse is a daily Lunar prayer, adoration or salutation which complements and counterbalances Aleister Crowley's Solar adoration **'Liber Resh vel Helios'** (http://mysteria.com/liber/L_200.txt).

Unlike Liber Resh, it is concerned with moonthly cycles rather than daily ones, and is thus to be performed but once nightly (Liber Resh is for dawn, noon, dusk and midnight), preferably on or near the rising of the moon. The first verse is for every night, the others are to be alternated according to the phase of the Moon. Thus use of this liber helps attune one to the natural cycles of the moon's course.

Unlike Liber Resh which aside from its Hebrew-Greek title deals solely with Egyptian deities, Liber Qoph draws from a variety of mythological and cultural pantheons to represent different aspects of the lunar goddess -*Greek, Egyptian, Mayan, Incan, Hindu, Celtic, Norse*. Primarily it is a prayer to the Greek three Fates, the Moirae (Norse Norns) -spinner, weaver, cutter- introducing also the fourth unseen face of this traditionally triple Goddess, and Her function as a hidden fourth Fate. In the Sabbatical tradition there is a secret fourth 'dark road' from the 3-way crossroads Hekate traditionally inhabits. (Many thanks to Alexander Blok and Alobar Greywalker for the initial inspiration to include this Fourth phase).

The purpose of this work is balancing the solar energies of Liber Resh vel Helios with lunar energies, as complementary metaphors for the conscious and subconscious mind.

Thus the title: Resh is the Hebrew letter which corresponds with the Sun astrologically and the Sun tarot card and is symbolised by the front of the head. Qoph is the Hebrew letter which corresponds with the Moon astrologically and the lunar High Priestess tarot card and is symbolised by the *back of the head*.

Similarly in ancient Hindu texts the *Ajna* ('third eye') chakra is considered solar and the *Bindu* chakra on the back of the head is considered lunar, even as physiologically (yes, science!) the *Cerebrum* or conscious 'rational' mind is in the front of the head and the *Cerebellum* concerned with subconscious dreams and visions is located in the back of the head. The subconscious reflects the conscious mind in much the same way as the moon reflects the light of the sun -thus in the human head the alchemical metaphor of the Hieros Gamos or 'sacred marriage' of sun and moon is physiologically embodied.

These solar and lunar energies can be united in the pineal gland in the very centre (from every direction: front-back, left-right, up-down) of the head, the gland which is actually physiologically responsible for our natural sense of time by tracking the light of the sun and the moon.

By traditional Hebrew Gematria, the letter Resh =200 and the letter Qoph =100, which is also a number associated with the lunar Goddess Hekate as in Ancient Greek the prefix 'Hecat' usually refers to a hundred (e.g. the Hecatochirons or hundred-handed giants)

200 + 100 = 300, the value of Shin, the Hebrew letter of fire and spirit. Thus the raising of the kundalini fire to the head and union of the ida and pingala solar and lunar energies in the centre of the brain, the pineal gland (the physiological 'third eye') causes the energy to fountain up through the Sahasrara crown chakra into Union with the All.

This liber, intended to be read aloud daily, helps bring subconscious strata to conscious attention and attunes us to the cycles and rhythms of the moon's phases. Combined with daily practise of Liber Resh it can aid this union of the solar and lunar energies within the centre of the brain.

It is particularly pertinent in our modern world where electric light interferes with the natural functions of the pineal gland.

It is recommended that whenever possible the work be read outdoors, under the light of the moon.

However unlike Liber Resh for which the sun should be faced directly, *Liber Qoph vel Hekate* should be read with the moon behind you, so as to absorb its subtle energies in through the Bindu Chakra on the Qoph or back of the head.

Hail Hekate!

-*Orryelle Defenestrate-Bascule*
Full lunar eclipse, July 2000.

ADDENDUM:

Moonths after the writing of this Liber regular practise of the adorations began to effect my dreaming (subconscious). I awoke one full moon from a lunar dreamscape with the realisation that there are four lunar '*Ar*'s worshipped in the work:

*A*Riadne, *A*Rianhrod, *A*Rachne, *A*Rtemis - even as there are four forms of the solar *RA* adored daily in Liber Resh vel Helios. Presumably practise of the two complementary works brought this subconscious strata to my conscious attention, even as the light of the moon *Ar* reflects (even linguistically) the light of the Sun *Ra*.

APPENDIX D

THE 13TH-TRIBE WEAVING

The Global ANAHATA (Heart) Chakra Working
Glastonbury Tor UK, June 21st Summer Solstice 2003

Cultural representatives of the 12 Tribes or source-races of humanity, woven together by Heart Chakra piercings in a web of Unity in Diversity.

Photographs in this appendix copyright ©2003 Geothro

There are extensive illustrated accounts of The **Global Chakra Working**s online, indexed from the overarching vision at www.crossroads.wild.net.au/vision.htm

I have chosen to include this one here as it was probably the most intense and pivotal of our 7 group rituals at different sacred sites around the world which correspond energetically with human chakras.

Additionally both the symbolism employed, the web of synchronicity surrounding the working and the nature of the rite itself as a physical weaving, are all pertinent to *Spider Magic* and the concepts and currents within the body of this tome.

The weaving of the 13-point star-diamond of Ma-nifestat-ion was a symbolic demonstration that we are all one people, despite the blessing of cultural and spiritual differences -individual in our minds and beliefs, united in (by) our hearts.

In the Hindu traditions the right-hand path of asceticism employs Mandalas and Yantras (geometric diagrams) as a means to gnosis, while the Vama Marg or tantric 'left-hand path' -which is of a more feminine nature- uses the human body (sometimes including sexuality) as a means to gnosis.

(The terms right-hand and left-hand paths do not have the moral connotations of the West in the Hindu traditions -the terms are not about good or evil, merely different Ways to the same Source). So by creating a Mandala or Yantra between physical Bodies (via Chakra Piercings) we brought together the left and right hand paths. These were just one pair of the many apparent dualities we United in this multi-layered Weaving of the Middle Way...

PART I:
Gathering and Preparations for The 13th-Tribe Weaving:

The wyrd path of signs, synchronicitys and omens leading into the 13th-Tribe Weaving itself was as amazing as the working. How likely is it that a traveling Australian would be able to find representatives of all the source cultures of humanity, willing to be ritually woven together in England? And most of these representatives were located/revealed in the fortnight just before the actual working! - Recorded here, from my journals at the time, is the strange flow of synchronicity in the process which confirmed that this ritual was, 'Meant to Be':

The first week in Glastonbury was difficult. My mission seemed nigh impossible: to find the rest of the tribal representatives -only seven were confirmed!- of the twelve source races of humanity, to be woven together by piercings in the chest (one of the less important methods of Anahata chakra activation in the rite but the one which I expected to meet most resistance) in the 13th-Tribe Weaving. I was only a few moonths into my travels in a foreign country (as an Australian in the UK) and had only two weeks left for my task.

Every day I was spending many hours (before the days of wifi everywhere) in overpriced email cafes sending out messages to various groups, online notice-boards and individuals attempting to find the last few cultural representatives needed for the 13th-Tribe Weaving.

As the solstice drew closer I became quite concerned that the 13th Tribe Weaving wasn't going to come together in time, although there were several people flying in within a week from far places to participate. I felt like I should have engaged more thoroughly in the process of finding the right people earlier, it was such a major and important working imminent.

However it became obvious later that the gathering could only really be done at the last minute like this, as the very first candidates

I found -last year- actually pulled out due to big changes in their lives.

I began to understand why I had felt to invoke the Messenger-God Hermes in London recently -

attaching small wings to my ears as I had done when first calling this deity years ago on my first fly agaric trip- for I was caught in a web of intensifying Communications needed to bring the vision of the physical 13-pointed web into Ma-nifestat-ion.

Ultimately most of the contact work had to be done in person - after all how many people would respond to emails from some weirdo wanting to pierce their chest and weave them into a geometric web with 11 other cultural representatives, without at least some idea of the magical currents and symbols involved?

I was thankful that there were some Silver Dusk astral in-it-I-ates and Horus-Maat Lodge members I had been corresponding with for some time who were into the idea enough to come from afar, but began to worry that they would be wasting their time and money if I couldn't find the last few initiates...

And all this while coming off a recent temporary marijuana habit, beginning the gradual process of cleansing (caffeine was next!) towards the working.

During this period I kept finding tiny spiders on myself. The first one that swung down from my head in front of my eyes was brushed away instinctively -crushed accidentally before I realised what it was. The second time -later the same day- I began the same reactive motion then realised and stopped, carefully removing it by silken strand instead. I took this as an indication of the care and delicacy that would be necessary to execute the heart-chakra weaving and its preparations.

At least one spider a day continued to alight upon my person! I was very glad to have synchronistically met Mark and Daphne of the *Planetary Art Network (PAN)* in London and taken a lift up to Glastonbury with them.

Sharing the vision of the 13-star through their work with the 13-moon calendar of the Mayans, they were very encouraging and Mark introduced me to many people in the Glastonbury community -and some people further out such as Simon who ended up participating- who aided and supported the process greatly.

I kept being told by cosmic locals (and there is no shortage of them in Glastonbury town) that it would come together, somehow, if it was meant to be, and I found this alternately reassuring and frustrating according to my mood! I knew there was still a lot of practical work to be done to make it happen, but there were many wondrous synchronicitys and omens along the way which gave me hope whenever I was beginning to wonder...

Primary amongst these was meeting David. He immediately resonated with my vision (in fact it brought tears to his eyes) and offered his land 20 minutes or so out of town as a place for us all (when the others begin to arrive) to camp while preparing for the rite. His property is at 'Wagg' on the tip of the tail of the Dog, 13th land formation in the geomantic Glastonbury Zodiac which reflects the constellations above, and thus a very apt place for the 13th Tribe to gather...

Well he took me out there for a preview and I was blown away! What a beautiful place...

Lush gardens and fields (where we could camp) around a gorgeous round-house thatch-roofed stone temple. When he showed me its interior I understood his resonance with our vision -it seemed almost made for this work:

The round house has as its ceiling wooden beams forming a hexagram/six-pointed star (or 'Star of David' in this case I guess!) - which is the symbol (in the Hindu system) of both the Anahata (heart) Chakra our working was focused upon, and also the primary corresponding sephira Tiphereth on the Hebrew Tree of Life.

There are 13 pillars forming the round framework of the temple, and each bears a small painting of one of the formations of the Glastonbury Zodiac in the Somerset landscape, inc. the 13th: -the Dog -which I now discovered used to be the Unicorn before major earthworks (to disguise it?)- the area where the temple itself is located in Wagg. I related the (black) dog also to Hekate as a lunar congruent of Arachne, the spider-Goddess I was more familiar with as the 13th sign of the Zodiac, and to Sirius (the 'Dog Star').

The altars in the temple were resplendent with artefacts and talismans from all over the World, including a porcelain face of AkhNaten and a large white ostrich feather (symbol of our patroness Maat of ancient Egypt, though David was then unconscious of this).

There were other little synchronous details I noticed later: the calendar on the wall with various mandalas from different cultures, and the one for the current month of June (inc. our solstice working) was the Anahata Chakra mandala.

So I returned to Glastonbury town recharged and full of fresh hope, though days later with potential tribal representatives pulling out (by email) even as I found others, I began to despair.

I was doing extensive daily yoga, breathing exercises and meditation and managed to (mostly) stay relaxed, but did start considering contingency plans if the weaving as planned didn't come together...

Ultimately I had to just go with the flow and TRUST that the rite would come together somehow if (and how) it was meant to. This was a major part of my own personal transition from the WILL of the Manipura (solar plexus) chakra to the LOVE, feeling and intuition of the Anahata (heart) chakra. Ultimately it was about balance between these energies, as I knew that I still had to project my Will somewhat to make it happen, but also trust in the flow and allow the changes as they came...

Thus I gained a new understanding of the Thelemic axiom, *'Love under Will'*...

On the full moon (Friday the 13th) just one week before the Summer Solstice, the energies began to pick up. I chilled out and played some violin at a small fireside gathering at the bottom of Glastonbury Tor.

The following evening I had promised (in emails) to be on the Tor from 6pm onwards to meet those arriving for the working and its' preparations. In the meantime there was a week-early (nearest full moon) Druidic Solstice ceremony on the Tor that afternoon, which I attended: about 200 robed eco-priests from O.B.O.D, *the Order of Bards, Ovates and Druids* whose abbreviated title has a strange resonance with my own initials (Ob and Od being also primal serpents of both Jewish and Vodoun pantheons).

Just after they closed their celebratory circle I stepped in before dispersal and announced our own imminent solstice rite, inviting their attendance and if anyone was interested in further participation come and speak to me about it. Well only two did (Druids generally being into only their own tradition) but one of them -Kieron- ended up being the Celtic-Germanic tribal representative in the weaving.

When a few days earlier previous candidate Puck had expressed by email that he couldn't participate after all, I was not particularly worried about that one as in terms of blood-links at least it was the easiest representative to find in Celtic lands. But it was good that we ended up with someone well versed in traditional Celtic lore who had a lot to offer towards the rite's design and execution, and also actually lived in Glastonbury.

Not many of those expected that night turned up until a few days later, but we had a first small circle on the magical Tor with a magnificent sunset as a backdrop. Starshadow -an email contact from the global Horus Maat Lodge had driven up from Milton Keynes and chanted the chakra tones with Jasmine, Natasha, Adam, and myself. He returned home to show the tones to the rest of his coven (six members) so they would all know them when returning on Solstice day to give their voices and support to the working.

This night was also my first flesh-meeting with Silver Dusk astral initiate Adam Trimurti, and we resonated well in person. Funnily enough, he and Natasha -the Cutter of threads for the rite, whom I had met in a fetish club in London the year before- had both flown in from Montreal Canada that day, yet didn't meet until they both arrived at Glastonbury Tor. Listening to them chatting together in French gave me a good feeling about the multicultural threads of the weaving beginning to draw together.

A good start, but I still felt a bit aghast at how it could all still coagulate in the mere week remaining...

The next day I walked into the Glastonbury town backpackers pub to use their email machine there to contact Marios (amongst others expected to arrive soon), wondering where he was. Well, he was there on the backpackers email machine, emailing me that he had arrived!

Marios had told me earlier in Edinburgh that he felt the weaving had its own momentum, and the right people would appear. At times I wondered about this, but ultimately it did seem to be the case...

A major turning point was meeting Bayard. Of all the cultural representatives I needed to find, the one that had me most stumped was the one for the Kalahari Bushmen/ Pygmy tribes. As a separate type of people from the other African tribes, they needed to be represented by an individual with cultural resonance (if not direct blood-links) with these specific peoples.

How on earth was I to find such a person? I had emailed several people who had been involved with various groups aiding the survival of the bushmen what with current gold-mining on their lands, to no avail, and though one person who had spent many months living with the bushmen was suggested to me by several different (and unconnected sources) it turned out she was currently in Mexico.

Then one wyrd day I had a sudden feeling to talk to a negro man I had seen around Glastonbury town a few times, whom I had felt a good vibe from. I approached him outside the magical red and white sacred springs, discovering he had indeed grown up in Africa, and after a brief expression of our intent for Solstice inquired if he knew anything about the Kalahari bushmen. He shook his head but before disappointment set in I said with little expectation, 'What about the Pygmies?'

'Yes!' he said, 'My tribe lives next to their tribe. We speak each other's languages, know each other's cultures very well...'

On my further excited explanation of our ritual, he agreed to participate with an 'Okay, why not?' and said he could come out to the first real gathering that night at David's 13-pillared temple and gardens.

He had been hanging out with 'Baba', a dreadlocked traveller from Kathmandu who had agreed to represent the Siberian/Mongolian peoples in the weaving (Baba however did not turn up that night and remained evasive to the last...)

Meeting Bayard was one in a rapid-fire sequence of Magical synchronicitys that day. Another was meeting an American astral initiate of the Silver Dusk who had been hoping to attend the weaving as she would be in Europe (Belgium) for an operation as part of her (formerly his) ongoing gender transition. However doctors had told her that this would not be possible as they needed to keep close tabs on her for a few days after the operation which was just before Solstice.

So instead she unexpectedly came to Glastonbury before the Solstice, just for a day, and we didn't have time to arrange any contact point.

However we still met by 'chance' just as she was leaving to catch her bus back out of town! Not only that, but - funny considering my own trip with hermaphroditism also- we met on the road between the two holy wells of Glastonbury, the female (iron-rich) red waters and the male (zinc-rich) white waters. She did not know of these so I told her as she was about to rush off to catch her bus, and she drank from and washed her face in each, then hurried off towards her operation! ...

The first gathering at David's was wonderful. His partner Susan cooked a delicious meal for everyone then we gathered around the bonfire, those who did not already know each other beginning to. There was a good feeling that we had all come together from afar to do this special thing together. We had a short but powerful initial chakra-tone chanting session in the Roundhouse. Bayard had to go to London next day but promised to return for the Solstice rite.

The next four days were mostly blissful, though challenging at times. Each morning we would all do yoga together, each sharing our favourite exercises and asanas (from Hindu, Tibetan, Egyptian and personal sources and systems) with the group and stretching and bending in new ways and directions.

Various mantras were also shared.

Evenings were long chanting and meditation sessions (breaking the tones colours and other qualities down into individual chakra work then rebuilding the octave/spectrum) in the intensifying atmosphere of the candle-lit roundhouse. The energy and the affinity between us grew progressively. We went from eating fruit and nuts to just fruit juices and water then back to nuts and grains. Of course this and all the sitting still brought up various aches and pains and problems for people, but in the sharing and open environment we had co-created all flowed out and on quite smoothly...

That seven of us formed the foundations of the rite is significant in that seven and thirteen are the sacred or mystic numbers of the Mayans, the Jews and several other ancient cultures, and have a strange interconnected resonance with each other. There was a simple clay sculpture in the roundhouse of seven people around in a circle arm in arm.

More joined us for the last few days, and the energy stepped up yet another level. It was coming together, the absence of several of the tribal representatives still was mostly ignored as generally the work seemed to be flowing onwards...

Towards the end of our stay at David's, Kieron and Adam were initiated (veiled back-to-back) into the Horus-Maat Lodge by Evan (from Australia) Marios (from Scotland) and I.

I was amazed by the spiritual, magical and religious as well as cultural and sub-cultural diversity of the people who were assembling: we had everything from post-Chaos-Magic Mayan daykeepers to Thelemic Maat-ians, Luciferian Witches, a Houngan (Vodoun priest), and our host on the land was a mystic Christian. And we were all co-habiting and co-operating with respect and peace. True Unity in Diversity, of beliefs and traditions as well as races and colours...

A few days away from the distractions of town and I began to feel very high from the fasting, daily yoga, chanting and breathing exercises, and the general feeling of sharing, truth and trust.

Our representative of the Mayan, Incan and other southern/central-American peoples –Simon, who lives half his time in Mexico- turned up with an interesting story: only hours after I had rang him (on Mark's recommendation) about the Weaving he had found a huge snake (much bigger than he'd ever known to exist in his semi-suburban area) trapped in a net in a neighbour's garden. He had disentangled the man-length venomous serpent and carried it (very carefully with hand clasped behind jaw) back out to the forest. The 'Serpent-Handler' constellation lies opposite that of Arachne in the heavens, and is considered by Astronomers to be the 13th sign of the zodiac.

The snake was certainly a potent symbol for the energies we were dealing with, both on an individual level as we began to stir our kundalini serpents with voice vibration and visualisation, and also the serpent/dragon energies of the Earth, the Gaian Kundalini we are resonating with in these global chakra workings. These two layers of serpent fire were also the current concern of the Mayan calendar Kin group who met up with us on our second-last night at David's sanctuary.

They had no venue that moon (they met every thirteen days), so because of the resonance of their own work with ours, the circles were overlapped, with us all chanting the chakra tones together after some general discussion of synchronicity, personal sharing and presentation of ritual intent. A few misunderstandings arose, one Kin person in particular unsure of our methods and/or motives and challenging aspects of our proposals. This was ultimately effective in getting any doubts out for contemplation and consolidating our purpose, will and love.

After the Kin group left (most expressing their support and appreciation, and several ended up participating in the solstice rite as elemental-sacrament bearers) we continued our work for a while beginning to nut out a basic framework for the over-all ritual by collating and arranging the ideas and possibilities that had come up so far from our workshops and discussions.

As those who were too tired to maintain focus drifted off one by one, there ended up being just four of us left by the dwindling fire, still discussing the opening circle-casting. Once we realised this -that there were four of us discussing the four directions and elements, as perceived by the four basic human types of red, white, yellow and black (before each sub-divided into three to form the twelve tribes) -the basic shamanic colours of most primitive cultures- the pattern clarified:

We decided to cast each direction from four different cultural viewpoints, after creating an initial four-path Crossroads vevé. The other three participants still up were aptly red, white and black representatives respectively, and we realised there was as yet no yellow -the three Asian representatives were not consolidated (though the elusive Baba still assured his participation when briefly seen in town).

It then occurred to me that there was a general lack of Asian culture and magic in our work and space so far. Even the altars in the roundhouse contained no real oriental artefacts or talismans, though most other cultures were represented. We had done no Asian mantras, rites, dances, postures or prayers...

While this was of course partly because we as yet had no Asian (inc. Chinese, South-East Asian and Japanese, Siberian and Mongolian) representatives attendant, it worked both ways and that if perhaps we did some Asian ritual the right people would appear...

So after the four quarters opening map was established and its self-designated priests and callers retired, I crept into the property's office to crawl the wwweb in the dawn hours, searching for information to increase my somewhat scant knowledge of Asian (disincluding India) cultures and magic.

I was mostly looking for an Asian quarter-casting, but in the search came up with several sites concerning *Kwan Yin*. She being an appropriate Asian (Chinese and Tibetan Buddhist, and also with a Japanese equivalent Kwannon) deity to invoke for Heart Chakra work -as a Goddess of Mercy, Healing and Compassion, I entered one of her wwweb portals. The first site I opened began with, 'Quan Yin's Birthday -19th June' and I realised with awe that this day had begun that very morning as I looked at the site...

So I finally went to catch just a few hours' sleep, knowing that the growing group's morning activity would include a bit of an improvisational Asian rite and birthday party for Quan Yin.

The Puja to Her I had extracted from the web was a water-blessing, appropriate as our rite on aeonic cusp concerned Aquarius, the Water-Bearer (as glyphed in its 'double current' symbol). The solstice ritual would be upon the Tor, which is the spiral throat of the Aquarian Phoenix shape in the
Somerset landscape (below its corresponding constellation above). Evan put a photo of a Quan Yin statuette in the centre of the circle next to the special curvaceous golden glass water vessel Sunbird had given me for the rite, Natasha contributed a Chinese fan, and we chanted, 'Na Mo Quan Yin Boddhissatva' as each in turn bowed to Her.

Then, primarily because it was really the only Chinese we knew (as a result of the SilKMilK Magizain's magical launch on Chinese new year) we began chanting the Chinese words for happiness, while drinking the blessed water, which I realised later was an apt mantra for a (happy) birthday celebration!

After the short morning puja to Quan Yin a few of us went on various missions into Glastonbury town. I went to connect with a few people and hopefully bump into some kind of Chinese mage or sage! I tried the Chinese herbalist, who although western seemed a possibility with his cultural resonance and oriental acupuncture practises. But he was too busy to even hear my proposal.

I began to feel very depressed, having slept little that morning and on a low ebb in the purgative process of the fasting. It seemed like the working could not possibly come together with several representatives still missing only a few days before the solstice.

I knew it was getting desperate when the others went into a Chinese restaurant to see if they could find any Asian representatives there. It was not just any Asian we needed, but someone who could relate to both the intent and methods of the work and was into ritual or spirituality. I stayed in the car, feeling very down; sure enough they returned saying the staff there just wanted to take their orders, and added (they were still fasting too) that the food smelled really good.

We began to drive out of town -my impossible mission apparently aborted- and passed two people hitching on the far side of the road. They were obviously wanting to go in the opposite direction from us, but I suddenly felt a very strong and pretty inexplicable urge to communicate with them.

I asked Kieron to stop the car, got out and walked back, began to tell the thin bald bearded man on the corner —he said his name was Andy- about our ritual. I got a really good feeling from him, a calmness and centred-ness.

He was very interested in the ritual, and revealed he had indeed spent most of a year in Japan recently and resonated strongly with their culture. Halfway through the conversation -which was already being interrupted by the other hitchhiker (who in typical cosmic Glastonbury style was telling me what alien race I was from because I had snakeskin tights on, and that because my jumper was red I was into blood sacrifice)- they got a lift, so I quickly wrote down the phone no. of where Andy was hoping to get to that night for further discussion later.

I got back into the car feeling a bit lighter. When I rang Andy later that night he confirmed my intuitions in that although he had not practiced ritual magic as such he was a very experienced meditator, having done several Vipasana courses, etc., and would therefore have the necessary focus to be involved, in addition to the gentle enthusiasm and understanding he had already demonstrated. So in such work it seems very valid to trust crazy hunches; Intuition seems an attribute of the general emotional open-ness of an activated heart chakra...

The other Asian representative that miraculously manifested that same (Quan Yin birth)day was Louie, Mark's returned housemate who was also a meditator, having set upon this path in Tibet. He joined our chanting circle that night, and enjoyed it but expressed anxiety that his severe back problems may make participation difficult, although he hoped to transcend that. The idea of him being in pain and needing to step out or sit down when we were all interwoven certainly gave me reservations also, despite the encroaching desperation of the situation.

When he rang next morning to cancel I was simultaneously disappointed and relieved. Simon and Jasmine went round to his house later that day to give him an extended (massage and Reiki) healing, which all seemed part of the Anahata journey also.

We had all gone into town together this last day before the Solstice. Half-way in we stopped -two carloads full- at the ancient Yew Tree next to the old church at Compton Dundon. I climbed up then down inside this amazing gnarled hollow tree (estimated to be about 1700 years old!) and chanted through its various orifices and openings while the others joined me while encircling it. Oddly the earth below me felt and sounded hollow underfoot, resounding to my stamping feet like a big bass drum.

In Celtic and Norse traditions the Yew is the gateway to the Underworld, personally validated by how spaced out I felt after even this brief visit.

I found out weeks later that there is a grove nearby with a circle of the thirteen different trees of the Druidic lunar zodiac which our final weaving would be representing (amongst its other layers of multi-cultural symbology) -a shame we had not been aware of this at he time to visit but at least we resonated nearby. This whole area -including the ancient Yew- is part of the Gemini land formation in the Glastonbury Zodiac - most apt to our work in that the Aeonic Double Current of the Sacred Twins Horus and Maat was eminent to our purpose. I acknowledged them with mudra and mantra before we left the area.

Imagios of the Horus-Maat Lodge was picked up inGlastonbury town, having just flown in from The Czech Republic for the ritual. I had only discovered his local presence the night before due to yet another synchronicity, this one involving the very number of synchronicity itself. Usually I delete the contents of my bulk-mail folder without looking at them, as its where my email account automatically puts advertising (sometimes for both breast and penis enlargements in the same day) and other junk, but this day I checked it just because there were 23 messages. Sure enough, Imagios' message of arrival -wondering how to contact and meet up with us- was for some reason in that folder.

Imagios had come to Glastonbury to be a part of the rite but didn't expect to be a cultural representative, however thankfully he agreed to be a reserve, taking the missing part if Simon's half-Chinese friend Ben (a DJ from London) failed to turn up on the Solstice day itself! Although Imagios had no real resonance with Asian or South-East Asian cultures, he did have an appreciation of the intent of the work and an understanding of the magical currents involved, and we figured that at this stage (although a bit sad) having one 'token' cultural representative would be better than the whole thing not happening due to one absence. My friend Zya from Australia -whose words had helped inspire the vision of the global chakra workings- had hoped to participate but could not get to Europe in time. She being half-Malaysian, the South-East Asian representative being the only missing party kept suggesting to me that she was meant to be there, but I had to usher out this recurring thought pattern to allow psychic space for someone else to turn up for the part....

He did –half-Chinese London DJ Ben- but only on the Solstice day itself, much to our relief in the completion of the preparation of the work. Such a quickening!

Even on this final morning, there was much last-minute shuffling around, but somehow all the pieces fell into their right places in the End and it came together into full glorious Ma-nifestat-ion!:

These final adjustments were made after a wonderful raw food feast we broke our fast with the night before -figuring that we needed to maintain the health gained from our fasting but needed a burst of nutrition energy to give us the strength needed for the solstice ritual itself. It felt really good to all gather together -the most of us assembled so far- for this informal celebration on the eve of our Great Work. We were camped this final night in a field halfway between the Tor and Gog and Magog, the ancient Oaks of Avalon and guardians of the Gates to Faery.

Unfortunately most of us did not really get a long sleep on this final night, as by the time we had run through the ritual format again around the fire, there were only seven hours or so before our early rise to perform the slow Labyrinth-walk spiral up onto (/into!) the Tor next morning.

Personally I only got about two hours sleep, as I sat up for several after everyone else had retired, trying to work out how the hell I was going to weave a twelve-pointed star between everyone that could then be transformed at dusk into a thirteen-pointed star without unweaving and reweaving the whole thing. This had come up (fortunately!) in the discussion, an enquiry as to how exactly I was going to do this, to which I suddenly and rather drastically realised, 'I don't know yet!'

With everything else I had been co-ordinating, I had given little attention to such a practical consideration as to how the physical web itself was to be woven!

Miraculously, I worked out how to do it in an hour or so, and relievedly went to sleep for a short while...

After our early rise, Schwing who had offered to guide us through the Tor Labyrinth walk (half of the paths being obscured over time) didn't turn up anyway (I later found out he had a fever that day).

It was probably better for us this way as we were actually able to just chill our for several hours instead, preparing the finishing touches to costumes etc. in a more relaxed manner than expected.

It was very hot. The sun was beating down and we assembled in the shade at the base of one side of the Tor for a while, consolidating aspects of the rite.

I climbed back up to the top at about 1pm to see if anyone else had turned up. To my relief both Baba and Bayard (who had only just driven back up from London that morning, having retrieved from there a beautiful bark-woven patterned loincloth amongst other Pygmy artefacts) -the final representatives- were there, and we joined them, preparing the space in a crater-like dip in the grass near the medieval tower (which was unfortunately covered with scaffolding for repairs) at the Tor's summit.

Then Ben turned up too and the weaving seemed able to happen in full splendour after all, with genuine cultural representatives of all twelve tribes or source-races of humanity assembled.

While others also turned up to assist us -the four elemental sacrament-bearers and Venom the spinner/piercer of Fates three- there were last minute problems with some of the cultural representatives:

Baba revealed that he was not into being pierced and woven in, denying that he had known this was what was entailed although I had gone through it all with him several times over the last week when managing to locate him on town visits. He had seemed half-hearted (!) about it all along, so I wasn't surprised but obviously concerned by his withdrawal and at a loss as to what to do. Then as about to break down I suddenly realised that with Ben now present, Imagios could take Baba's place as Siberian-Mongolian representative. He agreed and confirmed that unlike the other Asian parts he was previously reserved for this was a culture he actually had some affinity with. Of course! –Czech is just on the edge of this region and has a similarly Slavic language- the last piece in an intricate puzzle fell into place!

My relief was however followed abruptly by another problem: Bayard also objected to the piercing aspect -not in his case from lack of commitment to our rite or its intent but simply because as a spiritual practice he never marked his body.

However my anguish was allayed by his suggestion that the thread could be attached to the talismanic panther fang which hung from a necklace over his heart. I agreed, and felt a surge of utmost relief and joy that everything could -and I was now finally sure would- go ahead as planned. With so many difficulties miraculously overcome already, amidst a flow of synchronicity and intuition which even upon my own exceptionally Wyrd Way was unprecedented, victory must surely be ours.

I would not expect weaving together all the cultures of this planet -even on a symbolic microcosmic level- to be an easy task! ...And indeed, there were many more ordeals -we called in the elements from each direction and culture and they came en force! -which would beset us in the actual execution of this momentous ritual, ordeals we would endure in our collective Love and Will to bring it to full Ma-nifestat-ion...

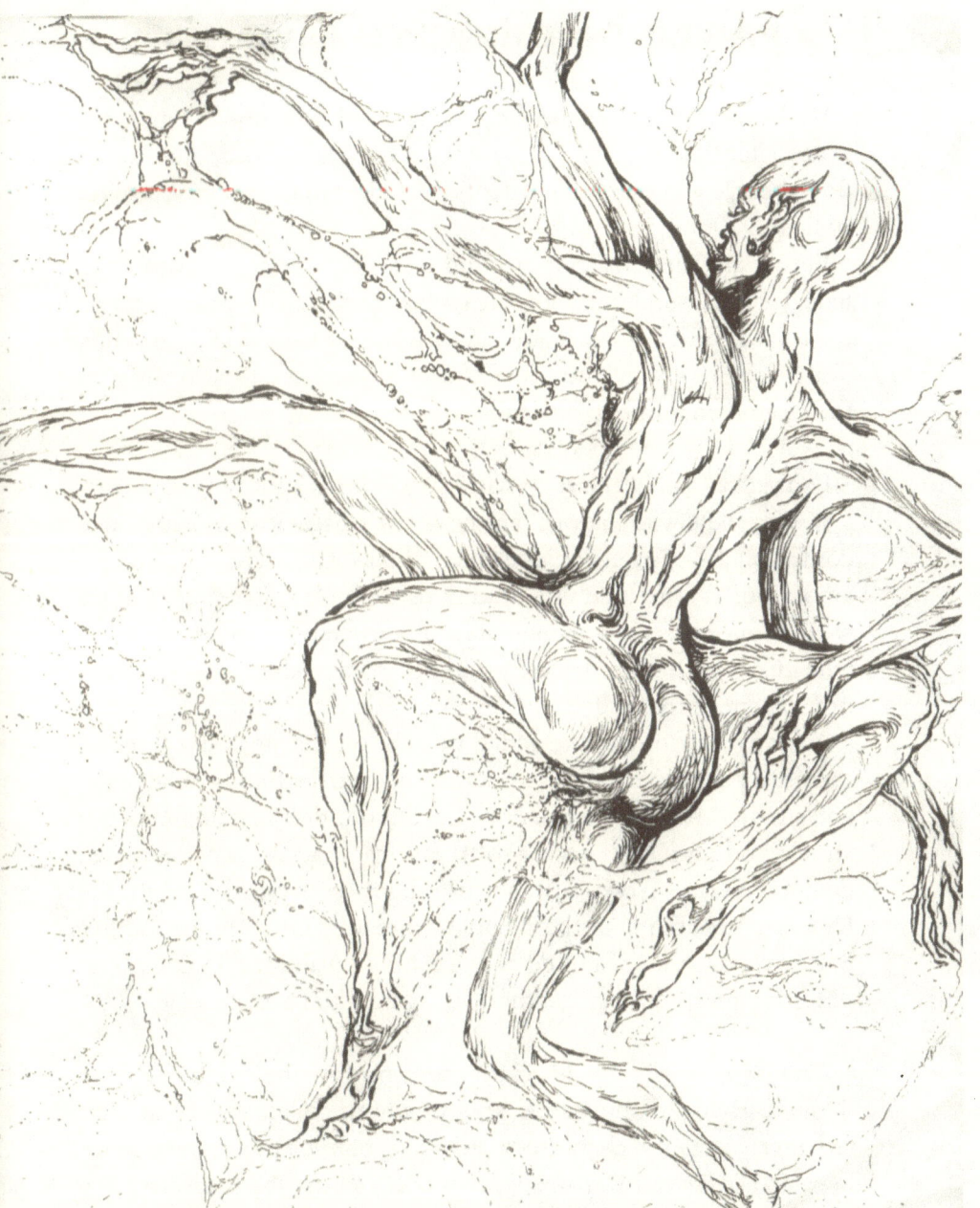

The Spider-Queen of Space weaves the 13-pointstar into Ma-nifestat-ion from afar...

A drawing I did soon after the ritual to show the wyrd and destined aspects of its manifestation.

PART II -THE PIERCING- DIVERSITY:

We began the 13th-Tribe Weaving ritual at around 4.30pm, a few hours later than expected what with all the last-minute adjustments. So the circle was cast and elements called just in time for the solstice peak at 5:20pm.

Before the circle-casting, we did a serpent-dance, weaving with linked arms around the whole area, snaking up and down and around the top of the hill- to welcome other solstice visitors to Glastonbury Tor to join in or watch our ritual if they wished, and to resonate with the dragon energies of the land.

Four altars had been set up with wooden poles forming triangular spaces, replete with various talismans from participants -with much confusion about directional- elemental correspondences due to the amount of different cultural traditions we were employing - but we worked out some kind of mutual flexible system somehow! -this was true Chaos-Order Magick, finding some kind of syncretic order/pattern from such a collection of diverse cultural traditions.

A funny altar touch was added by Sebekh, the small daughter of the ritual piercer Venom. She put her Unicorn doll on the earth altar, and insisted that my hermaphroditic spider-doll hanging above it should ride on it's back -so there we had a concise visual demonstration of two different paradigms converged- that of the Unicorn (apparently in the original geomantic Glastonbury Zodiac before earthworks 'disguised' it as a giant dog) and the Spider as two different interpretations of the 13th sign of the lunar zodiac.

We began by all crowding into the centre of the circle the altars defined, then linking hands and slowly uncoiling as we at first tentatively began to chant freeform tones, our voices unfurling as we began to snake our way in a human chain across the landscape. We wound our way around and up to the top of the Tor (sacred hill), gathering people as we went. Some were reticent but many people joined the lengthening human serpent, the diverse voices rising as we eventually coiled back into the parameters of the altars, forming a tightening human spiral. The sound expanded as the circle contracted, while we felt the vibrations of each other's voices on the backs of our necks and the energy crescendoed into a jubilant harmonious cacophony.

Releasing hands we moved out to the edge of the circle, the Twelve Tribal Representatives sitting in predesignated positions around the periphery. Other participants formed an outer loose circle around this.

The directional quarters were called by four representatives: of the eastern/yellow, western/white, northern/red and southern/black people, each direction by all four of these representatives according to corresponding elemental God/dess forms of these cultures.

Having never cast a circle before, the South-east Asian representative Andy -who was the Eastern candidate for the quarters- didn't realise that only one of the four Japanese elementals he was using was usually attributed to each direction. He very graciously called all of them from every direction - and that's pretty much what we got! (as will unfold...)

In the early afternoon it had been very hot, and I had worried we might all get sunstroke standing for hours in the shadeless grass 'crater' near the top of Glastonbury Tor. However soon after we began the rite proper, the sky clouded over, and continued to darken as we progressed. Cold wind came in and there were sporadic bursts of light rain.

The initiates representing the four shamanic colours moved to the centre of the circle, standing back to back. I spoke from Ra'en's tale of the Twelve Tribes:

'In the beginning, the first people lived together at the centre of the world.
One day a dream came. The people divided and went to the North or East or West or South...'

As I spoke each of the directions, the corresponding initiate began moving slowly out from the centre, sprinkling grains that were respectively red (north), yellow (east), white (west) and black (south). Thus we formed a four-coloured Crossroads Veve as the axis of the rite from the centre of the circle.

I continued:

'Each of these four nations ate from their new lands, and became a part of where they settled.
The Northern people became the colour of ice.
The Eastern people absorbed the colour of the rising sun.
The Western people were filled with the colour of blood, and the Southern people took the colour of Earth.
'In time, the four nations divided again each into 3 tribes. The white nation divided into the Western people-Celtic and Germanic, the Northern people- the Russian and Baltic, and the Eastern people-Greek and Roman, and Middle-Eastern peoples...'

As I spoke the name of each of these subdivisions, the tribal representative for each stood up from their positions around the periphery of the circle, joining the first who had now completed the Crossroads.

'The Eastern peoples divided into the North- Siberian and Mongolian, the East-Chinese, and the South -the mountain people of South-East Asia.
The Western people divided into the travelling people in the North (Aztec, Navajo, Kiowa, Lakota, Dakota, Nakota, Inuit, and their cousins), the farming people (Cherokee, Chippewa, Mohican, Mohawk, Iroquois, Hopi, Incan, Maya) in the West, and the Island people in the South (Maori, Polynesian, Hawaiian, Arawak, Caribbean).
The Southern Nation divided to the West-Pigmy and Bushmen; the South- the African; and the East- Aboriginal, New Guinean and Dravidian (India).
Each of these twelve tribes will learn to sing with the voice of their lands, and to feel the blood of the Land in their blood.
But the First people shall be lost...'

Then Venom as Spinner (the piercer who set the chakras or 'wheels' of the heart spinning), myself as Weaver and Natasha as Cutter of the threads came together in the centre of the circle.

We lined up and formed an Arachnean composite, a Kali-Arachne asana with our six arms (and two legs) waving and weaving together the energies of the Triple Goddess.

I had felt slightly strange about being a part of this feminine formation earlier -as initially my Australian friend Zya was going to take the role of the weaver/mother. And yet had I not woven together the rite into formation already, its physical completion being merely the coagulation of a long process? And having been initiated by three genetic women into Womanhood towards the end of my 9-moonth invocations of Goddess energies while taking oestrogen several years ago, I was not entirely unqualified to take the role of Priestess. Certainly I felt myself to be a Mother to the whole difficult process of birthing this grand ceremony on the physical.

Our formation of The Three Fates was echoed by the local elements. While several expressed later how a brilliant zig-zag of lightning flashed behind us at this time, Evan had also noticed a Crow fly in, circle high once around our three heads then fly off again. The Celtic correlative of the Three Fates are the **Morrigan** or Crow Goddesses, and we were on Celtic land...

The wide-ranging Diversity of cultures across this planet were exemplified by the words, songs and dances of the Twelve individual Tribal Representatives. Each in turn gave a short presentation of the essence of at least one of the sub-tribes within the basic types of people they were representing. This was also reflected visually to varying degrees, ranging from the elaborate Polish dress-pattern Christina had hand-sewn in the spaces between circles over the preceding week, to the woven bark pygmy laplap Bayard had brought, and body-painted tribal markings (Evan, Adam, Bayard), to the grass skirt woven by Jasmine to represent the Islander peoples.

I began the calling of the twelve tribes with Kieron, representative of the Celtic-Germanic peoples- in his traditional Druidic robes he offered some Celtic blessings and invocations then adopted some appropriate rune postures (e.g. Gifu/Gebo -Gift and Sacrifice) while intoning their names.

Then on to Marios as representative of the Eastern European and Middle-Eastern peoples - in traditional Greek (his own nationality) Toga with eastern belt he performed some European mantras and mudras.

I had not consciously thought about why I began with Kieron and proceeded thus around the circle, but realized even as the ritual naturally unfolded that we had begun with the peoples of the land we were upon, then moving east in a great symbolic arc across the globe as represented by the progression around our microcosmic global circle.

So Christina -representing the Baltic and Russian People- was next after Marios. She told a Polish folk tale then offered a small shot of vodka to each around the circle (very warming in the cold wind and light rain) while presenting them with a moral indictment as a postscript to the tale. These were assigned at random, and it was quite amusing who was told what: for example, I was instructed never to poke fun at other cultures, and especially not at my own. As the representative in the ritual of the 13th or syncretic global tribe, this was an oxymoron and a tall order indeed!

After each had performed their tribal representation, the twelve initiates went one by one over to Venom's space on the edge of the circle, to receive their ritual piercing while the next took centre-circle to dance their people.

I oversaw the moment of penetration in most cases, reminding people to draw up and feel all their fear and pain, and to release it when the piercing- rod went through their chest.

Most of the twelve had not had piercings before, so there was a good deal of fear and apprehension, which actually aided this process. It is a wonderful feeling of release when the needle sinks through the flesh, and any anxiety and tension about the act is dissolved in release and relief -this experience was expressed by several of the initiates.

Because we were operating as a microcosm within our ritual circle, I urged the tribal representatives to each feel and then release the fears and pains of their peoples also, especially those that they had with other peoples or cultures due to history's appalling inter-racial and inter-cultural wars and genocides.

When the piercing-rod had been pulled back through with their ring and sealed with small steel ball, I presented each of the initiates with a feather, confirming that their heart was now as light as this feather, as in the Egyptian mythos where the Goddess Maat (the Neter or Principle of Truth) weighs the hearts of the deceased against the feather (her hieroglyphic symbol) in Judgement of their spirits.

These were accepted with varying degrees of gratitude and relief, as some admitted later that they were not sure if they would pass this test of Judgement!

An amusing aspect of this was the presence of Venom's daughter Sebekh, named after the Egyptian crocodile God/dess who in some streams of tradition is the deity to whom the souls of those whose hearts weigh too heavy are fed to. I had mentioned this to most of the initiates, describing Venom's daughter Sebekh -whom I had not seen for several years- as being a strange pointy-toothed fairy-eating feral child; but to my amusement she now ironically appeared- and I don't know if Venom dressed her up that day deliberately due to the mythic resonances- as the sweetest looking angelic little girl, all in pink with little bows in her golden hair...

The feathers presented to the newly pierced initiates were particularly appropriate, for they were goose feathers from David's land, so not only did they represent Maat, Egyptian Goddess of Truth and Justice whose hieroglyph is the Feather which the Hearts of the deceased were weighed against, but also the Egyptian Earth-God Geb (represented by the Goose). Thus the Goose Feather symbolised not only Truth, but Truth Earthed, made Manifest within the physical World, which is what the ritual entire was all about -the Ma-nifestat-ion of the Ma(at)-I(ae)on.

Maat was acknowledged after each piercing with Her mudra (symbolic hand gesture), fingertips of one hand vertical intersecting the palm of the other hand horizontal in a gesture of Her Scales of Balance over the Heart. Venom and I performed this in conclusion of each ritual piercing, and most of the tribal representatives echoed the gesture spontaneously.

Venom as piercer, spinner of Fates Three and Priestess of Maat did a wonderful job, gently telling each initiate how to breathe with the piercing and waiting until they were settled and ready. Ironically she had just found a job that very day as a professional piercer, so what a wonderful way to sanctify this work, to provide these 13 piercings in full ritual context as prelude.

Her name seemed relevant to our rite, as the Venom of the Spider (she being one of the Three) is in the vodoun tradition the purifying poison (often symbolic of some sacrament) or ordeal which allows the initiate to enter trance for the ritual proper. Thus each cultural representative was purged and purified for the weaving ceremony which was to follow...

To represent Japan and South-East Asia, Andy laid down a silk cloth, sat upon it in lotus with a small Buddha figurine before him, and simply asked everyone to join him in silent meditation for a few minutes.

This was a welcome calm within the surrounding storm and the tumult of emotions being brought to the surface in our rite.

Representing China, Ben unwrapped from Chinese-character-adorned paper an I Ching coin and a mandarin fruit, which he gracefully offered a segment of to each of the other tribal representatives.

This gift-giving performed by several of the initiates seemed an integral part of the cultural exchange, though unplanned.

Imagios/Bennu represented the Siberian and Mongolian peoples by talking of their fly-agaric-imbibing reindeer shamans, in both English and Czech languages.

Representing the Farming Peoples of the South Americas, Simon affirmed our Kinship by acknowledging the Galactic Source, Hunab Ku, and with the Mayan greeting, 'InLakesh', meaning, 'I am another Yourself.' He then performed a graceful Cherokee harvest dance.

Adam did a more severe dance to represent the Hunting Peoples of the North. Placing a dog skull in the circle, he crouched low in warrior eye-paint, swayed and prowled about in ecstatic trance, howling in an improvised shamanic Death Dance which was very evocative.

This was then counter-pointed with The Dance of Life (below), a Native American dance and song shown to the group by Kieron. As most of us had practiced this with him during the preceding week's circles, we all joined in with the rotating swoop and gathering motion of this, weaving a web of intent into and out from our circle.

Because we were representing source races rather than more recent sub-divisions, some of the cultural archetypes seemed grouped strangely -for example Evan (left) representing both Australian (where he has lived for most of his life) and Dravidian peoples (interestingly he came to the UK via India, a trip planned before his role in the ritual had solidified).

So I painted the traditional Shivaite trident markings on his forehead in combination with the Aboriginal designs he had adorned his body with, and he performed a dance with story-telling which combined the Rainbow Serpent land mythology of the Australian Aboriginals with the kundalini serpents of the Dravidians. This also seemed apt for the whole concept behind the Global Chakra Workings, that of resonating the microcosms of our personal kundalini with that of the Earth.

Being also from Australia, I danced around the periphery of the circle clicking clapsticks while Evan spoke and danced his dreamtime tale, and Jasmine also accompanied on didgeridoo. This kind of hybrid representation brought us back to the whole multi-cultural cross-pollination the idea of the 13th Tribe represents, reminding us that we began all as one people and the layers of diversification only leads back to our origins as One People.

In fact the whole difficult process of finding the twelve initiates for the working had constantly reminded me of this -so far have we gone into cultural blending in the modern world that it would be nigh-impossible to find people to represent these ancient source races in any kind of pure way. Instead it was to do with resonances, reMembrances, and who did what reflected this global hybrid reality of the 13th Tribe as already very present.

For example, Jasmine (right) is half Scottish and half Negro, yet chose to represent the Islander people because this is the people whose culture she feels most resonance with.

She danced in grass skirt and flowers, but decided against singing the Hawaiian Pele (Volcano Goddess) invocation she had prepared because the elements were already so intense at that point, with rain and cold winds gusting through the circle. Personally I think some earth-fire could have warmed us right up at that point, but given the immediate effectiveness of everything else we were doing, perhaps she chose wisely!

Houngan Richard, though of white skin and celtic blood, knows the African traditions well as passed down into Haiti, where he was initiated as a Vodoun Priest several years ago. Shaking Assan -a shell-adorned gourd consecrated as sacred rattle- he evoked the Loa and primal energies of Ayida and Damballah Wedo, the Rainbow Serpent of the African Peoples. Like the Australian Almudj or Central American Kukulcan/Quetzalcoatl, this great Earth serpent can be seen as the kundalini of the Earth itself, coruscating through the rainbow spectrum of her chakras or sacred sites.

Bayard was the last to perform an individual rite, and spoke of the importance of drums and rhythm to the pygmies. Several others began to beat drums in time to his words, and the rain intensified.

Lightning flashed dramatically and booming thunder echoed the earthly beats. He spoke of the affiliation of drums and rain, and said that rain is a great blessing for the end of a ceremony.

Without wanting to disrupt his flow too much, I felt urged to whisper rather urgently that the ritual was only actually about halfway through -because Bayard had been unable to attend the circles and preparations all week he seemed unaware of this. The last thing we really needed was more rain to be called!

Too late it seemed as the thunder crashed and the sky darkened further. Bayard received his symbolic piercing (he does not mark his body in any way), the ring being attached to the panther fang he wore over his chest.

Under a blackening and pregnant sky, I went to circle's edge to receive my own -and the final- piercing, as Venom had to leave soon to begin her new piercing job (she also had not expected the ceremony to be so lengthy) that very day.

As I prepared myself -breathing deep in an attempt to still the tingling fire which was by now coursing through my nervous system- I stated aloud my intent to feel and release the accumulated fears and pains of all peoples and cultures, having suddenly realised this was my role as the representative of the global 13th Tribe of collective humanity. As Venom asked where I wanted it (each initiate had specified the depth and location of their individual piercing within the heart chakra area), I suddenly realised I should go for the left nipple rather than a mere surface piercing in the central chest, considering what I was taking on symbolically.

Sure enough this was very painful, as my nipples -already super-sensitive from my oestrogen intake years ago (a sensitivity deliberately magically retained) - were particularly sensitised lately from some of the kundalini yogas and massage techniques I had been employing recently to help bring my energy to the heart chakra area (what with the associations of the nipples with nurturing also).

Tears ran down my face and I was immediately swept into a sensation of ecstatic release. Many of the personal anxieties and tensions I had inadvertently accumulated in the difficult process of birthing this ritual were let go of, and I surrendered to the simplicity of Love and Truth.

With my own final ritual piercing the first half of the ceremony was complete, that of individual cultural expressions and purifications. Now it was time to proceed to the Weaving, the bringing together of these diverse strands in a Great Web of Unity.

As if testing on cue how much we really wanted to do this, the heavens split wide and cold rain now poured rather than trickled down. Shivering and reaching for cloaks and blankets, we huddled together around the circle. Those less involved in the rite fled for the scant shelter of the Tower a few hundred metres away, flattening themselves against its scaffolding-enfolded bulk in an attempt to escape the elemental onslaught. As hail now joined the water (Kieron later quipped that the spirits had taken his circle-casting cries of, 'Hail and welcome' too literally!), knuckle-sized pellets of Ice pummelling us, I saw several faces crossed with the thought of fleeing. But none of us dispersed, instead we came together at this point of ordeal, and joined hands. I was being rather explicitly reminded that in the Mayan 13-moon calendar which we were distinctly resonating with in our ritual it was Storm day! I had noticed this a week or so prior and wondered if this would be a problem weather-wise, then thought

'No, I shouldn't take it so literally, it probably just means there will be lots of intense 'stormy' energy raised...'

Well there was, but I guess I shouldn't have been surprised that the physical elements reflected this also, considering the very earthed nature of our ritual...

Another aspect I later contemplated in relation to this freak summer solstice storm was that of Odin and the Twelve Gods of Asgard, one of the many multi-cultural mythic resonances (Arthur and Twelve Knights, Dionysos and Twelve Greek Gods...) of the 12 and 13 point mandalas we were creating with our ritual. Odin -one of the main deities I had been invoking lately in ritual theatre while in Europe- is also Woden, ancient God of Storms...

I struck the sacred chime -which now quite wet had not quite the full resonance we had become used to at David's sanctuary- and announced the Muladhara (Base) Chakra and its colour red. Its attributes of survival and instinct hardly needed verbalisation at that point!

As we began the now-familiar chant of the base (and bass) Muladhara 'Ohh' tone, its resonance united us and began to stave off the elemental onslaught. A creeping warmth emanated from the collective vibration as we resonated it long and loud thirteen times. The sacrament-bearer of Earth proceeded around the circle, reaching under cloaks to anoint the base of each initiate's spine with sacred silken mud from beneath the Tor (the acquisition of this is another story...). Earthed, we stood in solidarity.

The hail had stopped by the time we reached the second chakra, nevertheless it was still raining hard and I wondered fleetingly whether to skip the chakra of water as we seemed to have more than enough of it already!

However, I did proceed with the Svadisthana, 'Oooh' tone and John -the sacrament-bearer of Water, daubed each initiate's already-slippery spine at the navel level with the sacred water from a Thousand Springs around the World as we collectively shifted up to this second tone (chanted 13 times) and the colour Orange. The resonant vibrations continued to charge and warm our quivering forms.

By the time we were a few breaths into the Manipura (solar plexus) chakra's powerful and radiant, 'Ahhh' tone and Anna -the sacrament-bearer of Fire- was smudging our spines at this new (golden) level with sage and copal, the rain had ceased.

Everyone was quite deep in trance now, eyes closed or turned downwards. I'm not sure why I looked up, but once I did I was so astounded that I stopped chanting long enough to draw everyone else's attention to the sky:

Although the rest of the sky as far as we could see (which was a considerable distance from high up on the Tor) was full of dark and brooding storm-clouds dripping rain, there was now a hole of clear light right above our circle, as if the resonance of our chanting and energy had parted the very heavens above us...!

The serpent-fire now successfully raised to the chakra of Manipura, I wiped the chime dry . and let it's fourth tone resound, announcing our collective arrival at full focus on the Anahata/Heart Chakra ...

PART III -THE WEAVING -UNITY:

Being the tone we had chanted the most in our preparatory circles, the Anahata chakra's long 'Aayyyyy' sound came in powerfully, and I saw eyes alight with bliss around the circle -we had reached the crux of the ritual.

As the tone continued, I took up a ball of thread and passed the end of it through the Anahata piercing of Evan, representative of Australian Aboriginal and Dravidian peoples. I put the ball itself on the ground, unravelling thread from it and carefully pulling it through the metal ring in the flesh of his chest...

I passed the loose end of the thread through the piercing of Christina opposite Evan in the circle, and spooling it on from the unravelling ball back to Richard next to Evan, and so forth dna kcaback and forth across the circle, moving sunwise from one person to the next on one side and moonwise on the other, hoping the method of weaving this complex mandala which I had determined on paper only the night before would work properly in practise?!

Because only a single thread not the whole ball of string could be passed through the piercings, I had to leave the ball at the beginning rather than tie off, so as I reached each new person more of the unravelling thread had to be passed through each piercing already threaded. So the weaving took a long time and a lot of care, especially as I began to web myself in, restricting my movements and requiring caution to not bump any of the lines of the star already woven. I was glad to feel the trust of the initiates in allowing this delicate slow process to unwind.

Throughout we continued to chant the Anahata chakra tone, its extended resonance deepening our gnosis as we began to slip into a timeless space. Sometimes this stream of constant sound would ebb or falter as a voice or two would lower or drop out to rest, then it would pick up again as another rejoined into its next powerful wave.

The outer ring of participants -including Starshadow and his coven who knew and had practised the tones- chanted with us, adding their voices, energy and support. Most of them had stayed with us even through the downpour.

The sacrament-bearer of Air circumnambulated around the outside of the inner circle, fanning air onto the Anahata area of the spines of the twelve initiates. I had wanted to find a wing for this action, and perfectly Adam had wings from a dove he had found - what better bird to symbolise the heart chakra's relationship with the element of Air?

I felt hyper-aware, totally blissed out yet extremely focused; several of the initiates expressed afterwards various stages of intense altered spaces during this part of the rite. I would look up from my weaving periodically to see expressions of elation, ecstasy and perhaps also some joyous surprise that the weaving actually seemed to be manifesting as planned despite all the obstacles along our way.

I felt immense love for everyone there.

With all the thread unspooling to be passed through piercings of the growing number of threaded initiates it became a little tangled, so Daphne stepped in from the outer circle and helped unravel it, passing it on to me as she did so.

When I reached Bayard as the last person to be woven into the web, there was nowhere to take the final thread to complete the 12-pointed star but to myself and take the centre. This I did, needing some direction from those encircled to find the very centre of the threads crisscrossing through the middle. Still we chanted the Anahata chakra tone, and I found myself awash in the waves of sound resounding all around me. I passed the end of the thread

through my nipple piercing (not then knowing that this nipple would a few weeks later become the abdomen of a tattooed spider, now at the centre of the web which it would later be on the edge of)...

And when the Web was thus complete, in its first -Solar- formation, there we stood resplendent, each initiate a petal of the twelve-petalled lotus of the Anahata Chakra of the planet. So too were we a fractal microcosm of the microcosm of the geomantic zodiac in the landscape, as it in turn reflects the macrocosmic web of Stars above, the solar zodiac, great Wheel of the Heavens.

The Glastonbury Zodiac is a series of animal and human figures in the Somerset landscape as seen from the air, below the constellations they echo. But the interesting thing is that apparently when the land formations were created in these shapes, they would not have been aligned with the corresponding zodiacal shapes in the sky as they are now, due to the slow rotation of this cosmic wheel across the heavens. Therefore it seems they were created then to activate now, 'when the Stars are aright'

Our rite felt like some great Key inserted into a cosmic double-lock as it slid into conjunction.

I had wondered earlier how that mysterious Fourth Fate I had recently written of would manifest in our working. She Who is the invisible yet implicate 'Splicer' -who in the dark phase joins Fates Spinner (waxing) Weaver (full) and Cutter (waning) full cycle - was suggested when Evan took up the ball of thread which lay at his feet where the weaving had begun, and tied it to the other end which hung down from my own Anahata piercing in the centre. This completed the twelve-pointed star, giving the final (and first!) point a double-strand (like all the others) triangle instead of a single representative strand!

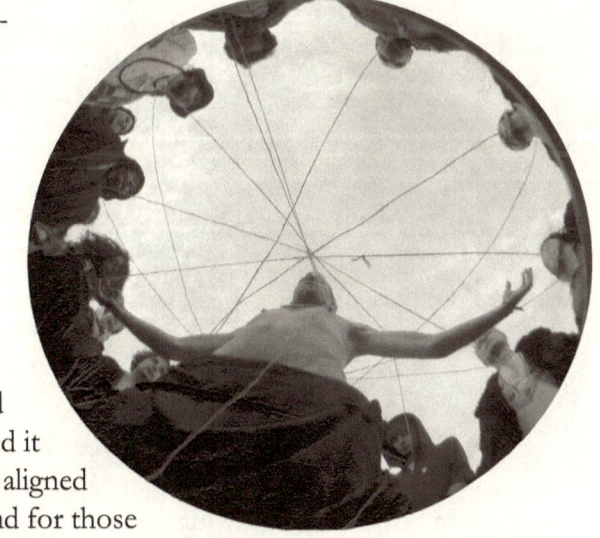

Once the twelve-pointed star was woven, we proceeded with an energetic exercise most of us had practised together in the preceding week, as instigated by Kieron. I guided it vocally to keep us aligned with each other and for those who had not done it before, especially in the outer circle. With deep inhalations we pulled the energy of the sun and the stars beyond down through the crowns of our heads, into our Anahata chakras.

Then we pulled the energy up from deep within the earth -Gaia's fiery core- also into our hearts. Here we mixed them in this central chakra, allowing the energy to expand as a ball of light, growing larger, brighter, larger as we breathed the stellar energies down and the telluric energies up -larger, brighter, larger until it could no longer be contained within our chests and burst forth into the centre of the circle, the individual balls of energy merging into one great central ball. In pre-planning, I had not intended to be in the centre of the circle at this point -because the energy was being directed at the centre itself not my presence within it. As it turned out with the 12-point star only being able to be completed with myself threaded in centrally, there I was anyway, and it felt fine if a little overwhelming, all that energy cascading around and through me. I found I was able to contain it for long enough til it was time to turn and release it out into the World.

People began calling out their intentions, what they were putting into the circle that they wanted to give out to the world - trust, truth, love, peace, understanding, open-ness and other such noble virtues, as well as a few funny personal quirky ones too. We all let the energy in the inner circle build up and up, the collective ball of light growing and growing until it too became uncontainable and burst out into the outer ring, then grew again, larger, brighter, larger, brighter, until...

...the bubble burst and all our Anahata energy, merged with that of the Earth Herself, went flying out into the World at large, helped in this propulsion by everyone in the outer ring turning on their heels and suddenly projecting outwards. An immense wave of release swept the circle- the joyous knowing that to give love does not deplete it but creates more exponentially and infinitely...

I noticed at this point and other energetic peaks in our ritual that the other people further up the Tor for solstice -although apparently mostly not paying too much conscious attention to our circle-responded with further ecstatic energy. Children were laughing and a tumult of excited voices rose in pitch and volume just a few seconds later as if feeling the first ripple of our projection.

We paused for a moment, allowing some silence to settle this formation before we moved into the final phase of the ritual.

After a while I began to narrate the conclusion of Rain's story:

'As the prophecy says:
In time, the twelve tribes will come in contact with each other and bring forth children who can sing the songs of more than one land.
First the four nations will meet amongst themselves, then each nation willmeet and mix. In time, a new people will arise, a people of the blood of all tribes, all nations. This people will be the rainbow people, and their children will sing all the songs of Earth.
In time, we will be one people again.'

Then -as the sun had began to set and a silver dusk descended at the end of the longest day of the year (summer solstice)- I stepped out from the centre, so that the twelve-pointed star became a thirteen- pointed star, I becoming its thirteenth point. This was the ritual transition -correlative with the even-ing of light and dark, night and day- from Solar phase to Lunar phase.

Now we formed a 13-pointed Star, a multi-layered Symbol representing:

*The 13-point star-diamond of Ma-nifestat-ion (outer star of illustration at left) channeled by Frater Achad

('Unity') on initial receipt of the Maat current, signifying it's earthing in this Aeon;

*The Lunar Zodiac of which Arachne is the Thirteenth sign;

*The 13-moon cycle of the year, as acknowledged in the calendars of the Mayans, the Druids, and other ancient cultures.

*The 13-baktun time-map of the Mayans, the Thirteenth point of which represents the final baktun/cycle from 1992 to 2012 -the Solar Age (glyph: AHAU);

*The Global Unity of all peoples and cultures as the Thirteenth Tribe.

We all leaned back to stretch the web into shape and fully feel the connections with each other -in a most tangible and physical way! (and of course on many other levels also with all the chanting and energetic work we had been doing together). It was really an incredible feeling, this multi-faceted joining.

'Unity in Diversity' I said, and each of the Twelve Tribal Representatives called out the Word, 'Unity', but each in their different languages, as researched where not already known - beginning with Kieron, Celtic-Germanic representative, calling out, 'Unity (English), Einheit (German)', then Marios representing Eastern Europe and the Middle East calling out, ´Omonoia (Greek), Achad (Hebrew)...´ and so on around the circle. When this was done I gave a nod and together, in Unison, we all cried out the Word, 'Unity' but each in the different language/s of the peoples and cultures we were representing, thus demonstrating the Diversity within that Unity (and the acceptance of that diversity being the only way of achieving true Unity). A simple but most effective exercise, and happiness radiated around the circle.

Then I gestured at the initiate to my right and he called out, 'M..', then the next who called, 'A', then, 'N', 'I', and so forth until we had collectively formed the thirteen-lettered Word, 'MANIFESTATION', at which point we all cried out the Word entire together.

For this is the Word in the outer rim of the 13-point star -diamond of Manifestation which Frater Achad -Crowley's magickal child- channelled upon initial contact with the current of Maat. And now we had truly Earthed -in full Ma-nifestat-ion- this current of Truth and Balance into our aeon, in a very physical way.

For Malkuth -the plane of physical reality- is the Daughter sephira and Maat (especially as 'Ma', the ancient Egyptian name of Her daughter form) is the Daughter of Earth in the aeonic formula YHVH, which completes the cycle, for 'The Ma-nifestat-Ion of Nuit is at an End' (AL I,66). Achad is the Hebrew word for Unity, and its numerical value in Hebrew (Qabalistic) Gematria is 13.

I struck the chime and we moved now up from the Anahata Chakra to the Vissudha (Throat) Chakra. After resonating so long on the single tone and note of the heart, it felt incredible to shift up to the slightly higher, 'Eeee' tone of the throat. It resonated with full power, as the chakra of Sound and Vibration should.

Thirteen times we sounded it, then with the signal of the chime on up to the Ajna (Third Eye) Chakra, and here for me the visions really kicked in:

Riding on the fluctuating subtle harmonics of the collective, 'mmm' tone humm, I saw the etheric web of connections spreading out from our immediate physical web. There were several Anahata group rituals linked with ours occurring simultaneously as well as numerous individuals tuning in across the globe. I felt these connections now, seeing a flash of a handful of ritualists at Boudica's Mound in Hampstead Heath, London, then a few more at the Serpent Mound in Ohio where I had performed a new moon rite with Nema and Tyger a few years earlier

With my mind's-eye I saw tenuous filaments of light stretching out across the globe from our circle to these, and to other, less locatable places and people, forming a fine lattice of subtle energies.

Suddenly I saw quite clearly the faces (especially eyes) of loved ones in Australia performing a linked rite. One of these was Kestral, and this made me smile for an actual Kestral hawk had been hovering over and near our circle on the Tor for much of the afternoon.

ARCANA XIX – The SUN
From **The Book of KAOS TAROT**

This hawk is also present in the original vision of the 13th-Tribe Weaving that I drew as the Sun card *(above)* of my Book of Kaos Tarot deck several years earlier, there representing the solar energies of Horus. I was laughing after the ritual about this being the Sun card, considering the extreme weather we had -although it was very hot for the first half of the day while we were setting up and preparing...

Other imagery in this picture has also clarified as the working unfolded -the Sun-lion (with mane of fire-serpents) was drawn to symbolise Egyptian Hrumachis, but is also akin to the stone lion head from whose mouth the sacred red water pours in Glastonbury's Chalice Well gardens opposite the Tor (which I had not yet seen when I drew it), in much the same way as the solar fire pours down into our circle in the image.

The web of stars beyond our sun -as in the card- I saw vividly as we concluded the Ajna tone and moved to the Bindu chakra at the back of the head, the, 'nnngg' sound fluctuating strangely with tongue held in back of throat. I felt the energy rush up to the back of my head, around and back down as this Kechari Mudra connected the energy circuit we had been establishing.

The lacework of light became more tenuous as it stretched off into infinity. I opened my eyes fleetingly to see deep trances all around, and it felt for a moment like we were going to collectively take off or dematerialise.

Some were beginning to sway slightly or even shake. It was hard to tell if it was kundalini, cold or both!

The sacrament-bearers and Natasha the cutter had been wonderful, keeping us supplied with water and as much warmth as possible (considering that the chest area still needed to be exposed) while we were woven together, but we had endured a lot.

We emerged into the high and resplendent, 'Ohh' tone of the Sahasrara (crown) chakra thousand-petalledlotus at the top of the octave and the energy fountained forth from the crowns of our heads.

Connection with the All. Unity uttermost shown...

Then it was back to the low bass, 'Ohh,' tone of the Muladhara (Base) Chakra to ground out and earth the energies. By this stage - after many hours of chanting and deep breathing, the piercings and the thread creating slight tension on these, and the bombardment of elements we had received from the extreme weather- we certainly needed it!

The energy descended as dramatically as the tone back to the bottom of the octave and our spines, and slowly we all sank to our knees, carefully so as not to put any strain on the delicate thread web between us.

It felt intense to be kneeling on the ground, then putting all our palms flat upon the grass, feeling the pulse of the Earth, grounding out the high energy we had raised, earthing our intentions into Manifestation. Several spoke these aloud as the rest continued the bass chant which droned in powerful waves of coagulation. Gaia felt very warm and responsive.

Eventually we slowly stood again and Natasha came in as the black-clad Cutter (the Crone Death of the Trinity of Fate) with her big pair of shears. Without hesitation ->Snip, snip<- she released us one by one from the Web.

I asked everyone to remember the Unity we shared, and that as we went back into our individual selves, identities and lives, to carry that with us. To know that though we are always AlOne, yet we are All One...

The feeling of relief and release was immense. After being united in such an intense and tangible way for so long, one could really appreciate the joy of individual Self and Being again!

The physical sensations of such were a reminder that the game of life is a special one, that we are, '...*Divided for love's sake, for the Chance of Union*' *(Crowley's Liber Al, 1,29)*, but also, '*United for Art's Sake, for the Chance of Division*' *(My Liber Pennae-Ultim-Atum, III,61)*. Both of these realities can be beautiful if appreciated fully with the knowledge and awareness of the other.

We jumped around, shook our limbs and bodies with regained freedom of movement, laughed and hugged one another joyously.

Knowing the energy could now scatter very quickly, I encouraged everyone to join hands once more to perform a final dragon-dance to end the rite as we had begun. Some were a bit reluctant but afterwards said they were glad we did this, for it distributed the energy more from the area where we did the rite, and involved others present on the Tor again.

It was a lot of fun. In linked serpent formation, we wound up and around the Tower atop the Tor -it felt great to be moving from that one spot where we had stood in such concentrated energy for so long. Many more joined us this time than the first serpent dance, and by the time we threaded jubilantly down back to the circle the human serpent was about 60 people long.

The random chanting was spread out over the sacred hill so that when we spiralled back into the centre, it was incredibly powerful as all the voices merged together, raised and peaked as we flung our hands high into the air in an upwards ecstatic spiral...

From here we began to disperse. Somehow amidst the ensuing elated chaos the four who began the rite managed to come together again briefly to thank and banish the elemental spirits in each direction.

The Global Anahata Chakra Rite was thus finished, a Great Work completed.

CODA / RESULTS:

A tangible Result: Returning to Glastonbury about a moonth after solstice (when I wrote most of this report, reminded by the locality of key elements) I was told by Claire (the sacrament-bearer of Earth in the rite) -at the Mayan Day-Out-of-Time (which I was a day late for) festival- that a 13-pointed star crop-circle had appeared somewhere near Avebury (also a part of the global heart chakra nexus and visited by several of us a few days after the weaving)!

Another interesting crop-circle with an eye in a vessica piscis similar to the design on the red chalice well lid in Glastonbury has manifested near the Serpent Mound in Ohio where a linked rite had been performed simultaneously with ours...

The ritual was also further earthed at a strange place called Morrigan's Mump, as suggested by a local Glastonbury witch who assurred us, 'That's the centre of the web round here.'

Well it wasn't much to look at, but there was certainly intense energy on that little mound, visited by four participants in the Anahata working - Evan, myself, Jasmine and Tekla, a visiting German woman who knew nothing of the rite beforehand but felt called to go up to the Tor that afternoon and then joined the outer ring of the rite.

A moonth or so later a 13-point star tattoo on my chest was also complete, the Memory of our rite etched for my life into my flesh, with all the design´s multi-layered symbolism contained therein. The spider over my nipple completes the web, the piercing received during the weaving extending from its abdomen, where the threads had connected me to the actual web on the Tor.

Imagios had come to the UK with the intent to be initiated into the Horus-Maat Lodge. Methinks he got more of an initiation than expected, being woven into the web of the 13th Tribe.

However two days later we endeavoured to perform the regular HML initiation ceremony also before he flew back to the Czech

Republic. This was done on the Tor in the same location as the solstice rite, and Jasmine was initiated with him, by the several Lodge-members who were still present.

The significant thing is that before even coming to the UK he had planned to -and did- take the magickal name 'Bennu' -the Egyptian name for the Phoenix- as a part of this ceremony, yet was unaware of the significance of the Phoenix to the locality:

In the Glastonbury zodiac of the Somerset landscape, the figure which encompasses the Glastonbury Tor is that of a great Phoenix for and below the constellation of Aquarius. Aquarius is the Water-bearer, and the sacred red and white springs are at the beak of the phoenix formation as seen from the air ; also perhaps they are the tears of the phoenix, traditionally reputed for their healing properties, just like Glastonbury's red and white springs which pour forth from the face area of the Phoenix land formation. The Tor itself is the throat of the Phoenix. There is evidence of an ancient Labyrinth on the Tor, a mystical spiral formation. Vultures have long spiral throats -physiologically- with which they break down flesh to feed to their young.

So besides the fiery solar aspect of the phoenix -correlating aeonically with Horus, the lord of Force and Fire; there is also the shadow of Maut the Vulture/Black Eagle -a form of Maat- implicit, to represent the *Double Current* (Aquarius sign as two ripples or waves) of our Aeon...

...And as the Silver Dusk descends about us so too within us something stirs. The Cosmic Day begun with the Golden Dawn now draws to its conclusion, for *'the Ma-nifestat-ion of Nuit is at an End'*...

...and as She Ma-nifests in our Ae(i)on, a Cosmic Night Begins, in the Balance...

APPENDIX E:

THE KALI-ARACHNE STATUE

ReTurning to Australia from India in late 2005 I was afire with devotion for the Great Mother of that ancient Mother-Land: Kali-Ma. Already taken with Her outer intensity and inner peace, in Her homeland I fell deeper into my devotion. Back in Melbourne, there was nowhere to worship. I was used to having temples on every block, and I immediately began to miss the fervent religious life of India. Of course I knew that Kali and Shiva and all of Them are everywhere, within and without, but I love the colour and joy of open regular worship, of deities housed in stone statues which you can see and feel and prostrate yourself before. As an artist as well as a mystic, I have never been content to just experience divinity on the astral or other inner planes, but to bring them into the World of Form.

The Indians seem to share this obsession, for although most of them know deity is ultimately beyond form, they have no problem with building beautiful and often surreal vessels on the outer for this interminable spirit to reside within.

I came back with a desire to build a temple, some kind of primarily-Hindu but multi-cultural holy house for the Gods and Goddesses. This seemed a gigantically ambitious goal -especially in terms of finances- I had not even a new (rented) home yet, let alone extra space for such extravagances, and I had no idea at first where to begin. I found myself visiting a warehouse-shop of Eastern antiques just to pray to the Ganesh and Durga statues in there...

The only temple near Melbourne I knew of where I felt any kind of potential for such a thing was 'Illuminature' out in the lush rainforests of the Dandenong Ranges; a large wooden space beneath share-house, it was used for various healing practises as well as the occasional pagan ritual, but was however kept bare of iconography and paraphernalia most of the time due to different people using it in different contexts at different times.

It was only a week or so after return to Australia that while I out there I was offered from the resident potter a lump of clay to play with. I really enjoyed making a small female figurine - the clay was wonderfully malleable, immediate and tactile, and I was able to bring my love of figurative drawing into three dimensions. My mother is a potter so although I had not used this medium for about a decade, the memory of childhood clay play returned and I found it natural.

A few days later I realised that the day that I had crafted this figure on was the Sabbat of Imbolc (in the southern hemisphere), when it is traditional to make 'bridey dolls', small female figures (usually with hay) of the Celtic Goddess of Fire and Inspiration, Bridgid. Well inspiration had certainly struck, for I now knew where to begin my Temple -from the centre, with a life-size statue of Kali-Ma.

This in itself was of course also ambitious -and I didn't realise quite how much so until I was a third or so of the way into the project, typically with a perhaps prematurely-set deadline for its completion; but it seemed affordable and acheivable. All I needed was a lot of clay, a lot of devotion, a lot of space and a lot of time (and I soon discovered, a lot of patience)...

It was several moonths after the initial inspiration -moonths of gradual integration back into my homeland- that I began work on the statue. I began with Her face.

I was delighted to discover that Durga Navaratri -the nine-night Hindu festival of the fierce mother Goddess who rides a lion or tiger (and is an aspect of Kali, or according to some traditions the reverse)- was to be celebrated with daily pujas in the Illuminature Temple. The priestess who had run such pujas for Navaratri around there for many years had recently begotten another child, so shifted the ceremonies from her house to the Temple, and would only facilitate every third night.

It was the eve before the Durga Navaratri that I heard of Tash's death -although then its finality was not yet confirmed.

She, a dearly beloved kin of our clan had upon arrival in India during Her first world-travels, had leapt into the Ganges and been swept away in the holy river's formidable current.

Only an hour or so after this news, whilst I was still in shock, another call came to the Temple and in haste the space began to be prepared there for an immanent birthing. But too late, for a follow-up message revealed the mother-to-be was now on her way to the Birthing Centre. Her child was born on the first day of the celebration of Durga, the primal Mother-Goddess of India.

I was facilitator of the third night -the last of the initial Kali phase of the Navaratri- and so dedicated the two-hour puja to Tash, praying that Ma Kali who presides over such transitions, take care of her passage (at that stage unsure whether it be just to the other side of the river or to The Other Side).

Just before the puja I sat in the Temple sculpting with clay.

Although I still was unsure how to create a stable infra-structure for the whole statue, I wanted to at least begin on this Kali day, and so moulded as a mask Her visage while chanting Her mantras. No conscious thought was aligned with this work, or rather play with clay, and it was only after the group puja with its dedication that her best friend Heidi and I looked back at it, then at each other with surprise and agreed that it resembled Tash. I finished the mask at dawn. After further defining the features it looked a lot less like Tash, but retained the uncanny resemblance in large brow and intense piercing eyes both celestial & telluric.

It soon occurred to me that Her hair should be snakes. It was only weeks later that a witch hosting my Tarot Conjuration workshop brought out some beautiful tanned snake-skins -with their heads still on them!- that she had acquired very cheaply, offering to resell them at the same price for her kin. And so after some sewing and stuffing, my statue acquired a Medusa-like element. It is thus several primal Goddesses rolled into one, since Arachne -as Mother of our local Magical clan in and around Melbourne- is also prevalent in the work. So I wanted to make four legs as well as the traditional four arms of Kali-Ma -a decision that later proved very anatomically challenging.

Kali is also very associated with serpents, particularly that energetic one She exemplifies as Shakti Kundalini. Making the serpent-locked head first, a significant factor in relation to the corrupted myth of Medusa occurred to me. Originally a powerful and benevolent Libyan Goddess, Medusa was demonised by the patriarchy and beheaded by their 'hero' Perseus, who obviously couldn't face the primal feminine. So by making the head first then the body and re-attaching it, I was restoring Her. And rather than turning others to stone, this Medusean head is stone (fired clay) itself.

Then there is Chinnamasta, a form of Kali who beheads Herself, but as a positive symbol of the abandonment of ego and intellectual mentation for pure being. I made the first hand on Dassura, the 'tenth day of Victory' after 9 days of 3-hour pujas for Durga Navaratri. The continuous chanting and ritual over the period had elevated my consciousness and after the final ceremony at dawn, I felt charged and -despite having risen so unnaturally early for the puja- spent the whole day sculpting.

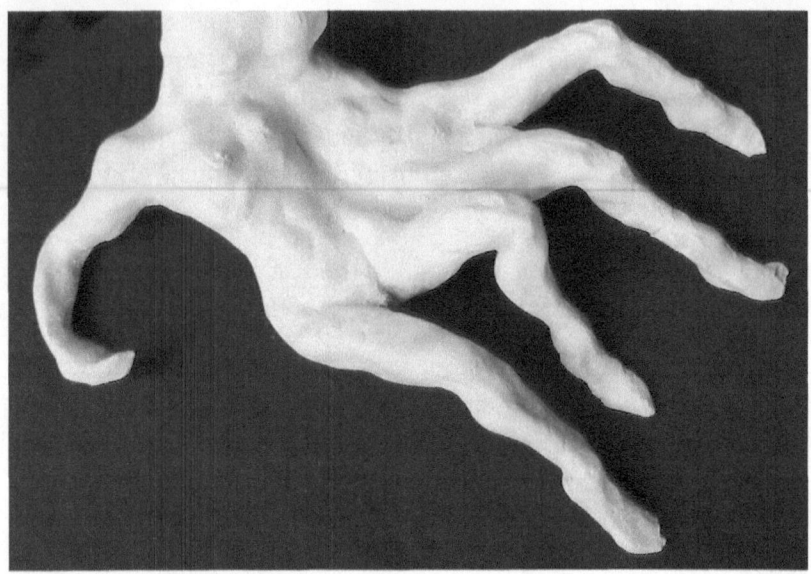

This introduced another whole element to the statue, for within each hand there are two figures, one male and one female, lying beside each other, their legs forming the fingers and one arm the thumb.

This was inspired partly by the tattoo of Pan upon my hand (my fingernails are His hooves), but the concept was now taken to another, more 3-dimensional level.

It didn't stop there however: Soon after making the first few of these hands (there are four for Her belt of severed hands as well as the four on the ends of Her arms), I saw a beautiful dance piece to Stravinsky's 'Rites of Spring' by the Chinese Shao Lin Dance troupe. The way the ten dancers performed their own individual movements yet were so interlinked as a whole, almost a single organism with independent parts- inspired me and by interval I was babbling excitingly to my partner about the visions the work had induced: I had seen my statue come to life, giant hands formed by two live figures each, and seven (I worked out the logistics later) dancers forming Her face.

To actually create and perform something like that would be no less than epic, and I had not felt to do any large-group performance work for quite some time; but the vision was too profound to ignore, although I did manage to mostly do so for 3 moonths or so before the time became ripe for its manifestation in the world of form.

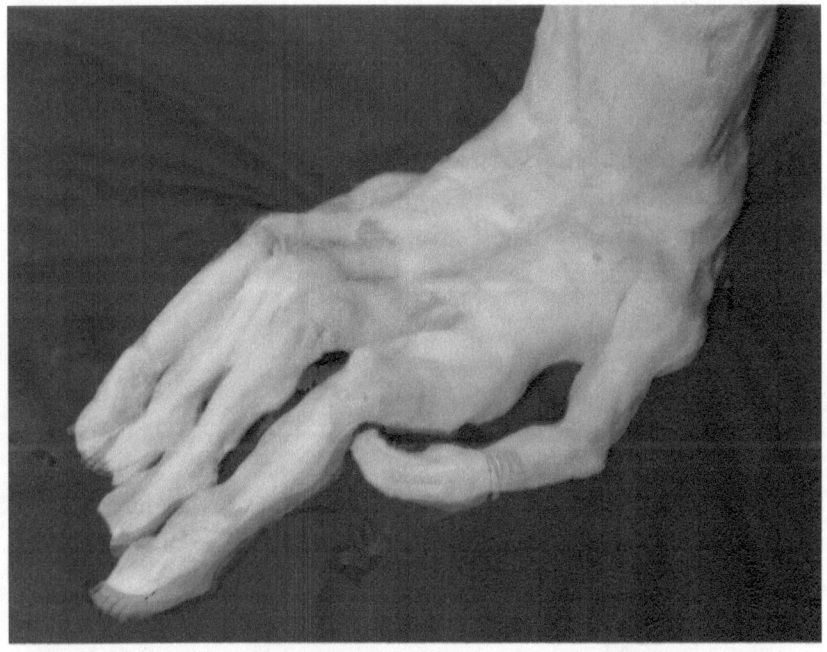

Still of two of the dancers -Heidi and Taz- overlaid with a clay hand of the Statue.

So the second edition of this book was launched simultaneously with the performance of this production- 'Loom o f Lila'- and the accompanying DVD (hardback only for this third edition) contains footage from the work.

Once the Ritual Dance was under way - performance dates set and rehearsals begun - I then also had a deadline for the statue -since She and film footage thereof were to be incorporated into the show and thus also a simultaneous deadline for the book and DVD- oh MahaKala, Great Lord of Time, why do I set myself up to learn your ways so harshly!?

I began to sculpt in earnest, with no real idea as to how to make something on that scale with a sound and solid structure -trial and error, and pure devotion.

Clay is such a wonderful medium. It is pure earth, then fired to become rock. Sculpting with it is direct manifestation from the raw matter of this planet -so different from all the less direct media, e.g. writing, drawing- I was accustomed to using when I rediscovered it. With all the video and editing work I had to do on computer, it was the perfect counterbalance from that abstraction, to shape the earth with my bare hands, feel its form changing and growing. For clay sculpture is far from just visual, it is totally tactile, and can become extremely sensuous, as one smooths the rippling 'flesh' as it forms, pressing like massage to define the subtleties of the musclature. For someone more used to working two-dimensionally however, it does have its difficulties -something may look perfect from one angle, then a slight turn or even a shifting light-source, and it may look quite wrong. Even using a mirror for reference was sometimes misleading, as it also flattens things out into a single surface, albeit one that forms can rotate within. I found I often needed to actually feel the human form, that of myself or another, to determine angles and degrees of curvature. So having my partner model in exchange for massages was helpful for both of us!

My partner returned from being away in time for me to do the back, which would have been extremely difficult without her. But for the bulk of the statue during a creative hermitage I only had myself as a reference, which was interesting. The statue being life-size, it was effective to be able to constantly make rough measurements against my own body. I have quite a feminine figure anyway, but obviously some adaptations had to be made. Halfway through this process, it occurred to me that it was yet another extended and subconsciously-activated result of some powerful magic begun many years prior:- my intent to womanifest my Anima. I have had many progressive results from this spell, several discussed in this book. I have mostly womanifested her within my self, reifying my latent hermaphroditism by taking oestrogen for nine moonths (culminating with a manifest Alchymic Wedding ceremony on Spring EquinoxuliuqE 2000), stretching my urethra and other progressive physical mutations, all combined with regular ritual evocation of my inner Goddess. Now She seemed to be womanifesting outside of my body, as a complementary reflection of it, yet a still very tangible one. I have always seen my anima as very arachnean, so the dawning perspective of this multi-limbed being as my divine feminine is a pleasing one. Of course She is much more than this, She is a deity incarnated on earth and in earth; but the personal microcosm of that is She as my anima and Fate, something explored at length in both the 'Loom of Lila' ritual dance and film, and in this book.

After making all the hands, some feet and two of Her arms, it occurred to me that I had better make a scale model of the whole sculpture so I could work out how all the pieces were going to fit together. This model alone - though only about a hand tall- took several long nights, and began to give m ean inkling of what was actually involved with the larger work.

This small Kali- Arachne model was begun ritually on a solar eclipse, invoking Atum it was crafted with the prime matter of the great kala and raw clay.

A week later it clicked that this was also the little puppet I needed for the beginning of the Loom of Lila dance, before I was revealed as the puppeteer dancing, until my own dance was revealed as the puppetry of the gigantic figure of Fate formed by dancers and film of the statue. How perfect that the first puppet should be a fractal of the larger puppeteer; so I detached Her secondary arms and legs, with holes to wire them back on at elbows and thighs to form a kinetic marionette.

Come the cold and wet of winter in the Dandenong Ranges, I would not have had the space needed to continue the work where I was living in Kallista, now that I was moving onto whole limbs and the abdomen, and also needed room to lay pieces out and see how they all fit together. But an opportunity came to move in to the bungalow near the Illuminature Temple, and I soon found myself in there sculpting every second night (all night). Mostly I didn't use the main temple space itself however, for an even better idea had occurred to me while in the adjoining sauna: this seemed the perfect place to make Kali, the

Goddess of Kundalini fire and the burning grounds. I wondered about the clay drying out too much, then realised I could keep it moist with my own sweat, which made the idea even better. So I spent probably too many hours in there, sweat trickling in rivulets onto my work, becoming faint sometimes when I knew it was time to get out, but was too obsessively engaged in my work to do so for a while.

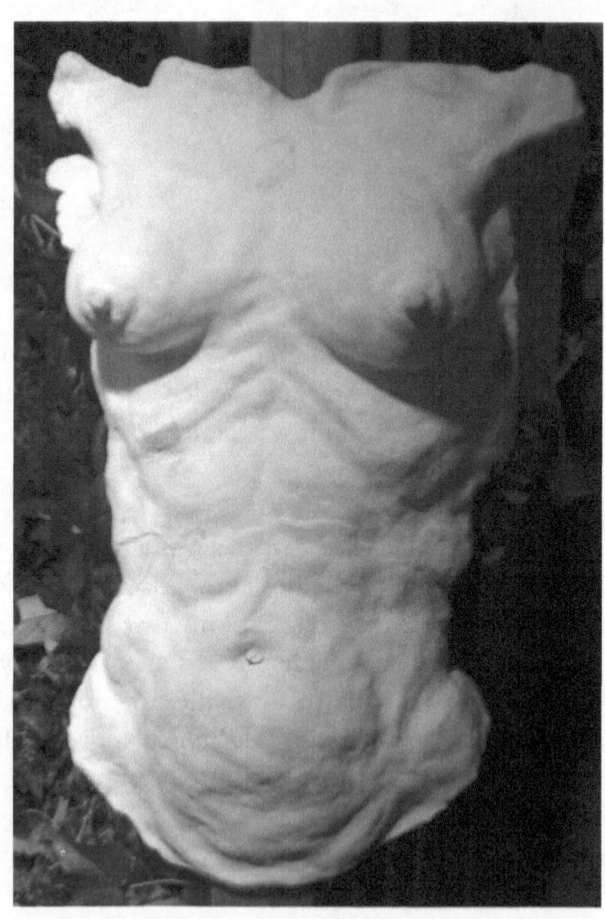

It was the perfect environment for it, the heat increasing my trance. The first time I chanted Her mantras

almost non-stop for hours, making Her first leg in there, pausing only to deep breathe, stretch or drink copious amounts of water. I found the most effective way to transfer a lot of my sweat onto the clay was to pick up the whole thigh-in-formation and rub it over my abdomen. Resultantly I also ended up covered in clay as well as Her in sweat -total transference!

Later when crafting Her abdomen I even began to use sweat from the corresponding parts of my own to moisten it. The clay on my body quickly began to dry out so I had a body treatment in the process- clay is very good for one, drawing out toxins and softening the skin.

It was during one of these extensive sauna gnosis sessions that the arachnean anima aspect began to clarify- for the relationship I had been deeply involved in for almost a year prior was in a state of dire uncertainty, and during her absence I reaffirmed my own inner Goddess, then realising that this was being reflected on the outer through my current creative processes. I felt complete in myself, knowing the joys of Art, and of devotion to the divine feminine whether embodied in flesh or clay, or ultimately discarnate, Kali as the all-pervading Mother of the Universe.

The more work I did on the statue, the more Art and Spirituality began to blur and blend into the same thing for me. The only way I could achieve something like this -crafting on this scale with an only semi-familiar medium and no real idea of correct procedure- was through unerring and total devotion. The whole time I was chanting mantras of Kali-Ma, imbibing the work with Her essence, praising Her name and invoking Her shakti into this earthen vessel.

When I wasn't sure how to go about something -how to approach joining a semi-dry arm to a wet shoulder-blade for instance- I just maintained my faith and let VishvaMata guide me. And mostly, things just worked. When occasionally something didn't, I would just keep chanting and try again another way.

Other deities made their presence known also- Giselle and I had done much Ancient Egyptian magic in the temple, Em'balming and mummifying people for restoration of the living, and much chanting of Sekhmet mantras, especially in the sauna. There are potent links between the lioness-headed One and Kali, for both are Goddesses of fire and destruction, yet also nurturing Mothers; and both sprung from the third eye of another deity to wreak havoc upon a humanity gone awry, both in their frenzies of bloodlust outreaching the control of their creators. Sekhmet was eventually pacified with the beer of the Gods, Kali by Shiva lying before Her, in total surrender -She could not resist His lack of resistance! -so both by divine intoxication. So I felt Sekhmet too in the sauna, then it occurred to me with sudden delight that Her traditional consort is Ptah, the divine potter!

Certainly there was a Pygmalion aspect to my work, obsessive as it was, and often rapturous. Like some kind of redeemed Oedipus, I fluctuated between faith in She who guides my hand as Mother, and She who as divinity enfleshed is akin to a lover. The transpersonal became personal, while maintaining its otherness.

I chanted traditional mantras praising the Lotus Feet of the Goddess, while adorning Her feet with their unfolding petals.

Colouring Kali-Arachne became quite a quandary for a while: I had made Her face initially with a gritty brown clay, but then for the hands switched to a fine white porcelain that was better for details. I enjoyed its smoothness so continued with this, thinking I would glaze or paint Her all black to bring the different pieces together. But I was unhappy with the black glaze when Her face was fired, and a layer of black oil paint didn't look any better- the matt blackness flattened Her contours, and even an added layer of blue-black for highlights didn't help much. The raw clay looked much better, more primal, but She couldn't be white, She whose very name means Blackness!

For some filming before a dance rehearsal, two fired clay hands had been placed in our ritual fire, the flames licking twixt fingers hypnotically. Seeing them a few days later, I realised that the effect was ideal: a mottled charcoal tone, and how perfect! -The Goddess of Kundalini fire and of the cremation Smashan would dance amidst the flames again...

This turned out to be the stupidest -yet incredibly liberating- idea...

I was about halfway through the statue when I finally got around to reading an essay on the Shri Yantra David Allen Hulse had sent me many moonths earlier (thank you David), and it seems it was the perfect time to do so: He wrote of the *Lalitasana*, one leg of the bright Goddess folded as if in meditation, the other outstretched dancing. I realized this was almost the same position as I had designed on the scale model for the secondary pair of legs, so decided to make them more exactly that on the large version.

It already felt like somewhat of a combination of Kali and Lalita, since She of the waxing moon represents the play of form ('Lila'), even as Kali of the waning is its glorious dissolution into the absolute. For it is a very manifest vision!

Then, further into David's essay I read of Kurukulle, a Hindu-come-Tibetan Goddess whose (4-legged!) form combines that of Lalita and Kali. She is a Goddess of love, bliss and ecstasy. What is more, Her name means, *'Mother of the Heartbeat Clan',* and in the 'Loom of Lila' ritual dance we had been forming the giant Kali-face of seven figures while performing the Sufi drum-breath (with a Sanskrit rather than Arabic mantra), which unites everyone not only by synchronizing our breath but also our heartbeats.

Om Kurukulle Hrih Svaha!

Throughout most of the process of creating the statue I was at peace, flowing with any difficulties and overcoming them easily enough. It was only towards the end of the process -when it came to actually putting together all the pieces- that I began to struggle.

TimE, Fate and Spider Magic

The first major accident was dramatic. I had initially planned to remove the head (rather than the face, which had already been made separately first) from the body, in honour of Chinnamasta (headless Kali) and so that I could -when wearing Her face as a mask in the final scene of 'Loom of Lila'- step out from behind the statue taking its head with me (see DVD)...

However, I made Her entire back- from head to bottom- as one flowing continuous piece as the work became more fluid towards the end, wrapping parts to keep them wet for joining. I knew that I was going to have to break up this large piece to turn it over, and to fit it to front pieces and limbs, as it was unmanageable whole and fragile unfired.

I was reticent to cut the head away from the body, and tried to lift and turn the whole back piece as one before it was even fully dry. The head fell off and smashed into five pieces on the ground. I saw it cracking off but could not save at is as I had my hands full with the rest of it. That was the first time I became upset during the work, though I still recovered quickly and managed to patch it back together okay with some improvisation.

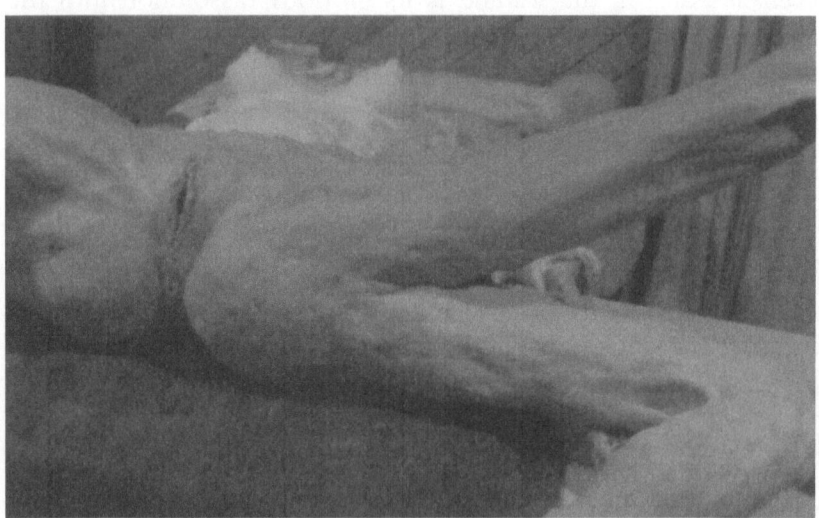

The second break was even more devastating: I had built three of the legs together onto the bottom of the statue, and while this time

I broke one off deliberately to move the piece, its components were in separate stages of dryness and it still crumbled when I lifted it, a leg and a half smashing on the floor. The half-leg I patched up with joining pieces, made roughly then carved to size and shape when they reached the same state of dryness as the limb they fitted into. The other was irretrievable, and I had to make it again and even - due to proximity to my exhibition opening- have it fired separately and joined on later. While my heart leapt and I was most upset when this accident occurred, I recovered very quickly and adapted, even though it meant the first public exhibition of the work would be of it in pieces.

By the third major break -the top of an arm- I barely flinched. Of course I still cared greatly about this object/subject I had put so much blood sweat and tears (literally) into, but I had reached a strange state of simultaneous utter sanctity and non-attachment.

It was all too delicate to be otherwise, like life itself...

It was all just a part of the process now. Shivaic surrender allowed me to exhibit Her horizontally on a tabletop, three-legged and disjointed, birthing the smaller scale-model puppet.

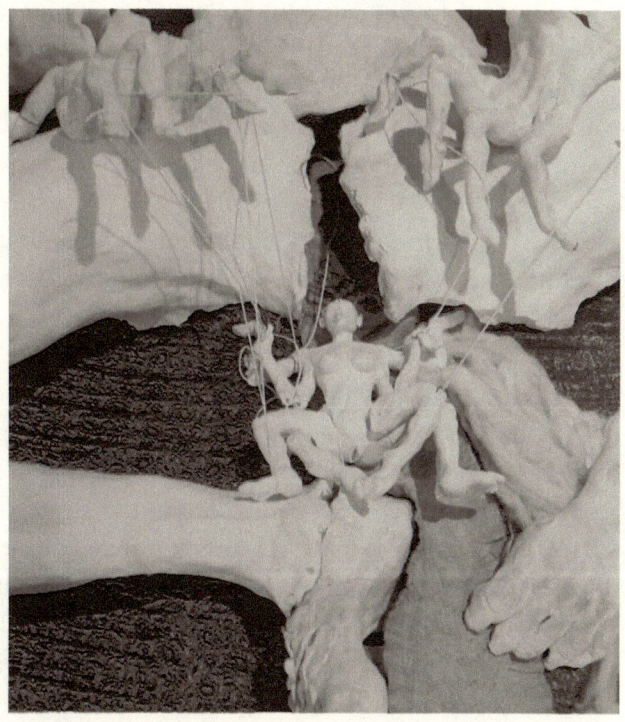

But I knew that I had to have Her standing for Loom of Lila, and began to realize this was impossible without help.

My friend Taz came to my rescue, welding together a metal skeleton as vital structural support.

I'm not sure if he would have begun if he'd realised quite what was involved, for the angles of clay pieces joining front and back and multiple limbs fluidly connecting was specific and required constant readjustment, and it was all heavy and awkward, difficult without a structure to already hang Her on. We became less particular about it as the Loom loomed...

We had a rehearsal for the ritual dance on the Saturday before Tuesday's first performance, and had planned to ritually roast the statue afterwards. I was up all the night before and on into the day glueing pieces together with a rather toxic 'fireproof' two-part glue. We did some more work on the armature after the rehearsal but progress was slow and burning Her whole seemed nigh impossible. So caught up in our attempts to prepare Her were we that by the time we realised we had no wood it was dark and creating a big enough fire seemed dubious. However it occurred to me that there was a large party at friend and cast-member Kali's (apt!) house nearby, so why not burn Her in the fire they would surely have there.

I loaded the various pieces and unfinished mainframe into the back of Hunna's car and off we went. There, amidst a handful of chanting and drumming mystics and many bewildered partygoers in the backyard, Raphael and I hoisted most of the statue, held loosely on metal frame, onto a huge fire I had built up further for the ritual, with a mantra to the Goddess of the Smashan. Without Her forelegs She was able to straddle the pile of flaming logs and embers, supported by more logs I had piled around strategically.

The flames licked Her yoni and the extended crack above it, leaping up over Her belly and breasts. It was a bizarre and beautiful sight to see my precious work engulfed in flames, yet unharmed by them.

It had already been fired at temperatures much higher, yet it was still disconcerting to surrender Her to the pyre...

Sure enough the glue -which was only heat-resistant for a short period and I had no idea how to retrieve Her now She was immersed- did begin to crack and pieces to overlap and even break off and sink down into the embers. I was beyond being distraught about such things- I had given Her to the fire and how She survived or not was beyond my control. At last after what had become very hard and relentless work (difficult to stay in a spiritual space with toxic glue, screaming metal-grinder and several days with very little sleep) I was in deep ritual space again, and all I could do was watch in awe and chant to the great Goddess of death and birth, creation and destruction.

Naturally some of the people present wondered what it was all about, while others knew Kali and chanted along. At least some who were disturbed by the spectacle came to the Loom of Lila performance, and saw that what had appeared as death and destruction was actually just transformation, that

She was resurrected from the flames and became whole thereafter. In that pyre was the whole paradox of simultaneous mortality and immortality, ritually and microcosmically encapsulated in flaming stone, sinking over many hours into a horizontal position in a slow-motion cascade of burning limbs.

It was not, however, an easy rebirth by any means. While at the time it was an intoxicating and even necessary release from the pressures and preciousness of trying to complete the work in Time (ironic), the pyre did set me back considerably, as I could not retrieve Her til the embers died down next day.

Every glue joint dissolved and there were even several new breakages from pieces falling or unregulated temperature changes. The bizarre thing was that She did indeed go black, while we were chanting Kali mantras, then I went inside for a short while and when I returned She had gone white again- soot coating burning off again? Wyrd. She came out multi-hued, mostly off-white but with some patches of mottled black and various shades of charcoal grey and umber brown.

Together with all the cracks, the effect was appropriate for a Goddess of the burning-grounds, and quite beautiful if not black. In film and photographic work Her negative image has yielded the deep blue-black I associate with the Star- Mother. Perhaps as a manifestation of the void She has inverted into pale form...?

The final few days before Loom of Lila were insane: We almost gave up several times, but having got so close now after so much work, it seemed absurd to stop. Joints were not all accurate and metal gleamed through the cracks, and in the end Her limbs were attached with a strange expandable foam to the rough and now fire-buckled skeleton.

We actually had grinders and welders going in the theatre during set-up, dance warmups and even semi-rehearsals going on at the same time with various limbs scattered around the periphery of the stage and sparks flying. One of the theatre-caretakers

Palms of lower figure-hands

dropped by and rolled her eyes at the scenario but left without further comment. Ci Orse, Rose and Amordios Gobblyn-Smyth all helped Taz and I pull Her together under seething pressure, and I am vastly grateful for their help.

By this stage I only became mildly perturbed when I couldn't find the bottom half of Her face (which had split in twain in the fire) anywhere, and after scouring the fire's coals again, gave up and made a new one at dawn the night before the performance, after fixing the video edits for projection. It wasn't as good as the first face (interestingly the first thing I made- nothing of Her original form remained!) but sufficed. The first night of the dance performance went well despite some technical hitches and sleep deprivation.

Garlanded with flowers (thanks Ashe and Giselle!) the Kali-

Arachne statue had a powerful presence despite needing some re-angling and refinement...

Afterwards an audience member who had also been at the fire party approached me with the original face, saying he'd had a strange feeling to take it and meditate with it after seeing it by the fire with flames coming out its mouth...

All that had to be surrendered from my original intent on the first night of Loom of Lila was the last edition of this book, of which only an unfinished sample proof was perusable for mail-orders; and with last-minute printing and binding the full edition was available at the second show a few days later.

Once again MahaKala had constricted me in the severe contractions of birth.

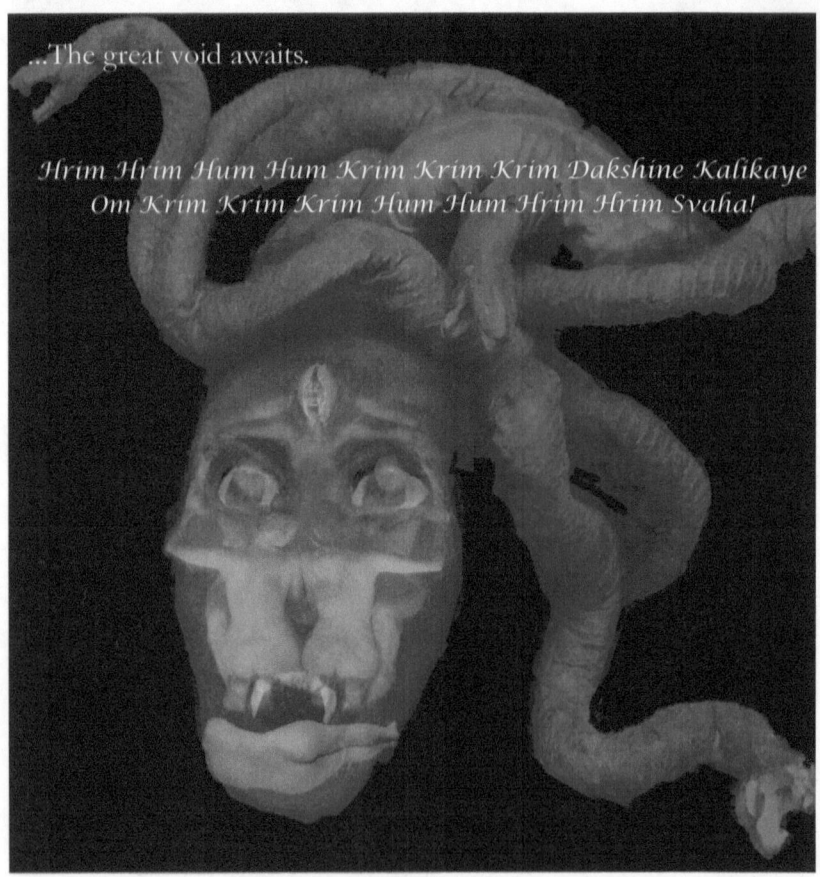

...The great void awaits.

Hrim Hrim Hum Hum Krim Krim Krim Dakshine Kalikaye Om Krim Krim Krim Hum Hum Hrim Hrim Svaha!

Is one of the Reasons (if reason here dwell)
Why people are so often afraid of spiders
That they resemble hands?
Legs drawn up, knuckleknees tight
Or sprawled to creep and crawl
Across a page, that inky scrawl
Of wyrd words, webbed into verse
Spiders like hands
Are purely tactile
Engines of touch, disembodied
Independent sensation
Unfettered by civilisation
Thoughtless Sense
Pure intention
Unbound yet binding

Or is it that they weave our Fates?
Hands of destiny, embodied, arachnean
Detached and miraculous
Masters of Vibration
Will we be trapped by their tendrilsense?
Will we be wrapped, in silk, with tenderness?

-Orryelle 2013

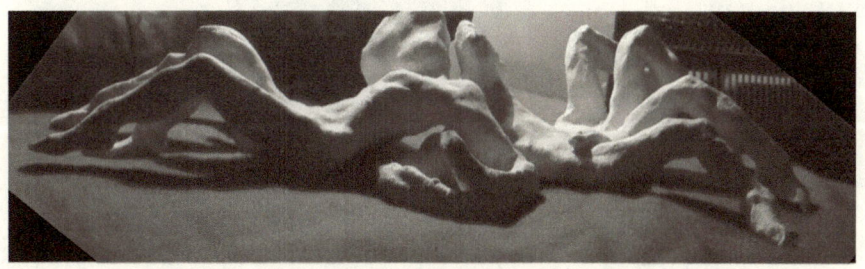

TimE, Fate and Spider Magic

LOOM of LILA

A *Texte-ile* by MetaMorphic Ritual Theatre Co.

The Ritual Dance Theatre *Loom of Lila* was the first production from MetaMorphic Ritual Theatre Company that has no dialogue or words in English (apart from sung lyrics on the final musical backing track, *Begotten*) -rather it relies on sound, imagery and movement to convey its concepts. Many of these are central to this book, which the last (2nd) edition of was launched with its second performance.

The Video of it on the DVD accompanying the hardback edition (also available separately from **iNSPiRALink.MultiMedia Press**) is a combination of live performance and effected material made for projection in the original show...

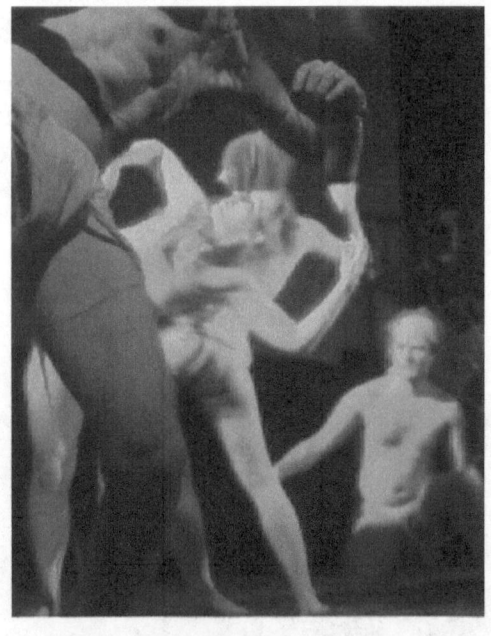

Loom of Lila expresses in form and movement the relationship of the individual to the collective, exploring also concepts of microcosm and macrocosm and Fate versus Free Will (and how this can be resolved), and the nature of Deification.

Dancers together form the face and hands of **Kali-Arachne**.

Individual dancers, expressing their free will,

break away from the composite figure to perform their own dances, yet these also ultimately weave back into the pattern of the whole. The fractal or holographic nature of reality is expressed through the forms and movements of individual figures echoing the larger movements of larger beings they are part of.

The composite face is created by the individuals who compose it, this being a visual and theatrical metaphor for the nature of deity: We believe in Gods/Goddesses -whether we call them this or less personalised names such as Fate, energies or 'collective consciousness'- and are therefore 'controlled' by them, yet they are a result of and created by our belief and energies.

We may struggle with our Fate, or dance with it and co-create our destiny, acknowledging our part within the collective reality, both being influenced by it and —with the language of our bodies and souls- influencing it.

The DVD containing *Loom of Lila* and other related **Metamorphic Ritual Theatre** footage comes with the hardback edition of this book, and is also available separately from **iNSPiRALink. MultiMedia Press:**

www.crossroads.wild.net.au/inspiral2.htm

Orryelle Defenestrate-Bascule is a ChaOrder Magickian and Baphometic avatar somewhat obsessed with physical reification and Manifestation.

While s/he does enjoy shamanic and astral journeys via occasional extreme entheogens and other deep trance work, s/he is not content to just travel to other dimensions, rather intent upon bringing back aspects thereof to the physical plane.

S/he is thus constantly reburbishing hir Temple, that is the physical form seen as a malleable tool: Physical mutations as magical acts (chakra piercing and weaving, Tattoo Tarot Tantra), Visual Art (drawing, painting, photography, video, sculpture), Esoterotica, Ritual Music (violin, voice) & Performancy, Dance; and Installation/Environment Sculpting.

As a vessel for these processes, hir **Metamorphic Ritual Theatre Company** present public rituals aiming to transform rather than merely entertain the audiences who thus be-come the initiates, sometimes being led through environmental installations (such as Labyrinths woven through the woods) while interacting directly with other 'characters'. Such ritual theatre is infused with universal symbology gleaned from Orryelle's studies of Alchemy and comparative mythologies (especially Egyptian, Hindu, Greek & Norse).

Other ongoing outlets of expression and initiation are endeavours such as *The HarleQuintet* (4 musicians channeling the Quintessence of Musick), *Well of Wyrd* and amorphous **Mutation Parlour, iNSPiRALink. Multimedia Press** including **SilKMilK MagiZain**; and the underlying/overflying *HermAphroditic ChAOrder of the Silver Dusk* -a lunar, artistic and intuitive apprehension of magic to counterpoint the solar, scientific and structured system of the *Hermetic Order of the Golden Dawn* ; employing a multicultural and multisubcultural blend of tradition and innovation.

Since 1999 the ChaOrder co-ordinated group rituals at various sacred site Global Chakras of the planet, culminating with the **Global Sahasrara (crown) Chakra Working** Dec. Solstice 2012.

Orryelle is also involved in **The Horus-Maat Lodge**, and is an initiate of the *AdiNath* and *Aghori* Tantric traditions.

In 1999-2000 he embarked on a 9-moonth quest of HermAphroditic reification via mantra, mudra, invocation and ritual estrogen intake, culminating in hir reified **Alchymic Marriage** as a WoManifest Wedding Ceremony with Self.

Orryelle's current (2014-) creative foci are the culmination of an extended Orphic Working (www.crossroads.wild.net.au/orpheus.htm) in multiple media, and the completion of the Tela Quadrivium, a fourfold book-web of Graphic Grimoires being progressively published by Fulgur Limited (http://fulgur.co.uk).

Each volume of this Quadrivium relates to a colour phase of Alchemy: Conjunctio, the Red Book (Fulgur 2008, sold out), Coagula the Gold Book (Fulgur 2011, sold out) and Solve the Black Book (Fulgur 2012). The final volume Distillatio the White/Colours Book (projected for 2015) will bring the journey full cycle as the tomes link up in a complex spiral mandala.

Portrait of Orryelle by
Heidi Valkyrie

TimE, Fate and Spider Magic

ReTurn, ReTurn, ReTurn
ReVerse, ReVerse, ReVerse

Please ReCycle this Product
Please ReProduce this Cycle

www.ingramcontent.com/pod-product-compliance
Lightning Source LLC
Chambersburg PA
CBHW021800220426
43662CB00006B/135